Praise for No Ordinary Love

"*No Ordinary Love* is a warning to our younger generations that abuse comes in many forms, and it is our compassion for others that will ultimately end the violence and help us understand that there is no easy escape."

— K.J. Harrowick, co-author of *I Know Why She Stayed* and co-founder and CTO of the *I Know Why She Stayed Initiative*

"A raw and unflinching look into the inner workings of an abusive relationship, this story will enrage and grip you in equal measure, sending you hurtling toward the uplifting climax."

—Justine Manzano, DOO of the *I Know Why She Stayed Initiative*

"*No Ordinary Love* looks through the eyes of an abuse survivor, and follows her through all of the stages of abuse and recovery. At times it is an incredibly painful read, but stick with it—it's well worth what you learn from the journey."

—Kasey Rogers, co-author of *I Know Why She Stayed* and co-founder and CEO of the *I Know Why She Stayed Initiative*

The *I Know Why She Stayed Initiative* was founded by authors Kasey Rogers and K. J. Harrowick and aims to provide resources and information to empower people who suffer from financial abuse.

'99% of women worldwide who are domestically abused are also financially abused. More than fifty thousand of those women die every year from domestic abuse, while many of those women stay in the abusive relationships because leaving means no home, no healthcare, no food, no finances of their own.' —iknowwhyshestayed.org

No Ordinary Love

BB Gabriel

Writing Brave Press
1940 Palmer Avenue, #1032
Larchmont NY 10538
www.writingbravepress.com

Distributed by IngramSpark and KDP

Copyright © 2025 by Robbin Gabriel

All the necessary due diligence has been made to contact the copyright holders. Anyone who believes that their copyright to be infringed upon is welcome to contact the publisher.

The NO MORE Project—All rights reserved © 2025.
The use of The NO MORE Project's tools and resources has been approved by Lyndsey Dearlove, Director of Operations, NO MORE.

CASW ACTS—All rights reserved © 2025.
The use of CASW's resources and website link has been approved by Kate Hudson, Administrative Coordinator, Canadian Association of Social Workers.

All rights reserved. No part of this book may be reproduced in any form or by any electronic or mechanical means, including information storage and retrieval systems, without written permission from the author, except by a reviewer who may quote passages for review.

Cover Design: Karinna Klocko
Text Design: Melissa Williams Design
Copyeditor: Danielle Dyal

Library of Congress Cataloging-in-Publication Data available.
ISBN (Paperback) 978-1-0691213-0-1
ISBN (Ebook—EPUB) 978-1-0691213-1-8

First Edition

This story is based on true events. It represents the author's recollections of her lived experiences, along with memories and correspondence from others, during this period of time. To protect the privacy of individuals, certain details, such as names, characteristics, and locations, have been changed. Other details pertaining to events, dialogue, and timelines have also been adjusted to provide a more cohesive narrative.

This story depicts intimate partner violence, sexual assault, miscarriage, death, grief, substance abuse, and profanity. If at any point reading *No Ordinary Love* becomes overwhelming, please give yourself permission to skip a paragraph, a section, or, if needed, an entire chapter. Readers are strongly encouraged to seek professional support for their own personal situations requiring therapeutic, medical, or legal advice.

If you or someone you know is in immediate danger, please call 911 or the phone number for your local emergency services: police, fire, ambulance.

Global Resources

The NO MORE Foundation is dedicated to ending domestic and sexual violence by increasing awareness, inspiring action, and fueling culture change. They are a groundbreaking, global initiative comprised of the largest coalition of nonprofits, corporations, government agencies, media, schools, and individuals addressing domestic and sexual violence. NO MORE is committed to engaging, reaching, and working with people from diverse communities. They work to amplify and grow the movement to stop and prevent domestic and sexual violence around the world by creating and supporting innovative campaigns, partnerships, and tools that leverage the power of the media, entertainment, sports, technology, and collective action. With more than 1,400 allied organizations and over 40 state, local, and international chapters, NO MORE sparks grassroots activism, encouraging everyone—women and men, youth and adults, from all walks of life—to be part of the solution.

The NO MORE Global Directory is an international resource linking survivors of domestic and sexual violence to credible support services in more than 200 countries and territories worldwide. It includes specialized resources for all genders and sexual orientations.

The NO MORE Survivors Guide provides detailed information on recognizing all forms of abuse, accessing counselling, legal aid, and other resources, and finding inspiration to light the path toward a brighter future.

NO MORE Silence: Speak Your Truth Platform is a space for survivors to share their stories safely and anonymously, finding connection, understanding, and support from a global network.

All these and more are available at nomore.org

Canadian Resources

The Canadian Association of Social Workers (CASW) offers a vast list of resources for those who are or know someone who is seeking help for family and/or intimate partner violence in Canada: https://www.casw-acts.ca/en/resources/family-and-intimate-partner-violence

The above link includes: Canadian Women's Foundation, Women's Shelters Canada, National Action Plan on Violence Against Women and Gendered-Based Violence, Ending Violence Association of Canada, Families Canada, Government of Canada Intimate Partner Violence Against Men and Boys, Shelter Movers, 211, The Government of Canada Stop Family Violence Services, Government of Canada Gender-Based Violence Knowledge Centre, We Believe You, WeProtect Global Alliance, It's Your Business—A DIPV Workplace Toolkit, and Humane Canada: ACT to Keep Families Safe Online Learning Centre.

Resources can also be accessed from their homepage www.casw-acts.ca through the menu under 'Resources' then by selecting 'Family and Intimate Partner Violence Resources'.

Please note: the above resources/links may change and/or expire during the lifetime of this book. This list is not exhaustive in nature and is not a substitute for help someone may need.

Foreword

by Dr. Sandra Preston

Welcome to this important and engaging book. I met BB, the author, while teaching a course called Violence Against Women. It was one of the courses students could choose to take as part of their social work degree. I had worked for many years in the field in shelters and as a therapist helping women and their families escape and recover from the abuse of their partners (almost always male). This work led me to return to university for my PhD which again focused on the work of feminists to get violence against women recognized and addressed. All of this was influenced by my own experiences as a young woman experiencing violence from boyfriends and my first husband. In my work and research I learned that I was not alone. In fact, violence against women was epidemic and continues to be in Canada and around the world. In Canada in 2018, 44% of women reported experiencing intimate partner violence[1]. That means that if a woman has not experienced violence herself, she most certainly knows someone who has.

BB is someone who has experienced such violence. When I met her she was part of a group of young, beautiful, well-dressed women who sat together in my class. They all looked like models and in a program which focused on poverty and oppression, they stood out. Many students assumed they had lived easy, privileged lives. Fortunately, they were also very strong women who made it clear to the class that such assumptions prevented women, especially those who appeared to have everything, from getting the help they needed. They challenged the stereotypes about abuse - who was a victim and that abuse was much more than physical. BB has continued that work in writing this book.

From chapter to chapter we are taken on a journey. We are given the privilege of walking in the shoes of women who are experiencing violence at various stages of their lives. We also get the perspective of family and professionals, who often know that something is wrong but struggle to accept and assist in the realities of those who are trapped in violence and abuse. Circumstances that those who are experiencing it don't feel safe sharing. Sometimes people ask how anyone would 'let' themselves be abused. BB clearly illuminates how the world young women inhabit sets them up for violence and exploitation. We can feel how trapped young women can be and the danger they face. The usual question of "Why doesn't she just leave?" has a clear answer - she can't. Then when a woman does have the courage to leave, understanding it might end in her death, she is constantly haunted by the abuser who continues to fill up her life. BB brings this to the page as well, sharing it with us. It is one thing to read statistics, it is another to have those statistics made real and tangible as it is here. There is also hope in this book. For, when facing the tragedy that is violence against women, it is important to know that sometimes there is a light at the end of the tunnel.

BB has brought us a story that will help the reader understand violence against women at a personal level. This is an amazing accomplishment. I am proud that I had some small part in bringing this book to life. It should be read by anyone who has experienced, and/or wants to know more about the violence and abuse that women and girls face in our society. It isn't an easy read, but you will be happy you took the time to read it.

—-Dr. Sandra Preston, retired university professor.
Areas of expertise include the feminist movement in Canada, social policy and women's issues, social work practice with women, women abuse and mental health, and women's issues.

Dedicated to *she* who will no longer remain silent.

Chapter 1

Gabbi

My little sister is dying. But not before she sees British Columbia, for fuck's sake. Feelings flood my eyes at the thought of losing her, and I hastily wipe them away before turning around to see if she's still napping. Across the airplane aisle, she and Johnny are chatting. She notices me and waves. I blow her a kiss.

How ironic. To come full circle. Flying here, of all places, and with my family, of all people. But my little sister has never been. Since this might be our last chance, we planned a family trip. Four days exploring mainland BC then three days doing the same in Alberta's Rockies. "We" consists of the original five: Mom, Dad, me, Tara, and Bryanne—plus the sisters' misters: Vince, Warren, and Johnny. Half of our group is already there; the remaining four of us are about to land any minute now. The BC itinerary is yet to be determined, as Bryanne refused to make any plans until she knew how she'd feel after chemo earlier this week.

"Cabin crew, please take your seats for landing."

As the plane begins its descent, I sense *him*.

The grumble of the engines rattle the memories loose. My hands and feet go cold. A baby wails. My heart races. My breath attempts to catch up. The nauseating smell of bathroom deodorizer wafts through the aisles. I startle when the woman beside me bumps my elbow off the armrest. A flight attendant straps herself in. The coffee I finished more than an hour ago stings the back of my throat, more sour than bitter now.

Bitters—

No! My eyes squeeze shut. Not today. I want *him* out of my head. Out of my body. I tap my icy fingers on my temples. Breathe. I lower my right hand to my heart and take a deep breath, feeling the slow rise and fall of my chest as an ominous storm rolls around in my stomach. I glance at the barf bag tucked into the seat holder in front of me and brace myself.

You came back.

I try to swallow, but my mouth is dry. As the plane touches down, I resist *his* invasion as forcefully as the screeching brakes fight the tarmac.

"Ladies and gentlemen, WestJet welcomes you to Abbotsford. The local time is—"

Why did I come back here? I scan my surroundings. Take inventory of the passengers in my vicinity. It's fine. Deep breath. I've got this.

"For your safety and the safety of those around you, please remain . . ."

I'm safe. My family is safe. Another quick scan. I hear the clanking of seat belts being relieved of their duties. The family in front of us stands up against the flight attendant's orders. Overhead bins pop open in unison. Deep breath. I've got this. I turn to look out the window but instead see my husband's face and feel instantly grounded.

I exhale too loudly. Vince's eyes check in with mine. A smile warms my face.

"I love you, little bird." He squeezes my hand and unknowingly calms the storm in me.

It never once crossed my mind until now that I might be triggered. Throughout all the months we discussed and planned what could very possibly be our last family vacation together, *he* hadn't come up at all. The mere fact I hadn't thought of *him* until now is still proof of a remarkable feat. Definite progress.

Deep breath. It's been twenty years. I'm freer than I've ever been.

The stairs from the plane to the tarmac are steep. One wrong step could send me tumbling and skidding across hot asphalt. I hold the railings tightly until I'm safely on the ground and make my way to arrivals. Unfriendly memories reintroduce themselves the closer I get to the airport. *Welcome back to your cage*, they taunt.

"Excuse me, please." An eager, dark-haired woman pushes a wheelchair past us toward the plane just as my husband and I walk into arrivals. Clearly an airport employee en route to assist my sister. I turn around and look out the window back to the plane on the tarmac; my eyes search for Bryanne. In that moment, *his* voice is gone.

"I think they instructed them to wait on the plane until everyone else is off," Vince says.

I raise my chin to kiss him. "Okay, babe. Mind watching this stuff while I use the washroom?" He takes my carry-on bag and purse and takes a seat.

A few passengers linger around the tiny bistro waiting for coffees and snacks as I push my way into the bathroom. It's empty. I lock myself into the farthest stall from the door.

I haven't had an anxiety attack in years. What the hell is wrong with me?

When I exit the stall, the bathroom is still empty. I grab a sink and stare at myself in the mirror. I take note of my eyes. Blink a few times. They don't break contact with their reflection as I turn my face from side to side and press the backings of my diamond stud earrings to ensure their grip. I soften my gaze. Inhale. Exhale. In again. And out. As I tidy my messy bun and admire my custom created 'Rock Ridiculous' t-shirt, a little smile cracks through. I reapply some tinted lip gloss and massage it in. I collect my eyes one last time.

I've got this. I'm not a child this time; I'm thirty-nine years old. And I'm not alone—not on this trip, not ever again.

The memories are still waiting for me when I head to the baggage claim area of the tiny airport. I brace for a distressing game of flashback peekaboo. My vision glitches between the present moment and the past; I'd been in this very spot all those years ago when I'd fled for my life. My body struggles to discern my current, completely manageable unease from the residual toxic terror that nearly immobilized me the last time I stood here. I choose to notice the upsetting memories and feelings, acknowledge them, then let them move on. A dangerous departure then, but a safe arrival now.

I notice my little sister ahead waiting for me. I admire her beautiful, thick, long blonde hair and her Barbie-blue eyes. I note the layers upon layers of comfy clothes she's wearing to warm the body that's failing her. To the uninformed eye, no one would even know she's sick. Sometimes I can't even believe it.

"I love you so much, Honey B," I say, sitting down beside her. She laughs. Likely at my pet name for her: Honey Badger. Never was a pet name more appropriate. She's a fighter. And Honey B doesn't give a shit.

Bryanne looks me right in the eyes. "I love you, too, Gabbi." Our family is more connected than I ever thought possible. There is so much love. Deep, deep love.

God, please, don't let this be our last family trip as a whole.

A Jeep, our rental SUV driven by Johnny, pulls up out front of where Vince and Bryanne and I are waiting. The three of us gather our luggage.

"That'll eat up a lot of gas with all the driving around we'll be doing!" exclaims Vince.

Johnny hurries toward us to take Bryanne's carry-on suitcase from her.

"No, not this one," says Bryanne, as she pulls away an oversized bag housing her heated blanket. "I'm going to plug this into the USB port in the Jeep. I made sure to pick a rental that had one."

"Of course, you did," I say. "And I love benefiting from your type-A personality."

We laugh.

Vince tosses his duffle bag to the ground beside the trunk and relieves me of my large hard-top suitcase and its matching carry-on.

"Oh, geez," says Johnny, admiring the extent of our baggage. "I guess a little game of luggage Tetris is required." Digging into the trunk, he rearranges his backpack and Bryanne's small carry-on to make more room.

I cup my hands and blow hot air into them.

"We've got this. You girls get in and get warm," says Vince.

"I Googled October weather here," says Bryanne. "Apparently, umbrella season's in full bloom." She pats a tall handle sticking out of her purse. "And, yes, I'll share mine with you, Gabbi. Johnny packed his own."

Of course, he did. I look up at the gloomy sky. "What makes you think I didn't bring one?"

"Did you?" asks Bryanne.

We both giggle.

"Let's get in, B. It's ten degrees out, at best, and the air's as damp as towel-dried hair."

"Yup, I'm chilled to the bone," Bryanne says. "And that's pretty much all I consist of these days." The awkwardness for her audience is a small price to pay for the relief her dark humour grants her.

From the backseat, the SUV is spacious, clean, and comfy.

"Straight to Squamish?" Johnny asks while plunking the destination into the navigation system.

"No!" Bryanne and I shout simultaneously.

"Coffee—" she starts.

"—and something to eat—" I add.

"—first!" we finish together.

Johnny starts driving away from the airport, and I settle into the roomy seat and look out the window.

12009.

My street address from over two decades ago suddenly dominates my mind. What the hell? That can't possibly be the correct address. But I know it is. Without prompt or query, without any attempt to recall it. Inadvertently remembering such an arbitrary fact strikes me as highly suspicious. I try but am slow to conjure up what I ate for dinner last night, for Pete's sake. No. I didn't "remember" that address. *He* planted that memory.

Stewart Street. 12009 Stewart Street.

Can't be. But it is. And it pulls me. Draws me in. Slowly but steadily, like quicksand. Against my will, everything in my being needs to go there. 12009. I feel it calling me. Can see the L-shaped, two-storey building, smell the mixture of detergents and dryer sheets from the main floor communal laundry room. I taste orange Kool-Aid. I feel the sand starting to suffocate me. The compulsion to go there and see it now with my grownup eyes, to show my family, to tell my story—it's almost overpowering. If I don't go back, if they don't see it, too, was it ever really real? What if I try to introduce my family to this concealed part of my past, this part of myself, but the physical building fails me, too, like everything and everyone else from its time failed me so long ago? What if a Starbucks is in its place? Like it never existed. Like that part of my life and that part of me never existed. I feel like an addict being pulled back to my drug of choice. But I didn't choose that. Did I ever have a choice? The perfect storm can come for anyone.

"Hello? Earth to Gabbi? Anybody home?"

Bryanne touches my knee. I flinch. We're sharing her heated blanket.

I look at her. "What?"

"Where were you just now?" She squints her eyes.

I shrug. Visiting Hell. Looking past her, out her window, I try figuring out where we are. "Burnaby? We're already in Burnaby?" I blurt out. I can't believe I missed it. So lost in the past, I didn't even notice the city sign for Maple Ridge as we passed it in the present. Tears come.

Stop it. Don't be silly. A little part of me wants to beg Johnny to turn the car around. Plea with them to go back there with me. Brave it together. In this family, nobody fights alone. Not anymore, anyway. This little part of me wants to show and tell. *Look. This is it. This is where we lived. This is where a part of me died.*

"Grouse Mountain," says Bryanne.

"What?"

"We're meeting Mom, Dad, Tara, and Warren at Grouse Mountain."

"Only twenty-six minutes away," adds Johnny from the driver's seat.

"What's wrong?" asks Bryanne.

"Nothing. I just wanted to show you guys something, but we already passed it." 12009. I consider Google Earth. No. Let it be. Let it still be there; let it be gone. I remember the secrets it keeps.

"Oh. Well, let's see whatever it is on our way back on Monday."

"Okay."

Please come back and get me. Please save me; take me with you. Please don't leave me here any longer.

Chapter 2

Alex

My drive to and from work was long, an hour minimum each way. I passed the time listening to audio books or singing along to the radio. The daily two-hour commute brought me some peace; I absorbed the oranges and pinks and purples as the sun rolled over the hills, waking the bright yellow canola fields, brightening the wide-open Alberta prairie sky. Cows and horses stretched and grazed, a coyote stalked a deer, and the occasional moose got far too close. I considered myself a city girl by night who had access to the country highlights by day. As I always left home in the early mornings when it was still dark outside, the drive allowed me to fully awaken and prepare for my guaranteed-to-be-crazy day counselling kindergarten through Grade 12 students struggling with social, emotional, and familial issues.

Despite the sense of peace I felt for most of the drive, the last twenty minutes always carpooled anxiety. My refusal to wake up any earlier than 6 a.m. meant I risked being late every single day. By the time I approached the hay plant, anxiety had climbed into the back seat. As I passed the cemetery on the hill at the very outskirts of the little town, it rode shotgun. At the bend in the road by the graveyard, I picked up speed, ignoring the posted 80 km/h to make it on time. When the speed limit dropped down again to 50 km/h, I was grateful no school-zone speed limit was posted.

I glanced at the time as I put my car in park at the finish line. 7:55

a.m. Excellent. I apprehensively scoped out the staff room window. Jane waved in my direction. Spotted arriving "early." Fabulous. Proud, I acknowledged Jane with a grin. I grabbed my coffee and purse as I exited and shut my car door. Never one to make more than one trip, regardless of the size of the load, I leaned in to grab my laptop and lunch bag from the trunk, and my work cell and notebook fell out of my purse. I straightened and tucked my wild, frizzy hair behind my ears.

"Alex."

Startled, I dropped my coffee cup to the ground. I sighed and closed my eyes long enough to grieve my coffee's premature death then turned to see Jane approaching me.

"Morning," she greeted. "I'm glad I caught you before the bell." She held out a folded note.

"What's that?" I asked, as I picked up my empty cup.

Jane thrust the note into my hand. "It's heartbreaking. Read it."

I unfolded the handwritten note and read it. My heart swelled. I looked up at Jane. "Jesus. Who wrote this?"

"I'm not entirely sure. I have a new student in my class. I found it on the floor by her desk," Jane explained. "I planned on referring her to you anyway, actually."

"Oh?" I retrieved my phone and notebook, swung my laptop bag over my shoulder, and slammed the trunk. My lunch had rolled out of reach, and I wasn't about to waste any more time grasping at air trying to dig it out. I rarely ate lunch anyway. Crises didn't allow breaks.

Jane continued, "Well, I've been keeping an eye on her for the last few weeks. She's always distracted, totally withdrawn, and I catch her tearing up a lot. Sometimes in class, sometimes by her locker. I tried to speak with her after class one day, but she hurried out and straight into the bathroom. She didn't come out for so long I finally gave up. I tried the following few days after class, but she always heads straight to the washroom and stays in there for the entire lunch break. I think she's eating her lunches in there. Like, in a stall. Anyway, yesterday I found that note." Jane looked at her watch. "I've got to go. Chat more later."

I headed for the main entrance of the school after Jane, who walked faster, ahead of me. The bell rang as I burst through the door.

Still technically on time. I rushed down the hall greeting staff members on the way to my office. I tried three keys before finding my office door's perfect match. As I pushed it open, it shoveled a clear path through the pile of referral forms and "I Want to See You" appointment request slips. I hadn't yet turned on the light, and already my day was overflowing. I tossed my laptop bag on my chair and tucked my purse on the shelf behind my desk. My work area looked like a Post-it note factory; my telephone flashed and beeped like R2-D2.

A head popped in my office doorway. "Good morning, Alex. Looks like it'll be another busy day for you."

Nothing got by Jessica.

Jessica turned on the lights and studied the thermostat. "It's as hot as a sauna in here. Do you realize it's set at twenty-five degrees?"

I turned on the space heater under my desk. "Sure do. Would you mind turning it up to twenty-six for me, please? My feet are like two ice blocks."

Ignoring the request, Jessica picked up the counselling requests and scanned the names. "I bet you have poor circulation."

"Thanks. I'll look into that. Is there something I can help you with?"

"Oh, I just wanted to fill you in on some juicy student gossip." Although a self-proclaimed secret keeper, Jessica only shared secrets. And although it was true that Jessica knew the most gossip, I knew the most truth. The deepest, darkest, most painful truths. I knew more about the students than Jessica ever would.

The second bell rang.

"Sorry. I've got to get these names to the office," I said, as I grabbed my appointment book and a handful of blank appointment slips. "Catch me later."

Not long after Jessica left my office entered the sigh of a little voice: "Hi." A young girl stood in the doorway wrapping her uneven, seemingly self-chopped hair around her finger. Her tights were filthy and missing knees. She was an adorable disaster.

"Hi, love," I said.

"Can me and my sister talk to you?"

I nodded and patted the spot beside me on the couch.

The young girl waved to collect her sibling from the hallway, and together they inched their way over to join me. The youngest girl chomped a huge wad of gum like it was a chunk out of her bike tire. As the eldest got closer to me, her chin tilted downward.

I collected her with a small smile and scrunched-up nose.

The youngest girl plopped her bum down on the couch and released a sigh far too loud to come from such a teeny person. Her big sister stood in between us.

"What's your name?" I asked.

"Kristen," said the eldest.

"What grade are you girls in?"

"I'm in Grade Two. Rosslynn's in Grade One."

"Nice to meet you."

"We hate Hanson."

I kept on my best curious face.

"Mom's new boyfriend."

"What don't you like about him?"

"He's really mean to us."

"How so?"

"He calls us names . . . and other stuff."

Blending families wasn't easy. For most kids, the hardest part about the separation of their families was adjusting to their parents dating new people.

I gathered as much information as I could from Kristen, but she didn't give much for me to go on without me reading between the lines. Rosslynn let her big sister do most of the talking. I needed more. I explained to the girls that their mother had to provide consent for them to see me and asked if it would be okay for me to give her a call.

"You gots to call before Hanson gets home from work," said Rosslynn.

"I can do that." I noticed a high school client pacing back and forth outside my door. I refocused my attention on the sisters. "Okay, girls. I'll give your mom a call right after I see what that big kid out there needs, okay?"

Both girls looked out to the hallway and nodded.

"Now, chop, chop, back to class."

Rosslynn giggled. "You're funny. I like you."

"I like you, too. Now hurry, hurry, scurry, scurry."

After Rosslyn and Kristen left, I went to the door of my office to beckon in the high school student, but the girl had disappeared.

I stepped out and looked both ways down the hall to be sure then returned to my desk to call the sisters' mother.

"I just . . . I don't really think it's a good idea," the woman said, sounding scattered.

A pit grew in my stomach.

"Oftentimes, just being able to talk about their feelings with someone outside of their family is helpful," I said.

"Well . . . yes . . . that makes sense, I guess. But . . . well . . . I don't know . . . Um . . . ya, no . . . they just can't. You can't. I'm sorry . . . it's just not going to be possible. I'm . . . I'm sorry."

Click. The line went dead.

The convoluted conversation made me fear the family had something to hide. But without more information or parental consent, there was nothing more I could do for now.

The lunch bell rang. Having a little free time to eat, I raised my fork to my mouth.

"I was right!"

Startled, I stabbed myself in the cheek with the fork, smearing salad dressing across my face.

Jane looked practically hysterical as she marched through my office door and right up to my desk, where I sat, salad momentarily forgotten in front of me. "It's definitely hers. The new girl I told you about this morning. I didn't know for sure, but the first creative writing assignment I gave my class was due today." She flapped a stapled bunch of papers in her right hand. "Check this out," she said, handing it over. "I read it as soon as the bell rang and put two and two together. That note was definitely hers. Poor kid."

I glanced down at the title page. A shiver prickled up my spine.

"I thought you should have it right away so you had a chance to read it before you start your afternoon."

I couldn't take my eyes off the title page.

Jane pursed her lips. "I strongly suggested she see you, but she adamantly refused. At first, she said she didn't want to miss any class time. But when I suggested she could probably see you over lunch break, or after school, she started crying and said she doesn't trust counsellors at all, or anyone, for that matter. So, I'm hoping you'll find a way to work your magic."

I took the papers, and Jane headed back out of my office, but when she reached the door, she stopped and turned back. "Honestly, Alex," she paused, "I don't know how you do your job. I could never."

"Thanks, Jane. That means a lot."

I always appreciated when people offered humble adoration. Because my job was hard. But my clients' lives were much harder, and I was uniquely equipped to help them—and not just because of my two degrees and close to a decade of therapeutic training. I didn't just talk the talk. I had also walked the walk. My office filing cabinet hid the pen-to-paper proof of my own painful past. Locked up safe and sound, it housed my decade-old top-secret diary, in which I had documented some of my most tender and traumatic times as a teenager.

Chapter 3

Katee

"Sean? Whadda you mean, he's going to kill me?"

I heard a gulp on the other end of the phone. "Katee, I swear, I'm telling the truth . . ."

"I believe you. But . . . what the hell should I do?" I rolled out the computer desk chair and sat down.

Sean resumed, "Whatever you do, hide. Hide good. We're still at the bar. He's fucking plastered. Ranting on and on about taking you out then fleeing Ontario for good. He's even plotting it out on some folded-up lined paper he pulled outta his pocket. He's a psycho. I'm trying to stall him. You've got at least two hours. He's making me bring him. We're coming to get you."

It was New Year's Eve, and I was nineteen years old. I hung up on Sean and called 911.

Operator:	"Emergency. Do you require police, fire, or ambulance?"
Me:	"Police? My ex-boyfriend is coming to kill me."
Operator:	"What is your location?"

Me:	"Well, I'm two hours away from him, but he's on his way here."
Operator:	"What's your name and location?"
Me:	"I'm at my parents' house." I provided the details.
Operator:	"Where is the suspect now?"
Me:	"He's at a bar in Burlington. Our mutual friend called to warn me. I'm so scared."
Operator:	"You're doing great, Katee. We will get you some help as soon as possible. Do you know which bar he's at?"
Me:	"No. Maybe Club Fifty-Four? They're having a big New Year's Eve party for their tenth anniversary. Or, actually, probably Philthy McNasty's . . .? But I'm not sure."
Operator:	"Were any weapons mentioned in the death threat?"
Me:	"I don't think so . . . but I didn't ask."
Operator:	"It's okay. You're doing great. Does he have access to any weapons?"
Me:	"He carries a large switchblade with him at all times."
Operator:	"OK. Did he say why he wants to kill you?"
Me:	"Because I won't take him back. And I'm dating someone new. Said if he can't have me, no one can. We broke up five months ago. He's really violent. If you check with the RCMP, you'll find reports from when we lived together."
Operator:	"OK. Was he charged for any of those domestic disturbances?"

Me:	"No. But for lots of other stuff over his life. He's spent lots of time in jail. But wouldn't there be records of the calls and incidents from BC that involve me?"
Operator:	"What's his name?"
	I provided his first, middle, and last name.
Operator:	"Do you know his birthday?"
Me:	"November twelfth." I gave the birth year.
Operator:	"OK, does he have access to a vehicle?"
Me:	"Pardon me?"
Operator:	"I need a description of the vehicle he's driving."
Me:	"Oh, yes. And I know the plate number." I provided the make, model, colour, and license plate details.
Operator:	"Who is that talking in the background?"
Me:	"My friend, Allison."
Operator:	"OK. Are you still safe? What's she's saying? What's going on?"
Me:	"Um, she's scared. She wants to leave. Go to her house."
Operator:	"The questions I'm asking are not slowing down police response. Does your ex know where Allison lives?"
Me:	"No. Her parents' place is even more in the middle of nowhere than mine. About ten-fifteen minutes from here. He's never been there. Would never find it."
Operator:	"OK. Do you have a way of getting to her house?"
Me:	"Yeah. She has a car."

Operator:	"OK. First, I need to get a description of your ex."
Me:	"He's white. Good-looking."
Operator:	"OK, how tall is he?"
Me:	"He's, like, six-one, six-two, tops. And muscular."
Operator:	"Any idea what he might be wearing?"
Me:	"He always wears this oversized, boxy, black leather jacket. Listen, my friend is freaking out. Says she'll leave without me if I don't hurry."
Operator:	"We're almost done. Any idea what else he might be wearing?"
Me:	"Um, I'm not sure. Likely light blue jeans with a silver wallet chain."
Operator:	"OK. So, you're going to Allison's house now?"
Me:	"Yeah."
Operator:	"What's her address and phone number so police can reach you?"
	I gave the operator the details.
Operator:	"OK. I've notified the Halton Regional Police Service. An officer will be dispatched as soon as possible. Get to Allison's house and stay there until police contact you. Call us back immediately if anything changes or you have any more information."

Chapter 4

Gabbi

We arrive at the parking lot at the base of Grouse Mountain to meet up with the rest of the family before spending the remainder of the day losing ourselves via exploration of North Vancouver and deep conversation.

"Look at them piling out of that clown car," snickers Johnny. He's pointing a few stalls down and a parking row closer to the payment machine he just returned from. "Glad we splurged and got a sizeable luxury vehicle."

I spot the rest of our family exiting their tiny two-door rental car; the comical scene does not disappoint. I watch as the four of them, three over six feet tall and my mom not far off—and my parents both senior citizens—struggle to unpack themselves from the sardine can of a car.

"Oh my gosh," I say as I hurry over to offer my mom a hand.

"Thanks, honey," she says, as she regains her balance and gives me a long hug. "I'm just thrilled to be spending this time with you. With all three of my girls."

"Me, too, Mom. It's exactly what we need."

She squeezes my hand twice.

I squeeze back once.

Warren greets Vince with a couple solid whacks on the back.

Bryanne listens to our dad's Ted Talk du jour. Johnny stands off at his usual spot on the perimeter of our gathering and nods awkwardly at the others as they say their hellos to him.

As we head back to the rental cars at the end of the day, Tara's boyfriend, Warren, suggests two more stops prior to heading to the hotel for the night.

"Just follow us," Warren says to Johnny. "I grew up in this area. I want to make a quick stop at a friend's place on our way to our last destination."

We arrive in a residential area and pull over behind the others at the curb in front of a huge house. Warren exits their rental car and signals us to wait in ours. "I'll just run in quick."

He disappears into the front door for several minutes and returns with a bag.

"Grabbed us some sneaky beverages from my buddy's place to enjoy at the surprise location." He passes out canned coolers.

We turn onto Capilano Road. A bit farther down the road I spot a sign for the Capilano River Regional Park. We turn in and experience a kilometer of tranquility.

The short drive is mythical, quickly turning the country's third largest urban area into a place so secluded and serene it seems we're in a world of make-believe. Lush golden light sprays the forest. Tall trees wave in the mist. Lady fern, twisted stalk, and moss in every shade of green imaginable blanket the ground. The colourful scenery is as diverse, vivid, and bold as a box of pencil crayons. So mystical that I half expect fairies to grace us with their presence at any moment. The road ends at the Capilano River Hatchery. The building is already closed for the day, but the magic of the forest remains fully alive around us.

We park the cars, crack some coolers, and head to the closest viewing platform. The autumn air feels cool and damp. We get to the edge and look upstream. Salmon leap out of the river. The canyon's banks are steep and appear slippery. Some areas are marked with danger signs and fenced off. Unsure as to what Bryanne's neuropathy will allow her to do, we choose to stick to a short, easy trail. Starting near the hatchery, we cross two bridges. At the first bridge, a handful of men are fly-fishing below. A tug of war breaks out between man and fish. The fisherman struggles. The fish wins.

An overly excitable, wet, and filthy dog playfully jumps at Warren, interrupting the show.

"Oh my goodness! He's so cute!" My sisters, our mom, and I all gush over the dog.

"He's a real chick magnet," his owner tells us. We agree but burst into laughter once our mom points out the dog's initial attraction to Warren.

As we continue our walk, scenic views of the river and steep-sided canyon are the promised reward, but the real gift is experiencing a little piece of Heaven on Earth together. This lush coastal rainforest feels like the kind of place capable of granting miracles. As we walk beneath towering Douglas fir and western red cedar trees, listening to the roar of the Capilano River, it's impossible to forget the heaviness surrounding our family even momentarily. Our uncharacteristic silence says it all. Bryanne gazes into the distance. The rest of us take turns binding her in this moment to our memories and exchanging ominous glances with one another. My mom shakes her head at me, and tears fill her eyes. I collect her hand and guide her forward for a private moment out of Bryanne's vicinity.

"I just feel so helpless," my mom says to me when we reach a safe distance out of earshot of the others.

"I know. But we'll love her through this, Mom."

She nods. We embrace.

Moss is literally everywhere. And I love moss. Always have. Feeling chilled to the bone, I imagine blanketing myself in it for warmth. The cold damp starts to get to all of us, especially Bryanne. Someone suggests leaving, but she says it's such an otherwise perfect moment she'll happily struggle through the increasing discomfort just a little longer. A bench beckons Bryanne's sore feet, and she asks for help getting to it for a much-needed rest.

Vince points out how this spot encompasses so many of my favourite things: moss; quality time; fall with its colours, crisp air, and required clothing; travel; road trips; animals; salmon; mountains; and fairies, even if invisible to the eye. He promises to end the night spoiling me with other favourites that top my list: pasta with copious amounts of spicy red sauce, cheese, and sparkling rose.

"This is one of the absolute best days of my life," I profess.

Vince pulls me close and whispers in my ear, "All of the best days of my life have been with you."

After we're finally in our respective rooms at the Fairmont Waterfront Vancouver and heading to bed, I realize I didn't think about Maple Ridge or *him* for the rest of the day. Not even once until this moment for a fleeting congratulation. My ex has caused my family and me enough devastation and damage for a lifetime. My thirty-five-year-old little sister doesn't have much life left. I will not allow *him* to infiltrate what cherished little time we still have with her.

Chapter 5

Alex

Jessica burst into my office. "Have you seen that girl yet?"

"Jesus. You scared me half to death." I put the lid on my pen and set it down.

Jessica peeked down both sides of the hallway before shutting my door behind her. "I've been trying to catch you all day. You're always so, so busy. Anywho, I finally saw your door open, so I thought I'd pop in and fill you in on the latest news." She walked over to the couches.

"Right," I said. "Were you wanting to refer a student to me?"

"Didn't Jane refer her to you at lunch? I saw her come in here. Somebody sure should. Just listen to this."

I joined Jessica in the seating area. "Okay. You've got my attention." I waited, clipboard in hand to take notes. "What's the student's name and grade?" I played dumb to ensure I didn't release any confidential information.

"That new girl in Jane's class."

I put on my best confused face.

"Grace. She's in Grade Twelve."

I jotted down the name, grade, and referral source.

"Apparently, she went from honour roll to dropout. How does something like that even happen? Top of her class to repeating the grade. Can you believe it? I heard she moved far away with a boy. Scandalous, right?"

I considered my next words carefully. "It's not so unbelievable. But how do you know any of this is actually true?"

"I knew you were going to ask that. So, I did some fact-checking first. Apparently, the girl's mother pulled some strings to get her in here—especially as a 'mature student.'" Jessica air quoted this. "She should have graduated last year. Her mom drives her in from out of district every day. Why? Why not just go back to her local high school? Very interesting."

I shrugged.

"Well." Jessica stood and headed to the door. "You'll have to keep me posted."

I had no intention of keeping Jessica posted. But I did intend to get to the truth of this gossip whirlwind. I couldn't help but wonder what had happened to this new girl. How had her situation gotten to this point? How had this young girl become the focus of such gossip and rumours? And so quickly? The girl's story sounded freakily familiar. To say I felt triggered was an understatement.

More and more often, I found myself stuck between feeling for the teens I worked with and feeling for their parents. I wouldn't relive my high school years for any amount of money, but parenting adolescents couldn't be easy, either. Lord knows I had been no treat. Truth be told, I'd been downright awful. But over the last decade, especially the last few years, I'd not only made more of an effort but had become intentional about nurturing my relationship with my own parents—my mother, specifically. Being in this profession, I knew the importance and value in healing old family wounds. My mom and I had been in a good place for the better part of a decade, but past hurts still lingered in both of our hearts. Never too late for awareness, I glanced at the clock then rang my mother.

"Hello?"

"Hi, Mom. How are you?"

"Alex, hello. I'm okay, I guess. How are you, sunshine?"

"I'm just shy of excellent, thanks," I replied.

My mother laughed. "Well, that's good."

"It's something I'm making an effort to say and thus put out to the universe."

"I see. Good idea."

We both chuckled.

"But more importantly," I paused, as I twisted the phone cord around my finger, "I'm calling to apologize, yet again, for being such an asshole as a teen." I couldn't help but tear up. "I had so many messed-up things happening to me at that time, Mom." I took a deep breath. "Things that in fairness you knew nothing about. Things I've still never told you guys—" I paused, but my mother remained silent, so I continued, "—and I didn't handle it well. I had so many confusing, mixed feelings, but anger felt safest, and I'm really sorry I took so much of that out on you." I shuffled some paperwork around my desk while I waited for my mom to respond.

After a long pause, my mother asked, "New kiddo on your caseload tugging at your heartstrings?"

"Yup." I sat back in my chair and swiveled it side to side.

"You know, honey, the truth is, I had so much I was struggling with at that time. Things I was running away from," she paused then said more quietly, "if you know what I mean."

My father must have been in earshot of her.

"Yes. I know that now."

"Well, I couldn't very well tell you then. You were all so young. It wasn't appropriate."

"I know, Mom. Of course, not."

"And I've come to realize how me not coping so well with my situation likely impacted my ability to be there for you. I didn't even notice things I normally would have, probably should have. I suppose I was neglectful in ways."

I couldn't believe what I was hearing. Joint ownership.

"Mom. You did the best you could. I know that now. Considering the magnitude and complexity of everything going on, neither one of us being privy to the struggles of the other, and both of us taking it personally."

"I wasn't focusing enough or noticing how you were feeling even though you had certainly expressed your unhappiness. But to me, it was like I had to walk carefully around you. I wasn't sure when you were feeling okay or when you were going to blow up and we were going to argue."

I mindlessly massaged my earlobe. "We were both just trying to survive, Mom. You pulled away; I lashed out. Maybe subconsciously my escalation was an attempt to show you just how big and overwhelming my feelings were for me. To be taken seriously. But, in turn, it backfired and made you pull in and away even more."

"Perhaps. But, honey, my recollection is more about where my brain was about my situation then. I was so caught up in all my angst that a lot of what was going on with you I guess was overlooked in a way because I was so shocked and devastated about what was going on with your father and her."

"I know that now, Mom. But I didn't know about that then."

"Do you remember that night?" My mother's voice had hardened.

"Vaguely. But it didn't make sense to me until Dad told me years later."

"Did you see them together in the basement?"

I took a deep breath. "No."

"I was so anxious and gutted. It had been going on for years. And still having to see her all the time after finding out? Watching her give you kids tons of attention and playing with you, hugging you? It felt like my feelings didn't matter."

"We didn't know, Mom."

"I know. That was just my headspace at the time."

"It was a perfect storm of individual, unrelated circumstances that forced us to simultaneously struggle separately in silence. We both felt powerless, hurt, anxious, and depressed. We both thought we were alone, invisible, broken, and that we weren't enough."

"Quite the team."

We broke into laughter.

I heard a knock at my office door and glanced at the time. My next client was early.

"Mom, thanks for being so raw and vulnerable. I really appreciate your honesty. Sharing your realization with me is so meaningful, so healing. I've spent years beating myself up about how awful I was . . ."

"You were just a kid, Magoo. You were just a kid."

"And you were just human, Mom."

"Oh, I almost forgot. Some mail came here for you. I put the two letters in a bigger envelope and posted it to you last week."

"Two? Bizarre. It's been years since anything has come there for me."

"Yup. They're both from your old work," my mom said. "I completely forgot about the first one until the second one showed up a week later."

"Old work?"

"Yup."

"Really? That's super weird." I couldn't think for the life of me what on earth my old work would need to contact me about. Pension stuff, maybe? A new job opportunity?

"Shit!" my mother yelled. Then she laughed. "Pun unintentional."

"What?"

"Miss Poopy Pants Moxie just shit on the floor in her sleep again."

"Another sneaky poo."

"Well, she's old. Thank God it's not diarrhea. I've got to let you go. I need to get her outside and get it cleaned up."

"You enjoy that. Love you, Mom. Thanks for the talk."

"It was helpful for me, too, Magoo. Love you."

Waiting on my doorstep when I arrived home from work sat a parcel. I treasured the rare occasion I received a package, or better, a card filled with loads of handwritten affection. For me, words of affirmation beat gifts almost every time. Receiving mail as a kid usually meant birthday or Christmas money. But as an adult, mail was almost always a request for money. A whack of never-ending bills and depressing monthly bank statements. But I still held childish hope when receiving mail.

I picked up the box and brought it inside. I recognized my mother's beautiful handwriting and excessive tape job. People always commented on doctors' awful penmanship but never the perfection of teachers'. After cutting through the superfluous security, I discovered a box full of goodies. It housed a thoughtful note written on cute cat stationary, a stunning table runner surely sewn by my mother, and a bag of dog treats with a sticker reading "Yoshi." Underneath it all, I found a bunch of my mother's leftover school stickers and something that looked completely out of place: two small white envelopes. Handwritten in pencil, they displayed my name followed by my parents' address in eerily familiar printing, certainly not the penmanship of any past colleagues.

I flipped over one of the letters and noticed unnervingly recognizable artwork. I dropped it as though scalded. It landed on the second letter. I picked up the first letter again and warily turned it over. More drawings. Hearts with stars in them. Flower vines framing the envelope. More hearts with stars. A treble clef and staff filled with music notes. The name of our song.

I released the letter to join its predecessor. I reached for my eyelashes and started twisting them between my middle finger and thumb. Why would *he* contact me after all this time? Thank God *he* thought I was still staying with my parents. Although I certainly didn't want *him* anywhere near them, either.

"Ouch," I said, pulling my hand away from my face. I'd tugged at my eyelashes too hard and plucked one out. I looked at it and saw its white bulb root. I flicked it to the floor before switching to tug at my eyebrows instead. Pulling them out never hurt.

Chapter 6

Katee

After calling 911, I couldn't help but wonder—why me? And how? How had I gotten myself into this mess? How had this somehow become my life? My endangered life.

Things in my life had started unraveling when I was fourteen, and the events over the years that followed groomed me for a predator and led me to this moment: fearing for my life at only nineteen years old.

I wasn't born Katee. I was born someone else. Becoming Katee was a slow, painful process, essential for survival. To understand how I got here—a terrified nineteen-year-old frantically calling 911 to report a threat against my life—we need to go back nearly six years in time. Back to when my family didn't so much resemble a modern-day Brady Bunch as we did a story on *The Jerry Springer Show*. Back to when things started happening that ultimately broke the person I used to be and forced me to become the person I was now.

If anyone ever asked me, not that anyone ever did, I would say part of me died a month after my fourteenth birthday, when my family kidnapped me from my home in the city and transported me against my will to butt-fart nowhere land. I had everything going for me in the city: I had a lifelong best friend I'd met at the diaper truck; I was the "it girl" in the most popular posse at school; and, of course, I had my Grade 6 boyfriend. Yes, we'd broken up in Grade 7 after a year-long steamy romance, but I knew one day I'd win him back. Until we moved so bloody far away.

It felt like everyone I'd ever known suddenly died. At first, I didn't really believe we were going to move. Like, I knew it was happening, but it didn't seem real. It seemed more of a fun game of sorts. A bigger house? With two additional bedrooms and bathrooms? And a sauna inside the house? And side-by-side double showers in the basement? Yes, please. I loved fantasizing about the possibilities this new dream home could offer even if I despised its extremely uncool country location. I would certainly not be riding a horse to and from school. No, sir.

But as time went on, and there were fewer rooms to empty and less boxes left to pack, I started getting seriously pissed off. How could my parents rip me away from everyone and everything I'd ever known my entire life? It made no sense. In fact, it was so stupid, I decided I'd have no part of it. I would stay. I'd live with a friend's family, at minimum to finish off the last three months of Grade 8 and enjoy the upcoming summer. Allowing this was the least my parents could do. Like, really, what kind of parents uprooted their kids in the middle of a school year? Especially a teacher mom? Unheard of. So, I would just stay back for a while. They owed me that.

But, apparently, they owed me nothing, not even the time to listen to my thoughts, feelings, wants, and needs. Every genius proposition I presented them with was met with a firm no and an insulting bribe. The first was the promise of a puppy—clever and tempting, as we weren't allowed a dog in the city. But I said no deal. They ignored me and named the new pup Shasta. Their next dumb bribe was that they would still allow me to attend my Grade 8 graduation trip with my old friends. That had never been *not* happening. I'd spent a whole year selling cheese to fundraise for that. Their final attempt before giving up on getting me onboard with the move was a promise to check out the closest town's theatre. I loved acting but refused to join a theatre that was a joke in comparison to the infamous Young People's Theatre of Toronto.

Clearly, nobody cared about me, much less the fact that they were literally destroying my life.

The dreaded day finally came, and as we drove farther and farther away, I lost the will to fight any longer. All I could muster were tears of futility, which extinguished the last flicker of my spark. I tried keeping track of where we were and how we were getting to wherever the hell we were going, but trying to read every road sign and make note of every turn just made my stomach toss. Everyone knew I suffered from car sickness, yet, clearly, no one cared. As the never-ending path to get there continued on and on, I felt more and more lost. I imagined tossing breadcrumbs out the window, but, of course, I didn't even have any snacks. I lay my sick, sweaty head on the cold window. When other cars passed ours, I made my most scared-looking face and mouthed the word *Help* in hopes they'd think I'd been kidnapped and rescue me. But they didn't care about me, either.

Even if anyone had cared about me, it wasn't like they'd have been able to find me. No one had heard of the tiny town we were moving to, much less actually been there. Its name was stupid, dumber than Mississippi, which at least all kids knew how to spell. There was no catchy tune to help with the spelling and pronunciation of this shithole. I vowed to refer to it as "the armpit of Ontario."

Speaking of tunes, we drove in complete silence. I asked my mom to turn on the radio in hopes that singing oldies together would lighten the sourpuss mood, but my mom refused.

After an hour of driving, we arrived. The new house was stuck smack dab in the middle of one hundred and eight acres with a driveway over a half mile long and the closest town a twenty-minute drive away. Everyone but me loved it.

My little sisters, pathetically easy to please and impress, were sold on getting a puppy and rooms of their own. Gullible, simple-minded amateurs. I, however, was banished to the main level of the house and assigned a room that wasn't even a bedroom. It was tiny and didn't even have a closet. But I'd agreed to it after considering its one advantage; it was right by the front door. So, in my fantasies about running away in the middle of the night, it was easy access for an escape. But between the pitch-black sky, the terrifying howls, and the fact that I no longer lived right by the city train line, my fantasies ended there.

After spending the entire weekend in bed, refusing to unpack, I woke up with puffy, swollen-shut eyes for my first day at my new school. As I still wasn't allowed to wear makeup, I cursed my parents for ruining any chance I might have had to possibly turn this shitty situation around by at least making some new, cool friends.

Although I refused to show it, I was totally terrified as I strutted my stuff into school and tried to find my classroom without looking like a total newbie. My new teacher called me up in front of the entire class. He told them where I'd moved from, bragged about my amazing grades from my last school, and told my classmates they should all aspire to be a stellar student like me. I nearly passed out from mortification. If that wasn't bad enough, a mean-looking girl at the back of the room loudly called me a citiot, and everyone laughed. Another kid shouted that I was a suck-up teacher's pet, and the class chanted, "Citiot suck-up, citiot suck-up." I fought back hot tears.

By the end of my first day, my fate was sealed. A girl had stolen my brand-new Nike shoes, another bribe from my parents, and worn them for gym class while I was forced to sit out because I didn't have any runners. Even the kind-looking kids avoided making eye contact; the girl seated next to me explained via a whisper that the two most popular girls had given warning shots to keep me a social pariah. Now that I was invisible, I remorsefully thought about whether there'd been any kids at my old school I had never really noticed. On the bus ride home, an older girl seated behind me spat gum in my hair, topping off the day.

I spent the remaining three months of the school year with my head down. I avoided going out for recess by volunteering to maintain the school fish tanks and help the custodian. It was official—no one liked me. I had become a complete loser, an absolute nobody. I counted down the days until my reprieve from this hell and welcomed the transition to the upgraded punishment of two summer months stuck at home, even though I felt no more visible or wanted there.

After about a year, I settled in okay, for the most part. But the truth was I never felt like I truly fit in, not at school and not at home. I bumped around between various cliques but made few close friends. I felt more and more distant from my family but managed to stay in my parents' good books most of the time.

My parents barely spoke to one another. Instead, they enmeshed themselves in my sisters' lives. Driving back and forth between Beth's tutoring and swim lessons and Leigh's horseback riding lessons and basketball games ate up all my parents' time. Even though they bitched about it non-stop, I sensed they secretly loved it. These time-consuming tasks not only kept our parents away from me but also from one another.

Also, my dad was still obsessed with our old church, yet in the months before our move, my mom suddenly refused to go or have any more contact with the churchgoers. My sisters and I had been forbidden, too. Secretly, I thanked God for this true blessing. Amen and adios.

I knew what love looked and felt like, and my parents' marriage certainly wasn't it. A divorce would have solved all their problems—and most certainly have solved mine. My parents were just not compatible. My dad always pawed at my mom for hugs and affection, yet my mom would quite literally cringe at his touch. It was painful to watch my father deflate after each failed attempt even though I selfishly preferred this to the gross alternative of disgusting parental public displays of affection. My dad once told me he'd known after the first night he and my mother met that she would never be the touchy-feely type of his dreams, yet he'd married her anyway.

Even on the rare occasions our whole family was home, my mother chose isolation in her bedroom over being with—sometimes even eating with—the rest of us. The house was full of seclusion, passive-aggressive sighs, silent treatments, and nasty negativity.

Overall, I felt unloved, and eventually, completely unlovable. Since I failed miserably to get love at home or from my female peers, I hungrily searched for it from boys at school. I began to obsess over the last time I'd felt special, beautiful, important, and seen and heard by someone. His name was Matt. He'd been my Grade 6 boyfriend, and I couldn't stop thinking about him. Yes, that had ended, like, three years before, but I knew it had been true love. I'd loved him, and he had loved me. Our love had been very grown up. We'd spent every recess together at school, we'd gone to every monthly preteen dance together and pocket danced the nights away, and on one occasion, we'd even broken out of our homes after our parents had gone to bed to meet up for a late-night rendezvous. We'd always held hands and often gotten in trouble from teachers for French kissing in the back field during lunch breaks. Grade 6 had been, hands down, the absolute best year of my entire life. I'd known how much Matt had loved me, and it had been a wonderful feeling I'd never felt before him or since.

So, that became my mission: to find true love again. I was determined. My search for love became an obsession.

Most of the boys teased me about my giantess height and bee-sting boobs, as they called them. When they saw me racing to class, they'd holler for me not to be late for the itty-bitty titty committee. And so, my struggle with body image issues began. To make matters worse, my first crush after moving to the armpit of Ontario teased me the worst. On top of that, there was an older boy on my bus who flirted hard with me in private—almost an hour each day on the way to school and almost an hour each day on the ride home—making me feel sexy and wanted, but in public, he teased me, too.

I wanted so badly to be loved that when a boy named Declan, who totally grossed me out, started hitting on me, I decided to suck it up. He dressed a little grungier than the other guys, and his hands were always dirty. He had little, beady eyes, lots of freckles, and awful teeth—all crooked, spaced apart, and discoloured from the chewing tobacco all the guys used. But I figured I could learn to love him. He didn't talk to me in public, but he didn't make fun of me in public, either. I considered that a win. Plus, he did this sweet thing where he'd leave notes for me under a specific desk in the science lab. He had the class right before me and would always leave a surprise for me to find. I was pretty sure it was love. That was, until the next semester when we finally had math class together.

"Katee."

The packed room and noisy chaos made it impossible for me to figure out who had called my name. As if playing a game of musical chairs, I watched seat after seat get snatched. Frantically, I turned to check the row behind me, and I heard my name again.

"Katee."

Someone waved from behind a group of guys.

"Sit down, clowns." The group of guys took their seats just as Declan stood up. "Katee, I saved this seat for you."

I felt every set of eyeballs in the classroom on me, raising my body temperature with their laser-beam focus. The classroom fell silent. Declan publicly wooing me by announcing he'd saved me a seat would go down in history. I couldn't believe it.

Declan patted the top of the empty desk beside him.

As the distance between us melted, I realized I couldn't feel my feet. I sat down and prayed my deodorant wouldn't fail me.

"Hey, you," Declan cooed.

I giggled and quickly faced forward in hopes that my cheeks could pull themselves together and cool down fast.

Declan put his hand on my desk.

Still feeling flushed, I gave him the side-eye.

He nodded toward his hand and wiggled his fingers.

Confused, I looked straight at him then saw his friends watching us.

Declan chuckled then grabbed my left hand and intertwined our fingers. "Glad we finally have a class together," he said.

I almost passed out from nerves. His huge hand felt so rough in mine. My own seemed so dainty, so delicate.

Declan smiled. "After a whole semester of being pen pals, we can finally take this to the next level."

I tingled in places I had never tingled in Grade 6. Maybe Matt hadn't been my first love after all. Maybe this was it. I nodded at Declan and squeezed his hand twice. He squeezed back once. I reminded myself that we weren't even official yet. But I knew today would be the day he'd ask me to be his girlfriend. It was finally happening.

Grateful Declan had my non-dominant hand, I turned my attention to the front of the class, where our teacher was writing a complex math problem on the chalkboard. As I copied down the equations, Declan pulled our hands over to his desk. A few seconds later, he pulled our hands down to his lap. Still faced forward, I didn't realize what hard, warm thing he placed my hand on next. Caught off guard, I turned to see his penis out of his jean zipper and him commanding the attention of his friends.

Boisterous laughter ensued.

I ripped my hand away as Declan pulled his textbook down to his lap.

The teacher barked orders like a courtroom judge.

Barely able to see Declan through my tears, I gave him the benefit of the doubt.

Declan smiled, showing off his mess of a mouth. "Well, I officially promote you from a tease to a slut." He winked. "Always a good girl, Katee-girl."

Who knew a worse fate existed than just being invisible?

A patient boy named Jonas pursued me next. I was hesitant because Jonas was in the same friend group as Declan. We agreed to keep things on the down-low at school but spent many months and countless hours on the phone in the evenings and on weekends. I had a proper crush on Jonas. I knew for sure this was the real deal this time.

One day, he asked me to come over to his house. I was shocked when my mother actually agreed under the conditions that his mother had to be home and she had to talk to her first. So freaking embarrassing, but also so totally worth it.

Turned out, Jonas's mom didn't care to supervise us, and we ended up in Jonas's bedroom with the door closed. Next thing I knew, his hard penis was out of his pants, and he suggested I take care of it. I'd never done anything sexual before and had no idea what the hell to do. I knew it was called a blow job, so that was exactly what I did. The next day, I was the one to get blown—blown off. Jonas told everyone at school that I quite literally blew air on his dick. What an idiotic slut, they said.

Being known as the official school slut forced me to look for love elsewhere. One day, a kid from the town's inner high school had a party. There, I met a boy named Marc. He made his desire for me very clear and very public. I loved it. It felt so good to be wanted outside of closed doors for once. And the more Marc chased me, the more other boys seemed to notice me, too. The "in-town" crowd seemed to really take to me and offered me the sense of belonging I'd spent the last two years trying so badly to find. I'd learned my lesson after my other boy experiences. So, when, after a house party one night, Marc started grinding his hard bulge into my backside while he spooned me on my new friend Arleen's boyfriend's couch—in Arleen's boyfriend's bedroom with Arlene and her boyfriend sleeping soundly in the bed beside us—I knew I had to find my voice, be firm, and say no.

"Come on, baby. You're killing me."

I sighed. "You're relentless. I've said no a million times. How many more will it take till you believe it?" I weaponized my elbow gently into his ribcage, threatening him to stay back. Drunk with drink, exhaustion, and frustration, I just wanted to sleep like the others.

"Please, Katee. Pretty please. Pretty please with pasta on top. I promise I'll be quick, it'll feel great, and we can pass out right after."

I chuckled with the clever promise of pasta. Maybe Marc did know me better than anyone else. "Sorry, hun, even spaghetti isn't going to make me change my mind tonight."

Marc grabbed my bum cheek and started kneading it.

I laughed again.

"You're mean, thinking my agony is funny."

"I'm sorry. It's just by doing that, you remind me of a cat."

"Well, you love cats."

"Not ones in heat."

Marc laughed, and his hardness bumped up against my butt. "Argh! I need you."

I stayed strong. Convictions and elbow.

"Come on. You're, like, the only sixteen-year-old virgin."

I wasn't sure that was true.

"Everyone else is doing it, babycakes."

I doubted that.

"Katee, I love you. You know I do."

My body tingled in response to his words, threatening to jump sides. This was the first time since Grade 6 that anyone had told me that. "You don't."

"I do."

"Marc, I won't." I decided the best way to put an end to this was to give a good reason. "I'm on my period."

"I don't care."

The thought twisted the tingles to cringe. Revolting. Boys were just gross. "We don't even have protection." With that, I lost the debate. I gave him the winning point. Hope.

Marc bounced up and off the couch. I'd never seen such a quick change in someone's mood. Before I could retract my lousy argument, he bolted out of the house in the middle of the night to acquire condoms from the twenty-four-hour gas station. I snuck upstairs and locked the door. When he returned and tapped on the basement window, I pretended to be sleeping. Eventually, the noise woke Arleen, and she got up and let him in. His pestering continued, and so did my stalling. Between the residual alcohol from one-too-many wild berry vodka coolers and the level of exhaustion the wee hours of the morning brought, I drifted off momentarily. And just then, Marc entered me. My eyes shot open from the pain. My yelp caused our friends to wake up and catch the end of the short-lived show. I may have stopped saying no, but I had never said yes. I'd really thought Marc was different, but once news got around that I got around, Marc, too, was done with me. And he, too, turned mean, like all the others had before him.

I felt dead inside. Everyone acted as though I was. I wondered if this was what being a ghost felt like. People couldn't see you, were afraid of you, or thought it fun to try to summon and then torture you for their entertainment. I faked sick for a week straight to stay home from school, making this believable by setting my alarm to wake me up before the rest of my family and raiding the fridge for condiments to make a realistic-looking vomit mixture in the toilet. Then I'd try falling back asleep on the bathroom floor in hopes that my mom would find me and let me stay home. By the second week, the trick got old, my mom got mad, and I begrudgingly went back to school. I spent all my non-instructional time locked in a bathroom stall.

Around this time, I pulled further away from my family. I spent most of my time at home in the shower attempting to scald myself clean or in my bedroom trying to sleep away my living nightmare. The papier-mâché of *Archie* comics covering the wainscoting of my bedroom didn't lighten my mood. Instead, they served as proof of yet another guy who couldn't make up his mind and pick just one girl to be true to. The ultra glamourous and sexy Calvin Klein ads bordering the edge of the ceiling made me feel even more trashy and whorish. How many times had my mother commented on my makeup, crop tops, and low-rise jeans? At the time, I'd thought her a ridiculous old person who didn't get fashion or being a teenager. But now I realized looking like that was asking for it. I couldn't stomach looking at my teddy bear, Ginger, or my baby pillow. They no longer provided comfort; they only intensified my shame and reminded me of my forever-lost innocence. I exiled them to a bin and shoved it under my bed.

My parents repeatedly asked what the hell was wrong with me. I kept getting in trouble for my feelings being too big. But they were too big for me, too. I didn't know what the hell to do with them. My family certainly had no clue or patience. How I, someone who felt all the feels, was born into a family of people who didn't seem to feel much of anything at all, was beyond me. More proof that I was the thing that didn't belong. They didn't seem to care about what was causing my feelings, they just wanted them gone. Probably wanted me gone, too.

I started skipping school to spend time with the in-town kids. My only friends. Most of them were either high-school dropouts or had already graduated high school who knew how many years ago. Arleen was the only one my age and the only one besides me still living at home with a parent. As she and I got closer, her mom, Marilyn, became my surrogate mom.

One night, my real mom and I got into a huge argument about my dropping grades, my questionable new acquaintances, and my increasing attitude.

"Katee! Enough! We've had enough of your shit!"

I had had enough of never being enough for anybody. I was sick with jealousy of my little sisters. I knew I'd never be Leigh, the golden child, and I'd never be Beth, the babied not-a-baby.

"Fine!" I didn't notice my clenched jaw until the pain tattled to my brain.

"This is our house. And if you don't want to be here, you're free to leave."

The next day after school, I skipped the bus home and marched straight into town. It wasn't meant to be long-term, but tenacious pride ensured I didn't go home for eight months.

I moved in with a young lady named Leslie who lived across the street from my in-town friend, Jack, Arleen's boyfriend. I'd met Leslie at one of Jack's infamous parties a few months earlier where she'd told me if I ever needed a place to stay, her home was open. The twenty-three-year-old and I shared a birthday, making us exactly seven years apart in age. Throughout my stay with Leslie, my education remained my top priority. But getting myself to school on the other side of town proved challenging, and getting my homework and studying done in the evenings became more and more difficult. Outside Arleen, my in-town friends ranged in age from nineteen to twenty-five, their education in their rearview mirror. Partying with them was hard to resist, and even when I did, the loud music, chatter, and laughter from downstairs was hard to tune out and often kept me up.

At school, teachers started approaching me. Sometimes they wanted to discuss academics: "Katee, I'm very concerned about the effect your attendance is having on your marks." Other times, they wanted to talk about the basics: "I didn't notice you eating lunch today. Do you have one?" They knew I didn't live at home anymore. The principal tried making me see the guidance counsellor. At first glance, I knew she wouldn't be able to help. She didn't have a clue. Every adult sided with my mom, anyway. I knew to them my home life didn't sound that bad. They assured me spats between mothers and teenage daughters were completely normal, rites of passage, that I ran hot while my mom ran cold. They claimed my mother was strict because she loved me and had high expectations because she believed in me, that her parental rigidity was necessary to balance my adolescent impulsivity. And they loved pointing out our shared stubborn streak.

Even though part of me prided myself on managing to stay gone for the better part of a year, deep down I missed my family and secretly wanted so badly for my mom to ask me to move back home. But she didn't, so I eventually swallowed my pride and asked her if I could return. She reluctantly agreed.

Once home again, life remained uneventful for almost a year. My mom was less strict but even more detached, likely knowing I could and would leave again if backed into a corner. Although I appreciated the autonomy I'd previously fought so hard to get, I found myself craving family connection even more. Not knowing how to go about getting it and feeling like it was a lost cause, I put all of myself into my new boyfriend, Ryan.

I definitely loved Ryan more than he loved me, if he ever really loved me at all. Three and a half years my senior made him of age to drink and go to bars, and he did so most nights. A bouncer who had previously let me into his bar confiscated my fake ID shortly after Ryan started dating me. Surely, Ryan had tipped off the bouncer, as he never wanted me tagging along to parties or bars. Although he liked to show me off as his girlfriend around town, our relationship mainly consisted of daytime activities and after-2-a.m. activities. He cheated on me all the time. Most times, I heard about his cheating through the grapevine, but a few times I overheard a girl in the background while he and I were on the phone arranging an after-closing-time hookup. One time, I even got a phone call from one of the girls.

"Is this Katee?"

"Yeah."

"I'm Allison," the girl said. "I'm Ryan's girlfriend."

Shock and worry whispered through me. "Umm, no. I'm his girlfriend. And have been for more than a year." But my body already knew this girl's truth and instantly backed her up.

"Yeah, yeah, babe. I know. You're his in-town girlfriend."

The title stung. But I supposed it was better than the alternative.

"He's friends with my brother."

I didn't know his friends. We always hung out alone.

"Listen, hun. Don't blame me. Boys'll be boys. Fuck 'em. Us girls need to stick together. Called as soon as I found out about you. Douchebag never heard of girl code. We'll show him."

When I still didn't believe her, Allison three-wayed Ryan and told me to stay quiet.

He answered on the third ring. "Yello?"

"Who the fuck is Katee?"

"Uh." The pause was palpable.

"Well?"

"Alli—"

"Yeah, fuckwad?"

Panic pumped my heart.

"Katee who?"

So that was the end of that.

Allison and I became fast friends. My heart still hurt from the breakup, but the fallout of yet another failed relationship gifted me something of value for once: a true best-friendship.

The following week, Allison tested positive for chlamydia, and she'd only slept with Ryan. Terrified, I wondered if what I'd thought was an awful, never-ending yeast infection was actually something more. Allison said it had to be. Plus, the stuff my mom had bought me from the pharmacy to treat yeast infections had yet to work. I freaked. Our family doctor was in the city. I couldn't tell my parents I needed them to make me an appointment and expect them to drive me an hour away to see him. What if it wasn't a bad yeast infection? Would he have to tell my parents the truth?

I took matters into my own hands, skipped school, and walked an hour into town to the hospital in the West End where they confirmed chlamydia. But that wasn't even close to the worst part. Ryan's mother was the receptionist in charge of medical records. With a less-than-impressed face, she assured a mortified me that a strict confidentiality clause bound her from disclosing any patient's personal medical information. But, she told me, I was required by law to provide the names of everyone with whom I'd been sexually active for contact-tracing purposes. I could have died right then and there.

A nurse eventually rescued me from the waiting area and took me to a private room where she asked me for a list of people with whom I'd been intimate. Thank God Ryan was the only person I'd been with since I'd lost my virginity to Marc over a year before, so no one else needed to be called. Just when I thought I might be able to walk away from this with my reputation unscathed, the doctor came back with a prescription. I couldn't get that filled. I had no money and didn't have access to our family's benefits details.

I found a hospital payphone.

My mother answered, already sounding annoyed. "Hello?"

"Mom?" I said, not recognizing my own childish voice.

"What?"

"Umm..."

My seemingly boundless pause was broken by my mother's irritable impatience. "What, Katee?"

"Ahh . . ." I looked around, not sure whether I was seeking privacy or someone to save me.

My mother offered her infamous sigh. "Your school already called. Said you skipped last block. I'm not impressed."

"Well, I had to."

"Why?"

"To see a doctor."

"What? Why? Where are you?"

"At the hospital."

"Are you okay?"

Hopeful my mother would find the real reason for my hospital visit preferable to the one she had likely jumped to first, I spat it out, "Mom, I have an STI."

"A what? Like, a sexually transmitted disease? Oh, for Christ's sake, Katee." My mom's subsequent silence scolded me more than her words ever could.

As I waited, I imagined the disease spreading further and further from its spoiled source. I assumed my hands and feet, numb with chill, were already infected. My heart beat so riotously, I feared once the disease reached it, the combination might kill me right on the spot.

"I'll pick you up in twenty-five minutes," said my mother before promptly hanging up.

Shame bubbled up from my stomach. I ran to the closest washroom, thrust open the stall door, and dropped to my knees.

"Dear God—"

I threw up. Tears filled my eyes.

"Please, God—"

Salivating too quickly to keep swallowing successfully, I spewed again, projecting my sins. This time, I missed the toilet bowl. If real, I knew God certainly condemned me now. I curled up, lay my hot cheek on the cold tile floor, and prayed for absolution.

The stall door whacked my hip.

"Honey?"

A woman stood over me. I hadn't heard anyone enter the washroom. I turned to hide my face in the ground and sobbed.

"Oh, honey," said the woman, as she squeezed herself into the suffocating stall and crouched down to stroke my hair. "What's wrong, love?"

I could only cry. Ugly cry.

The woman readjusted herself and curled around me. "Everything's going to be alright, hun. Everything's going to be alright."

I closed my eyes and remembered a time long ago when my mom had held and consoled me. She'd sang "You Are My Sunshine," a tribute to one of my pet names. Although I could hear my mother's soothing singing, all I could visualize was an empty chair in the middle of a pitch-black, empty room.

Ryan reached out a few days later saying he missed me. Against my better judgement, I agreed to meet up with him, as I had been so heartbroken and lonely. Very quickly, one thing led to another, and a friendly catchup turned into a make-out session. When Ryan started unzipping his pants, I had no choice but to do something to stop the progression.

"No," I said, barely a whisper. I tucked my hair behind my ears, straightened my shirt, and pulled away.

Ryan groped at me. "Come on, baby. I've missed you. He's missed you," he said, pouting and pulling my hand down to his crotch.

"We can't," I said more firmly this time. I lowered the passenger-side window of his truck and lit a cigarette.

"Cocktease."

Had he still not gotten the call from the nurse at the hospital clinic? Did he know he was still spreading a sexually transmitted disease to God knows how many girls?

Only on day four of my prescription, not even an impossibly difficult and embarrassing conversation could stop me from the threat of having to start back at square one with my body, the hospital, and my mom.

"We can't have sex. We have chlamydia."

He backed up against the driver's-side door as fast as if a snake had struck him. "The fuck we do." He zipped up his pants and pulled his shirt back over his head.

"We do. I got tested."

"Are you kidding me, Katee? You'd better be fucking kidding me."

"I'm not. We do."

"You mean you do. I don't got no sick disease, you disgusting, dirty slut."

"You do. You must. You're the only person I've been with."

He barked out a laugh. "Yeah, right. This your way of trying to trap me, you twisted fuck? Make sure no one else'll want me so you can keep me for yourself?"

The truck engine roared and the tires kicked up gravel that hit the side of it like hail.

I fastened my seatbelt. "You need to get meds, Ryan."

"I don't got to do nothing," he said, shaking his head while fumbling for a lighter for the cigarette hanging out of his mouth. He nearly veered us off the road. "There's nothing wrong with me."

"The doctor said most people don't even get symptoms. And left untreated, it can cause infertility."

"What?" The truck swerved, and he jerked us back straight. "I swear to God, Katee, if you caused my dick not to work right, I'll fucking ruin you."

I reached over and placed my hand on his knee.

"Get your filthy fucking paws off me!" His arm shot across and cracked my breastbone, pinning me tight against the seat.

Tears filled my eyes as he yanked his arm away from me.

"Get out," he said. "And don't ever contact me again."

I returned to taking multiple showers a day at the hottest temperature that lasted until the water ran cold. But even scrubbing until my skin nearly bled didn't wash away the visual of my body decaying from the inside out. The excessive showering eventually created a bald spot at the base of my high ponytail caused by the middle of my hair never getting the chance to fully dry. Being surrounded by my little sisters' purity and innocence when I felt so dirty and was literally diseased pained me. I was the gangrene of my family. If I wasn't cut off and disposed of like the soiled garbage I'd become, I'd infect the rest of them with sepsis.

This time, my mom damn well knew what was wrong with me. Perhaps because she thought it self-inflicted, she didn't care.

Chapter 7

Gabbi

At the end of the second day of our family trip, exhausted from a full day of touring Granville Island and the aquarium, we decide to agree on a plan for tomorrow prior to turning in for the night. We gather in the grandiose hotel lobby since none of our rooms comfortably fit all eight of us. It's an enormous open space with magnificent cathedral ceilings high enough to house the gods and make our tall family feel tiny. We congregate to three convenient, comfortable, full-size couches just inside the main entrance's revolving doors.

With everyone too tired to speak at the same time, for once, Mom takes the lead. "Should we go to the island tomorrow?"

Just like that, *he's* back. Poking at me from within. My stomach turns in on itself.

"Oooh," says Tara, "that would be nice." She glances at Warren, and he agrees.

My shoulders tense. I try massaging out the rocks.

Bryanne nods. "It's on my bucket list. How long would it take to see it properly?"

I struggle to unlock my phone. "Fuck!" The family chatter stops. I look up sheepishly. "What?"

My husband turns toward me. His eyes meet mine and search them. "You okay?"

I nod. He winks. The family chatter resumes.

I look back to my phone. "Just trying to look up driving times. I think we'd be pressed to see the best of the island during such a short trip."

My hands and feet grow uncomfortably cold. My frozen finger conjures a quick Google search for the website of Burnaby Blogger, as I refer to him, who has tracked and documented my ex-partner's criminal activity, freemen sovereignty rants, court shenanigans, and whereabouts for the better part of a decade. Burnaby Blogger is clearly not a fan of my ex, throwing shade at *him* from a safe distance, hidden behind a computer, protected with a generic username. Since discovering his blog, I've considered him an ally.

Needing the most recent updates, I quickly scroll through Burnaby Blogger's twenty-six pages and five hundred and eight posts only and all about *him*, my ex-partner. I need to know exactly where *he's* living. *His* fans, followers, and court records list the places *he's* lived most recently. I scan the list of towns. Shit. Practically the whole damn island.

Tara laughs. "Gabbi, day trips are super common. That's the only way I've ever done it."

"Us, too," Mom agrees. "We certainly don't need more than a day, hun."

I try to imagine how shot my nerves will be if I'm forced to spend an entire day in flight-fight-and-freeze mode. Exhaustion consumes me just thinking about it. I close my eyes and inhale slowly and deeply before continuing my essential internet research.

Burnaby Blogger shares countless excerpts of my ex's overwhelming fan support:

Please keep us posted as to when you'll be speaking on podcasts and radio shows. I swear man, I'm your biggest fan.

And another: *I'm not a psycho stalker. I just love watching you expose the corruption, prove the conspiracies, and take down the government. We need your knowledge now more than ever. The world needs you, our Savior.*

And another: *I'd love to send you some money. I've followed your work for years now. You're wildly popular in Europe. You share the best information and are by far the most often quoted leader of the movement. Hit me up and I'll send you some money.*

"Are we ordering in take-out and eating together in someone's room again?" Tara polls.

I hear my husband grumble. He's never one for lots of loud people in confined spaces.

Bryanne responds, "No. Way too smushy. Let's eat there tonight." She points to the hotel restaurant.

"I'm fine with whatever," I chime in.

"I'm taking you out tonight," states my husband quietly but decisively. He gestures to my phone. "Check out the menu at Nightingale."

Accepting the permission slip to briefly zone back out, I unlock my screen again. Jesus. Why do so many people think my ex is so important? Thousands write to *him*. Praise *him*. Encourage *him*. Stroke *his* dangerous ego. Are accomplices to *his* delinquency. I notice a post in which my ex-partner, a trusted cult leader, provides banking details and instructions, a way *his* followers can best support *his* "mission," *his* lunacy.

Unbelievable. But it wasn't. I knew *his* charm all too well. My ex had always had a way with people, knew how to be everyone's drug of choice.

Burnaby Blogger's most recent post is dated September 19. Exactly three weeks ago. The blogger writes that the last time my ex-partner was heard from was in a Facebook post, dated seven months ago. At that time, my ex himself stated *he* lived in a tent city in a small town in BC.

"Gabbi?" Bryanne's voice commands attention. "Is it possible to see . . .?" she names three towns—all of which were named in my ex's Facebook post—and each one hits me like a gut punch.

Fuck, fuck, fuck. I raise my finger, requesting a minute, and pull up a map of the island. Aside from the fact that *he* was spotted living in all three of the locations Bryanne listed on her bucket list, to get to those places, we'd have to pass through two other places *he'd* been seen.

"N-N-No," I stutter. Pull it together. I clear my throat. "That's almost five hours of driving, not including any stops for sightseeing, food, washrooms, nor the length of the ferry both ways."

Dad interjects, "We can make a whole day of it, though. It'll be fine. We just do what we can do. Play it by ear."

I weigh the pros and cons of faking an illness while my family chatters excitedly about the possibilities. My husband tells me he's going to take our coats, the umbrella, and my purse to our room. He'll bring me back a glass of wine.

I direct my attention back to my phone, where my heart races my fingers to Facebook. I quickly unblock my ex and check *his* wall; *his* profile remains as open and unsecure as can be. Burnaby Blogger had stated my ex's last post was dated March 15, 2021, but now I see that was a typo. The cut-and-pasted post, my ex's actual Facebook post, is dated the previous year: March 15, 2020. That original post reads: *You haven't heard from me in over a year 'cause I had to stay offline while leading the tent city crusade. But I'm back! Stay tuned to hear all about the sordid affair to expose the corrupt and educate the blind. I love you all and have missed you! Time to get caught up and take down the house!*

My ex's profile claims *he* currently lives on the island.

The room blurs. The background noise muffles and mutes.

Crack!

I gasp and jump. Luckily, everyone's eyes are on the source of the commotion instead of my over-the-top reaction. Someone dropped their phone on the marble floor.

Just breathe.

"Apparently, on Sundays, the first ferry departs at seven a.m., and they run every two hours until nine p.m.," says Mom. "Plenty of time to hit all three spots if we take the first ferry over and the last one back." She looks at me with concerned brows and mouths, *You okay?*

I swallow, nod, and smile at her.

Lightheaded and dizzy, I focus on five things I can see: coffee cup in my hand, sign for the washroom, concierge desk, my family, my loving husband back with a much-needed glass of wine. I take a not-so-classy gulp. What if my ex walks into the hotel doors right now? We're sitting ducks. I look for an emergency exit. Hypervigilant of the happenings behind me, I shift my position so my back is to the wall instead of the busy check-in counter and elevators. I scan my surroundings.

Stop it. I'm a therapist, for God's sake. Pull it together. Practice what I preach. I focus on four things I can hear: a shrieking kid, my father's voice, faint background music, and the tap from my nail on my wine glass.

The panic attacks can't be happening again. I conquered them years ago. Come on. Regression is not an option. Three things I can feel: air entering my nose and filling my lungs, the soft suede couch underneath me, my jeans, a little pull in them. Although certainly more grounded, the strong sense of danger lingers. The body doesn't forget.

I grab my scarf and bring it to my nose. I inhale the flowery sweet scent of my perfume. I pull my ponytail over my face and breathe in the smell of the shampoo in my hair. The one thing I taste is bile at the base of my throat. I take a sip of wine.

"Well," interrupts my mom, "the island is a no-go."

Oh, thank God.

"The first two ferries to Victoria tomorrow are already sold out, and the only return time still available is three p.m."

Bryanne's face sinks. "Really? I didn't realize it could completely sell out."

Tara looks at me and gives me a playful eyeroll. "I did suggest we plan out our days ahead of time."

Mom continues, "I guess because it's Thanksgiving Sunday. It's also an hour and thirty-five minutes each way—and we have to arrive at the terminal thirty to sixty minutes prior to our scheduled departure. So, if everyone's okay with only going to Victoria, I guess we could still check it out, but even that would only give us just under two hours to explore."

"It's fine," says Bryanne. "No stress, no drama. Let's just do something else." She is likely still disappointed but putting on her notorious fine face.

Halleluiah. Suddenly aware of the urgency to lose my creepy Cheshire Cat smile, I break the family eye contact and look down at my phone. I unlock it again. Oops. I almost forgot to re-block my ex on Facebook. We've never been "friends" on there, but before I discovered I could block *him* without being Facebook friends with *him*, my ex sent the odd intimidating and unnerving message to my private account. Before I block *him* again, I scroll a little further down the rabbit hole. Link to the GoFundMe account Burnaby Blogger referenced. Never-ending court battle rants. Freemen on the land and sovereign citizen movement garbage. Free-living preaching. Video blogging and "Truth Radio" lightbulb ideas. Copious ego-stroking comments mixed in with a shockingly incredible amount of "fan" feedback.

I check *his* albums. *His* full collection of stolen social media pictures of the women *he's* conquered is still boastfully displayed: trophies to *him*, hostages for us. Remarkably not reported to Facebook by one of us long ago. Although triggered and tempted, I certainly don't whistleblow. How else would I keep tabs on *his* whereabouts? Stalking works both ways, from either end of the safety continuum.

Where has *he* been? My ex is not someone to go into hiding. *He's* an instigator, a loudmouth, a proud rule breaker and shit disturber. A year and a half is a long time for someone that full of himself to remain completely radio silent. Especially during a pandemic, which *he* would certainly believe to be a global, multi-governmental conspiracy. Many of *his* followers added comments and asked questions about *his* thoughts on the pandemic in response to *his* final post. All went unanswered. Could *he* be dead?

I re-block *him* and go back to the blogger's website.

Burnaby Blogger writes: *While he explicitly promised us he was going to soon be back in action, the old him revitalized, it was just a lie. If he started a blog, I've not found it. I've searched for him in vain on Google, Twitter, Facebook, YouTube, I've even dug into British Columbia court records to see if he's in jail. Drawn a blank on all of them. Maybe the government assassins finally caught up with him and he's buried under a landfill somewhere.*

A girl can hope.

Chapter 8

Alex

I yelped after accidentally plucking another eyelash out by its root. I must have mindlessly retreated to twisting lashes over brows.

"Jesus, Alex. Pull it together," I said out loud. It had been years since *he'd* made contact. So long that perhaps I'd let my guard down too much, become a little too comfortable.

But my life with *him* hadn't been all bad. We'd had many good times, great times even. Ninety percent of the time, our relationship had felt like a fairytale, but that other ten percent . . . I didn't want to think about it, about *him*. Yet my ex had somehow slithered *his* way back into my life once again. I felt kind of bad for *him*. How sad to never get over someone, always pine for them, obsess over them, beg for them. And sober *him* had always meant well. Hadn't *he*? I knew firsthand what past trauma could do to a person. I knew the toll childhood trauma could take on its victims—even its grown-up survivors. I held empathy for *him*. Okay, maybe not empathy. But sympathy? Ugh. I didn't know what to think or how to feel.

I picked back up one of the letters and examined the drawings, admiring *his* raw skill. Such a talented artist. Hopefully, *he* was no longer wasting *his* gift. I poked my finger through the top corner and ripped in a little before thinking better of it. Wine first.

Once I prepared myself to the best of my ability, I took the letters to the couch and snuggled up to read them beside my snoozing guard dog, Yoshi.

> Hi Sweetie,
>
> Long time no talk. I can't believe how many years it's been since I last saw you, heard your voice, and felt your body next to mine. I've never stopped loving and missing you. I thought after how things ended with us nothing could get any worse. Boy was I wrong. I should have come to find you that fateful night instead and maybe I wouldn't have gotten into trouble and wound up back in jail. I'll explain it all to you if you come visit me.
>
> I think of you when I go to sleep and at night when I'm half asleep I can almost feel you, it seems so real, when I wake up, I get a real hot feeling in my chest, almost crying I think of you, all day I'm reminded of you. You are driving me nuts, I wish I could forget you, but I can't, I never will, I hope you love me forever. I need you back. Just thinking of you is what is keeping me going. Will you visit me, write to me, help me cope with these problems I'm having? I need you more than you'll ever

know. I wish you were mine and not whoever's you are now. What a nightmare.

I hope someday you will put on my ring and love me again. You need to be your own person now and I understand that. I'll be waiting for you for as long as it takes. I love you, babe. For real.

Why don't you write me a letter and tell me all your true feelings, even about whoever you're with now, I can take it. Please talk to me, be my friend again. I need a true friend; I don't have any more.

All my love forever.

P.S. You will NEVER be replaceable.

The first letter seemed harmless. Just talk of a heartbroken man. But I knew how to read between the lines. I opened the second one.

Bitter Sweetheart,

I don't know why you haven't written back. Are you mad at me? I need you to write because that's all I have. You don't understand how much I need to keep in touch with you. Every night I think of you. Every morning I'm up at 4:30

or 5 am thinking of you. I'm going crazy. I still really love you and can't stop. Love me back and write to me. I'm not asking for much.

I don't know what you might have heard from the goofs around town over the last year and a bit, but they're all lies. I didn't hit that woman in the face. And the guy who charged me with aggravated assault sucker punched me first. But I got my revenge. The crown attorney tried to make a deal with me, three months if I pled guilty to aggravated assault. But I was already in jail for 6 months at that point, so I said no. I didn't take the deal because I thought I could beat it. Guess after staying out so long I forgot how corrupt the system really is. I chose to have a jury trial. That girl testified at the preliminary hearing that I hit her. That slut was so drunk she couldn't possibly know or even remember that night. But the crown won, and I got two years plus a day for the aggravated assault charges. But I don't care cause I stuck to my principles. Yeah, I'm stubborn!

Then I got all mixed up in the suspicious death of an inmate. His name was Henry. He was a new guy, never in jail before. He came into my part of the jail. A few minutes later he went down to the floor having a seizure. I resuscitated him, but unfortunately, he died four or five days later in hospital. The institution then put me in segregation. They stopped me from talking to the police or a lawyer for thirty days. They took my food away and my clothing and bedding. They tried really hard to fuck with me, but you know . . . I fight back.

After I did my time in that hellhole, I got moved from Maplehurst to Hamilton Wentworth Detention Centre. Things got a lot worse at Maplehurst, with the guards. I was beaten up pretty good, and they didn't feed me for about eighteen days straight, while in the hole. I pressed charges against the officers, then they threatened me, the big 'or else' speech, I guess those dumb fuckers just don't know me well enough, eh? So, I caused what they called a one-man riot. I pulled the fire sprinkler in my cell, flooded it and about six other cells too. I put a big spotlight on all the bullshit they were doing to me, over the suspicious death of Henry

The administration at Maplehurst shipped me out to stop the abuse.

But once I got here, it wasn't too long until the guards took me out of 'main population' and put me in 'medical observation' segregation cells, because I'm in a wheelchair now. I've been asking to see a specialist for six months, to get more tests done. They put me in this cell and took all my privileges away, it even took me two weeks to get to use a phone to call my lawyer. I'm going to sue the correctional services for not providing me with adequate medical treatment and letting me suffer for months. I couldn't begin to make you understand just how much my life sucks right now. I'll get through this shit and bounce back in no time. Just watch me.

I'll explain it all clearer to you if you come see me. I want to see you. OK? I'm not asking for much. I love you and I think about you every day. You're haunting my dreams again. I spend hours just trying to think of what to say to you to prove how I still feel about you. I'm not going to ever get you back and that's just the way it is, but I'm not sure I'll ever get you out *of my head. Or that I even want to. I miss you still and more each day. I need to hear from you soon.*

P.S. Reuniting after such a long time apart would show an exceptional example of your love for me. My love for you. Us. Please just think about it.

Damn I miss you.

Within you, without you.

Love you unconditionally forever.

The blinds still drawn from the night before served a new purpose, keeping my secrets hidden from the outside world. Concealing my misplaced shame. The house threatened doom, it had gotten so dark. But turning on the lights would illuminate the situation. Shine life into it. Highlight the hypocrisy in the room. I felt scared but also captivated. Hated *him* but also retained a soft spot for *him*. Saw the monster in *him* but also the wounded inner child. Held *him* accountable but also gave *him* passes. Crucified *him* publicly but also defended and excused *him*.

I looked over at Yoshi, now awake and judging me, too. I looked around the house. Never had it felt so oppositional, so ominous.

I turned on the TV for levity.

"Nope." I quickly turned off the TV. It figured that right when I received news from my ex, Sandra-fucking-Bullock would suddenly appear on the screen like a modern-day *I Dream of Jeannie* bombshell. Early in our relationship, *he* had told me Sandra Bullock was *his* celebrity crush since childhood. *He* practically orgasmed at the mere sight of the Hollywood star. At the time, I'd chosen to celebrate the silver lining; at least *he* only made me feel insecure in comparison to an untouchable celebrity and hadn't knocked my confidence by comparing me to any of *his* real-life flirty "femme fatales," as *he* referred to them. Every time Sandra Bullock had graced *him* with her presence on TV, *he* would remind me through orgasmic, breathy, dirty bedroom talk that if ever given the opportunity, *he'd* leave me for the celebrity without so much as a second thought or a millisecond of hesitation.

I reached toward the coffee table and grabbed a clementine from the fruit bowl. I punctured the orange skin and dug my thumb under the peel before carefully tearing it back. Pick. Pick. Pick. I took note of the fragrant mist as it squirted me. Such a soothing smell. I breathed in mindfully and deeply through my nose and exhaled with intention through my mouth. I pressed my sticky fingers together and smeared around the gooey texture. Gradually, I gouged, tore, and peeled the skin back around the centre of the clementine. I moved up to work on the top half and then down to finish the bottom half of the fruit, ensuring the peel remained in one piece. I slowly separated each sticky segment from its conjoined sibling and meticulously lined them up on the coffee table before grabbing a second clementine and eventually the last piece of fruit and repeating the process with each. Once all three clementines were stripped down to naked and separated sections and displayed in an ominous lineup, I grabbed the empty fruit bowl and swept the sticky cold mess into it. Then I picked up an intact peel and examined it carefully. Snakelike. I tossed it and the remaining two skins into the bowl with their insides, walked to the kitchen sink, and, using the backend of a spatula, bludgeoned the citrusy carcasses to a pulp.

Chapter 9

Katee

The last week of August, just before starting my Grade 12 year, just when I felt ready to give up—on love, on life, on everything—I met someone who changed all of it forever. He was crazy about me. He loved me. He believed I was perfect. He was my person. He was so cool. I felt like I was in *90210* or a music video or something. Like I was living the dream.

He had these eyes. Blue, but never the same shade. And they sparkled. Like the sparkle painted in the pupils of doll eyes. And his muscles? Drool-worthy! Goodness gracious, help me! And the way girls looked at him? It was embarrassing for them—for me! Like he was famous or something. He probably could've been. He had that "it" factor. He should've been a game-show host or something with that smile of his and his charm and charisma. People loved him, looked up to him. He was a natural leader. Everyone seemed to know him or want to know him. He knew who he was and liked who he was. Everything seemed to come easily to him. No stress. He commanded a room. He noticed little things and made them seem super important just by mentioning them or pointing them out, like an outfit or earrings or a certain look. Small things. Oh, and he had a car. His own car, not his parents'. A true panty dropper when living in the middle of nowhere land.

He dressed so well. He smelled expensive. I could have eaten him whole. Just looking at him made me feel a certain kind of way. I can't even explain it. It was like magic was being stored in my body, all tingly and warm. Electric. He was the first guy I ever physically wanted. I craved him like a drug.

And he chose me. I fell in love the night we met.

I met him late one night while hanging out at my friend James's apartment.

"Gross!" James came running out of his bedroom with wide eyes and a gaping mouth. "What the hell's the creamy stuff in your underwear, baby?"

James's girlfriend's olive-coloured face turned pimento red as she bolted out of the living room and into hers and James's bedroom. Three of us remained in the living room along with James; I didn't know either of the other two. We all looked up to see James's antagonizing facial expression. He flared his nostrils and wriggled his thick dark eyebrows like a rascal ready to rumble. His antics were sometimes side-splitting, other times annoying—the latter usually to the person being targeted, the former to the rest of the bystanders. Mostly, I thought he was funny. But whenever he chose to pick on me, humiliation consumed me in the form of nausea.

Still standing, he towered over the three of us sitting across his couches, appearing much taller than six-foot-three. With dark brown eyes and almost black hair, he was extremely handsome but far too immature for me.

As he was a close friend, I used to sleep over at his old place if it got too late to walk home to Leslie's house when I lived there a year ago. James and I would sleep in the same bed. The last time I'd stayed over, before he'd hooked up with his newest girlfriend, we'd had a sexual encounter of sorts. He'd started touching me under my pants in the middle of the night. I hadn't known whether or not he was actually awake, and because of this I hadn't known what I should do. So, I'd pretended to remain sleeping, and the touching had stopped. I'd never brought it up, and neither had he.

James's girlfriend reappeared at the living room entrance. "You're such an asshole!" She vanished again, slamming their bedroom door behind her.

James flapped his pinky and fourth finger together, making a snapping sound. "Don't be a slob and leave your dirty underwear lying in the middle of the floor then." He ran after her to continue agitating her.

With the only two people I knew out of the room, I scanned the two who remained. A ridiculously good-looking guy sat on the couch perpendicular to me. I'd never met him before, but I knew him to see him. He was friends with my ex-boyfriend, Ryan, as well as with my longtime crush, Anthony.

When I'd walked into James's place that day, he'd already been there. I'd noticed his height; thankfully, he was a few inches taller than me. His baby blue eyes shimmered like a Ken doll's, and his smile captivated me with its unique sparkle. For sure, he was older than me, but I couldn't tell by how much. I certainly didn't act seventeen, and having lived with Leslie—who'd been twenty-three at the time while I was sixteen—people assumed me older as well. Bouncers didn't expect someone her age to be hanging out with someone under the legal limit. I got into clubs easily. Leslie was twenty-four now, and this guy looked to be a couple years older than her. So, I guessed twenty-six, tops. Still, that would make him nine years my senior. Maybe it was a sign. My parents were nine years apart, too.

Squinting toward the bedroom, he heard something that made him stand up. The conflict in the bedroom had audibly escalated. "James," he called. His soft voice made him sound younger than I'd guessed. He walked over and knocked on the door.

James opened it. "Yeah, buddy?"

The mystery man let out a high-pitched chuckle. "Leave her alone already. It's probably just discharge, you goof. All girls get it. Just means they're about to ovulate."

I'd had no idea what "discharge" was before that point. I'd always felt embarrassed, assuming it only happened to me.

For the first time since I'd known James, I saw his face change colour. "Really?" His big eyes focused intently on the hot mystery man, my new crush.

"Yeah, really." Another adorable giggle.

I'd never heard anyone stand up to James. Especially not a guy.

But he did it in such a cool way. Apparently, I wasn't the only one to feel this. The other person in James's living room was a blonde girl sitting on the other side of the room from me. On hearing this conversation, she sat up straight and fixed her hair. When the cute guy sat back down on the couch and looked her way, she seductively dug her teeth into her lip, batted her mascara-crusted lashes at him, and twirled her hair teasingly. I almost threw up in my throat. Game on. I could feel my longtime crush on Anthony withering away the more I observed this mystery man.

Having never returned from their bedroom, I assumed James and his girlfriend had gone to bed. I waited it out. I refused to leave. The time had come to disprove the theory that blondes had more fun.

My competition got up. She stood in between me and the mystery man, intentionally putting her back to me. "Was nice to meet you."

I included myself in the conversation before he could respond to her. "See ya."

He glanced at me and laughed, clearly loving the attention. Then he turned his focus back to her. "Where ya goin', hun?"

She glared at me before curling her lower lip and flashing him an exaggerated sad face. "I have a ten-o'clock curfew."

I snickered. "That sucks. Nighty night, then." Since moving back home to my parents', I had a curfew, too, but I didn't care.

The blonde whipped her head around to glare at me. I smiled. With a huff, she stormed off down the long hallway and slammed the front door behind her.

He turned his head toward me. "So, where do ya live, cutie?" His eyes shimmered when he spoke.

"Out of town."

"You're the girl living with testy-Leslie, right?"

"Leslie? Ya. Not anymore, though." Even though she'd sort of earned her nickname, Leslie had always been good to me. She had taken me in and treated me like a daughter.

"Well? What happened?"

"I moved back to my parents'."

"All that freedom then back to jail, eh? Why'd you leave in the first place?"

"My mother hates me. She kicked me out."

"How could anyone hate someone as sweet as you?"

My cheeks burned. An intense but delightful heat expanded throughout my body.

He leaned his freshly shaven baby face toward me, stopping a couple inches from my lips. I gasped in a fresh breath of air.

He looked intently through my eyes and flirted with my soul for what seemed like forever then blinked and smiled. An imperfection. The upper tooth to the left of his big one had chipped, making it a little too short to reach its bottom partner. This made his smile even better.

He licked his lips then rested his top teeth on his bottom lip in a gentle bite. "Your parents clearly don't understand you. You're like the wind. And they can't cage that in."

On that couch, for the first time in my entire life, I felt like I belonged. To him.

He closed the two-inch gap between us and cushioned my bottom lip gently between his. I tasted cinnamon when his soft tongue touched mine, and a spark ignited, sending what felt like hot lava throughout my body. The strangest sensation began just above my upper thighs. The muscles pulsated. That area began feeling damp. I worried at first then remembered I must be about to ovulate. I didn't have to be embarrassed. He would understand. I'd had sex before, but I'd never experienced feelings like this before the actual intercourse began.

Somehow, we ended up on the floor, with me on top of him. The room was dimly lit by a small lamp behind us. It cast a deep yellow glow that made the room look warm. I felt so small with him. I'd grown tall before I'd filled out; a couple inches under six feet and only a hundred and fourteen pounds, I consisted of skin, no breasts, bone, and a huge bum. Although muscular, he had a bit of a stomach. It surprised me that it didn't turn me off. His body looked more like a man's, not like any of the boys' bodies I'd seen. It made me feel safe and protected. It cushioned me. My insecurity about my body vanished. He found a way to make me feel so good about myself. Beautiful, sexy, desirable. I'd found my forever love.

"I'm going to marry you one day," he said.

I envisioned us getting married by candlelight in the tiniest church in the world, possibly because of the romantic lighting in the small room we'd found ourselves in. After the ceremony, we'd dance barefoot on the beach until the sun began to rise, then we'd float away from land on a tube that read "Just Married." When we reached the yacht anchored just off the shore, he'd help me into it, and we'd sail far away. We would be together forever.

No one had ever understood me until the day I met him. My Prince Charming. He immediately made me his girlfriend. I found myself quickly and completely enmeshed, even after finding out his real age: thirty-one. Fourteen years my senior. I didn't care. He said age was just a number, and I was an old soul. As it had the first night we'd met, our relationship progressed at rapid speed. I started spending more and more time with him and less time with James, Allison, Arleen, or any of my other in-town friends, or respecting my curfew, which deepened the rift with my mother.

My family didn't care about me. In fact, they couldn't stand me. They were convinced there was something wrong with me. My mom was disappointed at how low my grades were. My boyfriend said that was ludicrous. When I showed him my report card with high eighties and nineties, he went crazy. He made all his friends look at it and bragged about how his girl was a goddamn genius.

My mom was always on me about skipping class. He said with my marks, I could definitely afford to skip more. Besides, didn't she know skipping class was a rite of passage—along with breaking curfew and underage drinking and experimenting with drugs? God, I was a teenager, he said. What did she expect? He said she wanted me to be a loser. He said she preferred when I didn't have any friends. He said she vilified me for having normal teenage experiences. He said more street smarts—not more book smarts—were precisely what I needed.

My mom said I was disgusting for smoking. My dad didn't like it, either, but he told me my mom used to smoke when she was young. So, what the hell? What a hypocrite. My boyfriend said he was surprised to hear my mom had ever been remotely cool. He said she was old now and clearly didn't know what was required of teens these days. Not only did he smoke, too, but he was old enough to buy cigarettes for us. Score.

My parents said my tongue piercing was repulsive. He thought it was super sexy. They hated my tattoo. My boyfriend was covered in tattoos. He said a blank canvas represented a blank brain. He thought my gargoyle moth was unique and the inspiration behind it cleverly fitting; it was symbolic of the constant pressure my mom put on me to be perfect without her acknowledging I was always trying my very best. He said I was simultaneously a work-in-progress and a masterpiece.

This guy. He just got me. He adored me. I could do no wrong, and it felt so right.

Lying on my futon couch in my bedroom, I looked up at the bottom of my bunk bed—it was just made of wooden supports tied together with thick white cotton ribbon, but I looked at them as if looking at the billion shining stars in the night's sky. As if he were right there beside me instead of on the other end of the phone.

"Geez, Katee. You're absolutely incredible. You know that? I've never met anyone as mind-blowing as you."

I twisted the phone cord around my index finger then pulled hard to release it. My cheeks ached as they throbbed and swelled in sync with my heart. I looked around my bedroom walls and saw validation from the smiling *Archie* characters and sex-craved Calvin Klein models stapled all over them. This was it, I thought. It was my turn to be loved.

"Really?" I asked sheepishly. A soft laugh escaped.

"A hundred percent, cutie." He took a deep breath then exhaled heavily. "I've been waiting my whole life for exactly you. You were made for me."

I felt a warm wave wash over my body so fast I worried I might throw up. "I . . . I . . ." Suddenly, there was so much spit in my mouth. I swallowed hard. "I really, really like you. Like . . . really."

The silence on the other end stretched so long I began to choke on it.

"Katee . . . I love you." I barely heard him. I doubted my ears. Before I could ask him to repeat himself, he said, "I will marry you one day."

We'd only been dating two weeks, but I could already see us on a beach at the tail end of a sunrise after dancing all night long with all our friends. The smell of the sea filled my nose and lungs. The rough sand smoothed my feet. I saw the anchored yacht in the distance and little inner tube a pool-length away from the shore. The moonlight captured a rope connecting the two. "Just Married," read a sign attached to the floaty.

"Katee?"

Grabbing my maroon throw, I pulled it up to my flushing neck. "Yes?" I managed.

He chuckled quietly. I felt my face match the colour of my blanket. "You're the best thing that's ever happened to me."

My cheeks clenched. Not knowing what to say or do, I gulped then said, "Ditto."

"But I have to tell you something."

But? But wasn't good. I tightened the phone cord around my finger until it went numb.

"I promise to marry you one day, but . . ."

I thought of all the *buts* I could live with: *but you need to be eighteen first; but you need to graduate university first; but you need to—*

"But I need to get divorced first."

I choked up a little of my dinner. "You're married?" I immediately regretted my stupidity and immaturity. Why wouldn't he be married? He was perfect. He was an adult. My stupid question would only remind him I was still a silly kid.

"It doesn't really count. We barely lasted a year."

Even Ryan and I had lasted longer than that. I guessed we'd both wound up at James's immediately after our relationships had ended. We'd both walked away from our awful exes and straight into one another's arms. Fake love to true love.

"It had to happen this way, Katee. I had to taste the bitter to fully appreciate the sweet."

Nothing about my home life made choosing between my boyfriend and my family a difficult decision. My family made me feel like an unwanted outsider. My boyfriend made me feel like a goddess and constantly bragged about me to his friends, telling them he was the luckiest man on the planet to have me for a girlfriend. Still insecure around others, I often thought his friends agreed with him to please him. Every girl seemed envious of how much he adored me. In fact, my boyfriend said jealousy explained why I'd lost my few in-town friends as quickly as I had. Even Allison and Arleen were slowly pulling away. He said they were simply too young and immature to be able to comprehend true love. Even to me, it all seemed too good to be true.

My mother made her disapproval of my boyfriend very clear. She tried to keep me from seeing him by taking back the slack she'd let out from my leash when I'd moved back home after living with Leslie. First, she tried denying me rides to and from town. But my boyfriend had a car of his own, so I didn't need to deal with my parents' we're-not-a-taxi-service rants anymore. Next, she tried grounding me for the stupidest little things so she could indefinitely shorten my curfew to 7 p.m. My boyfriend said I should no longer be forced to live by her overprotective rules as though I were still a child. He suggested I remind my mother that I'd already successfully left home once and I could easily move out again.

And so, the awful fights with my mother reached even lower lows. Screams, ugly cries, slamming doors. Awful words, silent treatments, uncontrollable fits of pure rage.

Come October, right as the leaves changed colour and fell to their deaths, I, too, struggled to hold on to my family tree. The five of us sat around the dining room table, in our usual spots, unaware it would be our last supper on the last night before I was dismembered from the family. Seated between my sisters and across from me, my mother started making her not-funny-at-all "jokes" about my midterm report card.

"How hard could it possibly be to get the other six percent, Katee? Are you skipping classes again? Forgetting to put your name on assignments? Don't get me wrong, these are good marks, but if you can get a ninety-four, then you're capable of getting the other six percent."

The only advantage I'd ever had over my sisters was my grades.

School had always come easily to me; I'd always been an outstanding student. But even that never seemed to satisfy, much less please, my mother. I came from a long line of overly educated perfectionistic teachers. My mother, my aunt, even my eighty-year-old grandmother had gone to university to become teachers. My eighty-seven-year-old grandfather had been a principal.

I cringed, lost control, and screamed, "God! It's never enough for you! You're impossible!"

My mother threw up her hands, burst into tears in performance of her "poor me pity party" act, and retreated to her bedroom. My middle sister Leigh and my father both went up to check on her, but she snubbed them and refused to come back down for dinner. So, my dad and sisters got pissed at me.

My father defended my mother.

I threatened to leave.

"Katee, you can't just come and go as you please. If you want to be a part of this family, you have to be physically and emotionally present."

"Dad, I'm not a baby anymore. I proved that by taking care of myself for almost a year."

A sigh escaped my father's mouth. "Honey, being a part of a family is more than just taking care of oneself. Your mother and I need you to be more respectful. We need you to want to join us in doing family things."

I laughed. "Family things? Like being dragged all around the province for Leigh's basketball tournaments and horseback riding? Or being forced to wait for Beth while she's at tutoring two days a week? We don't do any family things at all. All we do is revolve around their extra-curricular activities."

"Honey, you spend an awful lot of time with your friends."

"The only time I get to see my friends is if Mom or you are already making the drive into town to drop off or pick up one of the girls, only when it's convenient for everyone but me."

Leigh, my fifteen-year-old middle sister, was still attached to my mother by the umbilical cord. She scowled at me. "You're such a bitch, Katee. Why'd you even come home, huh? It was so nice without you here."

Beth, the youngest, piped in, "Just go back to wherever you were. It'd be nice to live in peace without you again."

My father turned to me. "Katee, something's gotta change. We can't live like this again. Your poor mother's nerves are shot. Go upstairs, and make things right."

"Screw you guys! And fuck her! It's her, not me! She hates me—she always has."

Red quickly coloured my dad's face. His nostrils flared. "Katee! Enough! You're the fucking problem here! No one else."

My heart paused a beat. Tears cooled my face. I'd only seen my father get upset a few times in my entire life.

I looked one last time at the three faces around the dinner table. Resentment. Hatred. Hurt. I ran to my room and slammed my door so hard I scared myself. I grabbed the phone. I had to dial the number three or four times because I couldn't see through my tears.

Someone answered, "Hello?"

I tried to whisper. "Babe?"

There was a slight pause. "Katee?"

"I can't stay here another second. I hate her."

"Don't worry, cutie. I'm coming to save you from that hellhole. Hold tight."

As I hung up, my mother burst into my room. "If you continue to slam my doors in my house, young lady, I'll take them right off." Wildfire blazed in her eyes. She looked demonic.

My eyes couldn't be more open. I shook in fear.

She noticed the phone still in my hand. "Who the hell are you lying to about me now?" She stormed over to me and yanked the phone out of the wall. She got right in my face. I could smell coffee on her breath.

I took a deep breath and spoke extra slowly, articulating each word and every syllable. "Screw you. I'm like the wind, and you can't cage me in. I don't need you."

Her mouth dropped open. "You ungrateful brat. Get out of my house. And this time, stay out."

With my body still vibrating, I fumbled to pack a bag as fast as I could. "For your information, you're not kicking me out. I was already leaving."

"Good. Your manfriend coming to rescue you?"

"He loves me. You wouldn't understand that."

"Oh, I get it."

My stomach started to turn. My palms clammed up. My heart felt like it had broken and its sharp pieces were cutting me on the inside. I lunged toward her. "Get the fuck out of my room!"

A look of satisfaction came over her face, instantly calming her. "This is my room. I pay the bills in this house. You get the fuck out of my room."

I burst past her and ran out the front door. As I searched my bag for my cigarettes, I heard the door open behind me.

"There is no smoking allowed on my property. Put that away until you're off it." With that, my mother closed the door. I heard it lock. We lived in the middle of one hundred and eight acres; we never locked the door when at home. I turned around to face the kitchen windows and lit my cigarette. I stood there smoking it as obviously as I could and blowing the smoke right at the house until I heard a car coming up the driveway.

Through the car window, I watched my boyfriend reach across the passenger seat and push open the passenger-side door. I jumped in the car and slammed it. He smiled and flashed me the sparkle from his chipped tooth. "I'll take care of you, cutie. I'll protect you." With my sisters peering out the front window, his tires spun a few times before getting traction.

I wondered how I'd gotten so lucky, but as we sped down my parents' long driveway, getting farther away from my family, my heart hurt as though they'd physically broken it, and I wondered when I'd become so unlovable.

"I used to fantasize about hiring someone to do a pretend home invasion," I said, as we waited at the end of the drive to turn onto the highway. Just when I wished the shameful words hadn't escaped my twisted mind, my boyfriend glanced at me, looking intrigued.

"Oh?" His impish grin encouraged me to continue.

"The bad guy would tie all of us up and tell my mother to choose two of her children to save, and that if she didn't pick, he'd kill us all. I just wanted to hear her say my sisters' names," I said, as we turned onto the highway.

"Okay. But why?"

"I once begged her to just admit that she loved my middle sister more than she loved me. I remember her response word for word. 'It's not that I love Leigh more, it's just that she's easier to love.'" My voice cracked as I started to cry.

He shook his head and put his hand on my lap. "Nothing is easier than loving you, Katee."

Even though we'd only been dating a little over a month, my boyfriend asked me to move in with him, into the spare bedroom he rented in his much older friend Patrick's house, while we looked for a place of our own. Patrick's house was infamous for the excessive partying that occurred there; it contained upwards of twenty people between the ages of twenty and fifty at any given time. We played crib, euchre, and bid whist. We drank and smoked, sang and danced. We ate. And everyone in the house stuck up for one another. It felt like how I imagined a real family would.

My boyfriend made me feel like a superstar. Every report card I brought home, my boyfriend whisked out of my hand and eagerly passed around the room. People couldn't believe my extraordinarily high marks. It felt so great to have so many people feel proud of me. They understood and appreciated the hard work and determination it had taken to get those marks.

After seeing my report card for the first time, one of our acquaintance's mouths dropped open. He slowly raised his eyes to meet mine. "Holy crap, Katee. This is outstanding. You sure are a smarty. The whole damn package. Got any friends like you for me?" He blushed then laughed.

Neither Allison nor Arleen would be caught dead in the presence of these hooligans. In fact, most of my boyfriend's friends said they had barely passed most of their classes; a few hadn't even graduated high school.

Here, I felt truly loved and accepted. Nobody here wanted me to change a single thing about myself. I felt content; I finally belonged.

Chapter 10

Gabbi

Leaving British Columbia feels bittersweet. To leave is to go farther from my ex but closer to the end of our family vacation. Mom, Dad, Tara, and Warren flew out earlier this morning. Bryanne, Johnny, Vince, and I fly later this afternoon. We're resting in our respective rooms.

I text Bryanne. *What time do you guys want to head back to the airport?*

Bryanne: *1p.m.?*

Me: *That early? Our flight's not till 4:40 p.m. and it's only an hour and a half away . . .*

Bryanne: *Just so we're not rushed. We also need to fill up and return the rental car.*

Plenty of time to satisfy this restless compulsion to drive by 12009.

Bryanne: *And didn't you want to show us somewhere?*

Bingo. I'll suggest we take a quick detour to check out Alouette Lake once we're on the road. We'll practically pass right by it. How I wish I could resist this urge.

Me: *Oh, right. Let's play it by ear.*

I spot a souvenir shop as soon as we enter the tiny airport. I peek in quickly on behalf of my sister.

"Can I help you find something, dear?"

I look up to see a lady sporting a vest exhibiting an impressive collection of dozens of one-of-a-kind button pins. Some display sayings and others itty-bitty pictures of who knows what. Totally endearing. I instantly adore her.

"Oh, no, that's okay. I was just seeing if you had a Vancouver magnet."

She scratches her head. "Nope. But I've got these beautiful Abbotsford berry ones on sale," she replies. Rising to her tippy toes, she awkwardly leans over the counter and fumbles to unstick a flamboyant piece of fridge jewelry guaranteed to devalue even the high-end appliance brands. She holds out the knick-knack and asks, "Did you know we're famous for our berries?"

Aw. Your pores make your nose look like a strawberry with all its seeds.

He's back.

"It has to be a Vancouver one. My sister and her husband collect magnets from every place they travel, but they didn't get a chance to find one there."

I thank her and start to hurry out, as if by doing so I might lose *him*. Then I think better of fleeing and choose to fight back, as I'm sick of *him* invading our family vacation—which *he's* already done five times in the four short days we've been here. "I hope you're buried in a lazy, shallow grave and your body now fertilizes the goddam berries," I spew under my breath. "Especially their seeds." A sinister smile takes over my face. Abbotsford berries: sweet as karma. Add that slogan to the gaudy magnets.

12009.

I stop abruptly, as though hitting an invisible wall. Oh . . . my . . . God. 12009. I can't believe I forgot. Again. I hold my breath to process this. A quick bark of laughter escapes with the air from my lungs. Unreal. Subconsciously intentional forgetfulness, I decide. I head toward the restrooms to buy a little time for reflection and weigh the gravity of my realization.

Vince exits the men's restroom just as I push on the women's door. "Hi." Any residual disappointment in myself drains out as I absorb the sight of him. I lovingly lunge at him, and we embrace. I pull away, place my hands on either side of his face, and cover it in loud exaggerated kisses.

"And yet, I still love you more," he teases and playfully bops me on the nose.

Strawberry-seed nose.

I deflate.

"We're all checked in. Johnny and I'll return the rental car. Shouldn't take too long."

"K."

He smiles. "I think your sister went to get a drink to take her neuropathy pills."

"If you see—"

"I'll let her know you're using the washroom."

I half smile and cross the threshold.

Enough is enough. I bend down to check under the stalls, ensuring I'm alone, then march to the mirror. I stare at myself, deeply inhale and exhale, and set an intention. I will listen to and fully experience all the mixed thoughts and feelings currently competing for space in my mind and body. I commit to patiently and compassionately loving them through their processes.

A little part of me thinks I'm abandoning a piece of myself. It pleads to be taken, too. Begs to be loved and deemed worthy of saving. This little part feels scared, lonely, helpless, and small.

You're not there anymore, little one. You're here. You're safe.

A bigger part of me thinks a huge opportunity is being missed to show the only tangible proof of my relationship—the place where I got so lost. It demands acknowledgement and justice. This bigger part feels angry, defensive, gutsy, and confrontational.

A dilapidated building, if it's even still there, is not going to help my family understand anything. It offers no justice. This is not the way.

But the part occupying the most space within me knows, without doubt, that all of this is an essential part of the journey. It reminds the other parts of me that things have been safe and far better than okay for a very long time now. It reassures these other parts of the strength of my family bonds, love, and connections.

This winning part feels evolved, empowered, and secure. It

soothes the other parts with motherly love, comfort, and a deep, deep knowing that things are going to continue to get exponentially better.

Yes, everything was very, very scary for a while back then, but things are safe now.

Yes, it was unfair and criminal; justice is deserved, but true healing only really happens from within. And happening it is. Have faith. I commit to figuring out a creative and clever way to reframe and reclaim 12009. Make it count for something positive and meaningful.

I look over both shoulders to confirm I'm still alone. I am. I engage my eyes in the mirror.

"Trust me," I say confidently. "This is absolute, unqualified, outright progress."

An idea excites me. Since Burnaby Blogger is fascinated in knowing *his* story, surely some people will be interested in knowing *mine*.

Everything around me seems to both spin and stand still. Silence and deafening chatter interrupt one another. My body buzzes with life. Euphoria fills my lungs. Power pumps through my veins. I feel high. I must write and share my story. The craving to do so feels palpable. The hunger insatiable. My revelation matures. I don't need to prove or defend my experience. I just need to share it. The missing piece has only ever been my own readiness.

I walk out of the bathroom dripping with confidence like I'm on a catwalk. I scan the busy crowd and spot Vince. He's talking to my sister. Johnny's off in oblivion. I can barely contain myself. I don't even want to try to. I imagine this is how it feels when people suddenly find the power of Jesus. Except I found the power of Me. Everything in my being is integrated, awakened, and fully alive.

"Babe?" I command my husband's attention. I make crazy eyes at him like I'm ready to pounce. This playful act always intrigues him.

"What?" Vince steps toward me, and his eyes match the excitement in mine. While I search for the words to respond, he slaps my ass, hard. "You look manic, hummingbird."

"I am elated!" I squeal.

"Excellent. Why?"

"Because I'm ready."

He knows exactly what I mean.

Chapter 11

Alex

Lunch time came and went, but my stomach stayed stubborn. Reluctantly, I gave in and drove down the street to source a pre-packaged, few-days'-old gas-station sandwich. A not-so-secret guilty pleasure of mine. My favourite: tuna, to which I added mustard.

As I exited the store, plastic container in hand, I stopped abruptly. Nuzzled next to my car, I spotted an old blue four-door Cavalier. Although parked in a legitimate spot, it infringed on my car's space.

I whipped my head around to scan my surroundings. Had *he* found me here? But *he* couldn't be out. Had *he* convinced someone to spy on me? Was I under surveillance again? Could this be an intimidation tactic? A warning shot? I spiraled down *his* drain.

"Excuse me."

I nearly fell off the walkway curb as a woman with a toddler in hand and a baby on hip brushed past me.

"Me, Mommy," said the toddler. "Me wanna do it." His arms were outstretched, reaching for something.

The woman handed the boy a key. "Carefully, Lucas," she said. "Don't be scratching the door again."

The toddler got busy puzzling the key into the lock, and his mother got busy buckling his baby sister in the car's back seat.

Silently, I scolded myself for my hysteria. Of course, it wasn't *him*. How many four-door sedan Chevrolet Cavaliers had been made in the late eighties-early nineties? Plus, *he'd* gotten rid of that old rust bucket nearly a decade before when we'd still been together. When things had still been good. Another lifetime ago.

This woman's archaic navy Cavalier had triggered unwelcome memories. But that letter, that damn letter in the mail from last week, that had found its way into this lifetime. To the here and now.

Back in the comfort of my office, I grounded myself after my parking-lot freak-out. Once calm, my hunger returned. I opened the plastic container housing my tuna sandwich and devoured it. Then I decided to collect more information on the new girl, Grace. I Googled her previous high school and searched the staff directory for the name of its guidance counsellor.

"Good morning, I. E. Callaghan Secondary School."

I cleared my throat. "Hello. Would I be able to speak with Petra, your guidance counsellor, please?"

I was connected to Petra and explained my reason for calling.

"My, my," Petra exclaimed. "That's a girl I thought lost forever."

"Yes, well, thankfully, she's found now," I said. "I'm hoping you'll help to fill in some gaps in my understanding of her history."

Petra snickered. "Wouldn't we all like to know? Secretive little thing she was. Ominous even. She refused to let anyone in. Thought she knew best."

I didn't like the direction this seemed to be heading. I tried to reroute it with a chuckle. "What teenager doesn't?" I asked playfully.

"She turned down all offers for help. She had many opportunities. I felt for her parents. She victimized them. The pain and suffering they endured? I can't even imagine. Spiteful little thing."

I wanted to crawl through the phone line and strangle this dreadful woman. "How so?" I asked through gritted teeth.

"Make no mistake about it," Petra said. "She chose to rebel. I assure you, her parents are good people. Maybe a little on the strict side, sure. But that's love. Tough love."

I rose to the young girl's defense. "I, for one, am hearing a lot of cause for concern," I said firmly, though with more annoyance than professionalism.

I heard a bell on Petra's end of the line.

"Apologies, but I've got to go. As I said, I'm quite shocked to hear she's resurfaced. But I wouldn't get your hopes up. If you suffer from a savior complex, consider this your warning. You cannot help this girl. Even if you could, she won't let you get close enough."

Feeling defeated before I'd even begun, I begged my brain to conjure up another way to gather more history.

A few minutes after Petra ended our call, my office phone rang.

"Alex?" said Doris. "I've got someone on the line for you. Call display says it's from I. E. Callaghan. Shall I put her through? Or send it to your voicemail?"

I looked at the time. I still had fifteen minutes until my next kid showed up. "Put her through, please." The line clicked, and I started, "Petra—"

"Oh, hello there. This isn't Petra, actually. I'm Mary. I'm a colleague of Petra's."

I grabbed a pen and notepad. "Hi, Mary. How can I help you?"

"I'm sorry to just cold call you like this. I hope I haven't crossed a line. But Petra just told me our sweet girl has resurfaced at your school."

"I'm sorry, Mary. Petra didn't mention you," I said.

"Oh, geez. No, it's me who's sorry. I'm a teacher at I. E. Callaghan Secondary School. I'm the one who tried to connect Grace with Petra in the first place."

Hope prickled my skin from the inside out. "I am so happy you called. But would it be okay if I called you back in a couple of minutes, please?" Under no circumstances would I talk with this woman until I verified her identity.

"Good. Very good. Yes, of course," said the woman.

"Great. Thank you." I hung up.

I couldn't help but get excited. Perhaps Mary held the key to this young girl's mysterious, vaulted past. Once a few minutes had passed, I redialed the school's number and was successfully put through to an English teacher named Mary.

"Hello?"

"Mary?" I asked. "Thanks for letting me call you back."

"Thank you, Alex. I appreciate you taking the time to talk with me. I'm over the moon to hear that Grace has resurfaced, safe and sound. What a miracle."

"Well, I'm hoping you might be able to provide the missing pieces to this puzzle. I'm trying to understand what might have been going on to cause her to drop out of high school."

"In short, I'm not sure. Despite observing many warning signs, I failed to figure out that very thing in time. I failed her."

"How do you mean?"

"My heart melted the day I met Grace. I adored her. I truly did. But I could hear her silent screams for help. Deafening and heartbreaking. The poor girl. Something clearly wasn't right. Someone had to help this kid. And fast. The most alarming thing I noticed was her peers targeting her. I witnessed this myself on numerous occasions. And once, I overheard a group of students talking about jumping Grace at lunch break in the smoking pit. I decided to hold her back in class that day to ensure no harm came to her. Afterwards, I reported the threat to the office. I used to follow her out to the bus area at the end of as many days as I could. You know, to ensure she didn't get beat up and such. I started noticing this James-Dean-looking guy, but much older, hanging around each afternoon to pick her up. He just looked like trouble. Leaning back against his car with a cancer stick hanging out of his mouth."

Mary explained she had reported her concerns countless times to all three administrators, following protocol. Nothing had been done. They'd repeatedly told Mary their hands were tied.

"After they confronted her, we never saw her again," said Mary, her tears audible. "I failed her." Mary sniffled.

"Oh, Mary," I said. "You did the best you could with the limited information and control you had."

"Please, promise me this. Don't give up on our girl."

"You summoned, madam?"

I jumped and turned to see my next client approaching my desk as I hung up the phone. "Richie. Yes, hello," I said. "I . . . I was actually hoping we could reschedule our session today. Is that—Would that be okay?"

"Most certainly. Consequently, this means math class is—"

I put my hand up to stop him walking any closer. "That—" I gagged back some regurgitated lunch. I tried again, "That cologne? Is that—?" I spun around and threw up in the garbage pail beside my desk.

Rouge diffused across Richie's previously proper expression. "Oh, shit. I mean, shoot! Shit, sorry. Dammit! Is it too much? Too strong?"

The assaultive stench of my ex's cologne—Eternity for Men by Calvin Klein—had brought back more than just my tuna sandwich.

I smeared the spittle left around my mouth with the back of my hand. "No, no, hun. I'm just super sensitive to smells." Not a lie. Not the whole truth.

"Dang. You're the reason for the new no-scent school signs."

I wasn't. "I am." I nodded. "Unfortunately, it's fragrance-free for me."

"You gonna report me to the air-pollution police?" Richie asked, backing away from me with his hands above his head.

An unexpected laugh stung my raw throat. "Not a stench snitch." I sourced some stale gum for my sour mouth.

"Promise I'll come 'au naturel' next time. No more razzle dazzle juice."

Chapter 12

Katee

He chose me. He could've had any girl he wanted, but he chose me. He made me feel like I was the only other person in the whole world, like I was the only one who mattered. I'd never felt like that before. I wasn't sure I'd ever feel like that again.

One evening, a couple of weeks after my boyfriend rescued me from my parents' house, my boyfriend, his friend Jay, and I were watching TV at Patrick's place. I was trying to study for a math exam I had the next day. The guys kept taking turns going in and out of the bathroom. At first, I didn't pay much attention to it, but then I realized it was happening more and more often. Just when I was about to check things out, my boyfriend approached me.

He batted his eyelashes and gave me his heart-melting smile. "Got something for ya."

"Really? What is it?"

He tossed me a small globe. "I give you the whole world."

This was most definitely the sweetest thing anyone had ever given to me.

He leaned in to kiss me. "I love you, cutie." The kiss was passionate. They all were. Our tongues slow danced in one another's mouths. There was no music playing, but he sang quietly to me between kisses: *"This is no ordinary love, no ordinary love."*

My entire body seemed to merge into his; we became one.

He released my lower lip, looked me in the eye, and said, "This is like no love I've ever heard about in my entire life."

I was in true bliss. My life was so perfect. My boyfriend went back to the bathroom. Wanting more affection, I followed him. The door gently clicked shut just as I got to it. I opened it and walked in. There were lines of white powder on the counter and a little bag about the size of a cracker containing more powder. I had never seen it before, but I assumed it was cocaine. Allison and I had just had an hour long talk the previous week about the rising cocaine use amongst some of our male friends. We were hysterical, shocked, and sad.

My boyfriend handed me a rolled-up bill. "Here you go." It was damp at one end. I felt totally freaked out, but I didn't know what else to do. If he was doing it, and some of my other guy friends were doing it, and they were all okay, I guessed it wouldn't kill me.

"I don't know how."

He giggled. "Hun, put the bill to your nose and lower it to the counter, then sniff hard."

I was terrified. I couldn't breathe right. My body started overheating, and I worried I'd pass out. What would the man of my dreams, my knight in shining armour, think about me if I chickened out? I was already fourteen years younger than him. I didn't want to make the age gap more obvious than it was already. I wasn't a child any longer.

I bent down and inhaled the line through my right nostril. Immediately, I choked and coughed. My nose burned, and a pungent, paint-fumes taste confiscated my nasal passage and throat. My head got hot, my body tingled, and for a moment I had trouble focusing on my surroundings. My throat started to close off. I struggled to swallow. My heart was pounding out of control. I looked in the mirror. My face was as white as the powder. My pupils alarmed me. For the first time since I'd met my boyfriend, I felt exceptionally unattractive.

I anxiously exited the bathroom. I heard a high-pitched giggle come from behind me. "Guess she actually is the girl next door," I heard my boyfriend say.

I had no idea what was happening to me. Would I choke to death?

My saliva accumulated in my mouth, and I concentrated on trying to swallow but couldn't. I ran to the bathroom to spit in the sink.

"Want another?"

"Oh, I'm good. I need to study now."

My boyfriend's face got serious. "I'm driving you to your parents' place. You're running out of clothes, and you don't have the rest of your books. We'll go quick, grab as much as you can, and we'll jet."

"Babe, I'm feeling really strange. I don't want to face my family right now."

He grabbed my hand. "You always look great, cutie. Let's go before it gets too late."

The entire drive out to my parents' house, my legs twitched, my feet felt uncomfortable, and my mind raced. We didn't speak a word the whole way there, but my boyfriend had a mysterious grin on his face. He drove a lot faster than usual. Maybe it just seemed that way because I was so high. Finally, we turned into their driveway. It was half a mile long; we drove up hills and bends before finally reaching the house. All the lights were out.

I grabbed my key and exited the car. I tiptoed up to the house. As I reached the door and went to press down the latch, it opened.

My mother stood in the doorway with a disapproving look on her face. "Why are you here?" She had only opened the door enough to see my eyes.

"I have a math exam tomorrow. I forgot some of my books." I pushed past her and to my bedroom, grabbed my books and a few pairs of fresh underwear, then bolted out the front door as fast as I'd entered it.

"Go!" I shouted to my boyfriend when I was back in the car. We pulled away so quickly I heard the loose gravel fly away from us.

I felt strange. My mother had totally noticed I was messed out of my tree. Now, she'd really hate me forever. I still couldn't swallow the entire way home. Was it possible I could die from this? If I did, everyone would think I was a cokehead even though that was the first time I'd ever tried the drug. I could have said no, but I hadn't.

For the first time in our two-month relationship, I was angry with my boyfriend. My lover, my protector. He'd exposed me to the other side. But worse? He'd forced me to go to my parents' house in the middle of the night, high out of my mind. I had a suspicion he'd wanted my mother to see me in that state, to ensure the deal was sealed. I chalked up my suspicion to the paranoia the drug provided.

Being in high school sucked. I felt like a child. The saving grace was my co-op placement: a cool cooperative education program my school offered Grade 11 and 12 students to provide two hundred and twenty hours of work experience in the community in exchange for four high school credits. I chose a bougie boutique downtown called Lovely Louise. It was a real job where I felt like a real adult—two days a week, anyway. Since it paid in credits, not paycheques, I didn't have an income. My boyfriend assured me he didn't care. He made lots of money tattooing. He promised to cover my costs until I graduated high school and could contribute financially.

While we searched for a cheap place of our own to rent, my boyfriend and I spent weekend mornings in the park people-watching. We'd pack lunches, a blanket to spread out on the grass, and cards to play games like bid whist, our favourite. But my favourite part of our weekends in the park, besides the hours of making out and receiving never-ending compliments, was looking through the classified section of the local paper.

"Oooh, babe, look at this one. Two bedrooms, one bath. And it's on the east side of downtown just off the main road, closer to my school."

My boyfriend sat beside me gathering fall leaves into a pretty pile of red, orange, yellow, and green. He smiled then kissed me. "You're so cute. It's just a crappy apartment. But since you're all mine now, you can have whichever one you like."

My cheeks started hurting from my perma-smile. "You forget. This is all new for me. I lived alone before but didn't get to pick the place. It's exciting."

"How many do you have circled?"

I dropped my chin and looked up at him with puppy-dog eyes. "Eight."

He let out one of his high-pitched giggles. "Alright, then." He unclipped his cell from his belt. "Let's start calling them."

I shrieked and did a little happy dance.

Within a few days, my boyfriend had rented us a place of our very own. It cost double what Patrick had been charging him, but we got more than double the alone space. I worried about how we'd afford it with me still in high school and the tattoo parlour my boyfriend had worked at having closed a few months back. But my boyfriend assured me he only needed to do four extra tattoos a month from home to make up the extra cash and he had a waitlist a mile long.

Our apartment was one of three units inside an old red-brick, two-storey house with cream-coloured shutters that hugged paned windows. Our front entrance spilled into our living room. A huge window on the left let in tons of natural light. Our large rectangular kitchen had plain white walls and laminate, square floor tiles. The right side housed a wall-to-wall counter with a white stove and white fridge but sadly no dishwasher. The left wall featured another big window. Past the kitchen, a short hallway led to a side door, our bathroom, and our bedroom. It was nothing special but really cute and all mine. It symbolized my independence. Living in the centre of downtown, I no longer needed to rely on anyone to get anywhere, and my friends could come over anytime. I finally felt free.

We couldn't move in until November first. We didn't have any furniture, so our landlord offered us a pull-out couch, a table, and an old TV to borrow until we got ourselves situated. We stayed in the spare room at Patrick's for the last bit of October. My boyfriend promised me a kitten if I accepted all responsibility for its care. He joked that he already had two dependents he was responsible for: his dog, Harley, and me.

Moving day. Anticipation filled every cell in my body. Aside from our clothing, we didn't have much to move, so I was surprised when Jay showed up with a U-Haul truck.

"Hey, lovebirds. You ready to get going?"

My boyfriend glanced at me, flashed a smile, and winked. "Sure are, man," he said to Jay.

I could barely contain my enthusiasm. I grabbed my boyfriend's hand and pulled him to the truck. "Hope our landlord already put the pull-out couch and TV he said he'd lend us in there. Babe? Can we go to the thrift store after to look for more furniture?"

My boyfriend chuckled. "Sure, cutie. But we'll do it after we get the rest of your stuff from your parents' place."

My excitement was instantly taken over by anxiety.

He cupped my cheeks, looked me in the eyes, then kissed my lips. "Don't worry. It's the last time you'll ever have to go there. Promise."

I'd had no contact with my family since the night I'd left over a month ago—aside from the brief exchange with my mom when I'd picked up my textbook a couple weeks back. "What if one of them is home?"

"It's a weekday. They'll be at work and school."

"What if someone stayed home sick?"

"They can't stop you from getting your stuff. If they try, they'll have to deal with me."

Exactly my worry.

The twenty-minute drive seemed to take an entire day. I would have preferred to open the car door and roll out onto the highway than to go anywhere in the general vicinity of my parents' house. Finally, we arrived at the bottom of the driveway.

Positive I was going to throw up, I made a suggestion. "Maybe I should just walk up in case someone's home."

My boyfriend nodded his head, signalling Jay to turn in. "It would take you thirty minutes just to get up there. Plus, you can't carry everything back down."

I closed my eyes and prayed everything would go smoothly. I felt the truck come to a stop.

My boyfriend and Jay opened the front doors, and the truck raised as they got out.

"Holy shit! Nice place. Why the hell would you wanna leave here, Katee?"

My boyfriend giggled. "Cause money can't buy her me." He and Jay both laughed.

The rear door opened beside me, and my boyfriend yanked my purse from my lap. I heard my keychain jingle. The house appeared to be empty. My shoulders dropped as I exhaled a breath that felt as though it had been trapped in my lungs since we'd left town.

My boyfriend had already unlocked the front door. "Come on, let's check this place out." He and Jay disappeared into my home. I got out of the truck and turned to look back down the driveway. Although the house sat a half mile off the highway, one could still make out the sound of passing traffic from down below. It was easy to mistake the noise of it for a car coming up to the house. The driveway climbed uphill from the road and was full of bends and turns. It was impossible to see incoming visitors until they made it all the way up to the house.

I had just finished throwing my last pair of shoes into a black garbage bag when my boyfriend and Jay entered my bedroom with a tool kit.

My boyfriend put it on my desk. "Let's get the bed first."

"The bed? We're not taking that, hun." I'd picked out that bed myself. When our family had moved from the city, none of us kids had wanted the office space on the main floor as our bedroom even though it would finally give us our own room. Our parents had made us a deal that whoever agreed to take the office space would get a new bed since we only had two beds from the two bedrooms we'd shared in our last home. I'd sealed the deal, and my parents had bought me the bed of my choice. It was technically a bunk bed, but the bottom bunk was a futon that could serve as a couch or fold out into a double bed.

"Like fuck we're not."

"Only the desk is actually mine. You guys can take it out to the truck."

My boyfriend laughed at me. "Would this stuff have been bought if it wasn't for you? Will this stuff be used anymore now that you're gone?"

"I guess not."

"Everyone else has their own bed and wardrobe?"

"Yes."

"Exactly. Without you, they don't need it. Without living here, you do."

"They'll be pissed, though."

"You can't be serious. They'll be happy there's nothing left to remind them of you."

A physical pain consumed my heart. It felt as though it was being squeezed so hard it might rupture. I thought about how perfect my family would be without me in it. My hands and feet started to get cold; in turn, they cooled off my aching heart.

"You're right. Fuck them." Through my tears, I began ripping my sheets, pillows, and duvet off my bed and shoving them into a black garbage bag. My boyfriend smiled, and he and Jay started dismantling my wardrobe.

I spent the entire drive back to town thinking about how my furniture would look in our new apartment. We had a huge wall-to-wall closet in our bedroom that could house all my boyfriend's clothing as well as anything we wanted to store. I would be able to have my wardrobe all to myself.

"Where should we put my desk, babe?"

"I'll need it for my work stuff. It'll go in front of the side kitchen window so I can get as much natural light as possible."

I reached up and around the sides of the passenger seat in front of me, squeezing his solid shoulders. "That makes perfect sense."

My boyfriend glanced at Jay in the driver's seat. "Pull over there on the right beside the bank." The truck came to a stop at Lovely Louise's. He turned around and smiled at me. "Have a good day, cutie."

"Babe, it's already after one. I can't just show up now for less than two hours."

"You have to stop missing so much, cutie," he said in a condescending voice. "If you don't get your act together, you won't graduate this year."

Confusion muted me. Every hour of work experience and school I had missed had been because of him. Why was he suddenly disappointed in me?

"Go on, little lady," said Jay. "We'll unpack the truck and get everything set up for you so it's ready when you get home."

Their condescending tones mortified me more than the fact that I was still a pathetic teenager being dropped off for school. I got out of the truck and entered Lovely Louise's, my head hanging in shame.

At three o'clock, my co-op supervisor dismissed me for the day.

I bit my lip. "I thought I'd stay until close today since I was so late getting here."

The silence was awkward. I fiddled with my hair to pass the time. I rarely saw my supervisor smile, and today was certainly no exception.

Annie stopped stamping the store's name onto the premium handled paper bags but didn't make eye contact. Her thin lips parted. "Katee, your shift with us finishes at three," she paused, examining me for so long I felt my head bob in exhaustion, "the same time your school finishes for the day. I realize you're not receiving a paycheque, but you are attempting to receive school credits for the time you put in here." She continued stamping the bags.

I took a deep breath and let out a sigh of submission. Although I hadn't meant it that way, it was exactly the kind of passive aggressive sigh my mother had used to get under my skin.

Folding the excess of my silver belt back and forth like an accordion, I also avoided eye contact. "I understand completely."

She crinkled her small sharp nose and displayed a patronizing frown. "Your tardiness and absenteeism don't demonstrate to me that you do. Tomorrow morning, try and remember that your day with us starts at half past eight." When I didn't move, she glanced up at me and smiled apathetically. "Well, get going, dear." She tilted her head in the direction of the back door, keeping her gaze on me. "Sounds as though you have some unpacking to do."

I grabbed my tattered pleather purse and got up to leave.

On my walk home, as I turned onto our street, I was glad not to see any visitor vehicles parked near our place. Up until this point, much of my boyfriend's and my relationship had been spent in the presence and homes of others. I felt ecstatic to finally have our own private space.

When I was a few houses away, I broke into a jog. I fumbled in my purse to get my keys but was unsuccessful in finding them. I realized my boyfriend must not have returned them to me after using them at my parents' earlier that morning. Luckily, our front door was unlocked. I took a deep breath to try and control my enthusiasm before entering our new home. Nothing made our age difference more painfully apparent than me getting overly excited at ridiculously childish things. Feelings contained, I opened the door.

On the borrowed pull-out couch to my right sat my boyfriend with a lit cigarette hanging out of his mouth. "Hiya, hun." He had draped one of his big knit blankets over the couch. Against the wall directly in front of me sat a huge fish tank; above it hung his snow monkey picture. In the corner to the left I saw the old TV our landlord had lent us; it was the kind you had to go right up to and turn the knobs on to change the channels and volume. To the left of it, under our near-floor-to-ten-foot-ceiling window, sat his red metal vintage Coca Cola cooler.

I turned to him. "It looks great in here. I just love it. Love you." I dropped my purse and headed toward the kitchen. On my left, just under our side window, was my desk: already covered with my boyfriend's tattoo equipment and supplies. I continued past the tiny hallway between our side door entrance and our bathroom and into our bedroom. My wardrobe and bed were reassembled and looked as though they'd been made to fit the room. I couldn't be happier—my very own place. This time was much different than the first time I had moved out of my parents' house. This time, I'd picked the house. All my things were in it.

I walked back through the kitchen to join my boyfriend on the couch. Something out of the corner of my eye caught my attention and stopped me. Our kitchen counter was overflowing with food. Nothing was in grocery store bags; everything was in bulk. I recognized all the brands as well as where they had come from: Costco. The closest Costco was over an hour away, and we didn't have a membership.

I picked up a familiar oversized jar of Prego pasta sauce. "Who got us this stuff?"

"I did."

I noticed a case of soup. "Yum. Tomato is my favourite. I always got my mom to get it for me. I'm the only one in the family who likes it."

"Anything for my girl."

I couldn't remember telling him about my love of tomato soup. Thinking about it, I couldn't remember ever eating tomato soup since knowing him.

I opened the fridge and saw the same kind of yogurt my family ate. "How did you have time to get all the way to Whitby today?"

"Guess I didn't."

Still crouched down, I looked up from the fridge in the direction of the living room. I took a step back from the cool air emanating from the fridge and shut the door. I stood there for a minute, arms crossed. Then I yanked open the freezer door. Chimichangas, the afterschool snack my sisters and I routinely ate and routinely fought over. I glanced back to the counter, trying to figure out how he knew all my favourite foods. Giving up, I grabbed a chimichanga out of the box, threw it on the counter, and reached for the cupboard.

"Oh, crap. Guess tomorrow we need to go to the thrift store and get some plates, eh?" I searched for a paper towel before realizing I'd have to heat up the chimichanga in the oven. "And a microwave, too, babe."

I heard a grunt of agreement from the other room. Never having cooked one in the oven before, I picked up the chimichanga to check the instructions: *bake at four hundred degrees Fahrenheit for twenty-five minutes or until golden brown.* I turned over the package before opening its wrapper; on the front was a big black "B" written in permanent marker. A sick feeling entered my stomach, bullying out the hunger. I marched out to confront my boyfriend.

"All this stuff? It's from my parents' house."

His eyes remained locked on the TV. "So?"

I moved directly in front of him to block his view.

He looked up at me. "What?"

I crossed my arms. "So, why'd you take it?"

"It's the least they can do. I've relieved them of the burden of feeding, housing, and clothing a teenager that technically they're still responsible for, for another year and a bit."

My cheeks grew warm. He smiled at me and patted the couch beside him. I walked over to him and sat down, taking a cigarette out of my pack. "Lighter, please?"

He looked to his right then left. "Oh, I used it to light the candle." He pointed across the room. "It's right there." Casting a romantic, soft light was a round-cake-sized beeswax candle. There was no mistaking it; it, too, came from my parents' house. I must have been so impressed with the fish tank when I'd first came home that I hadn't even noticed my parents' candle sitting underneath it.

A sigh escaped my mouth. I supposed the reasoning my boyfriend had given me for taking things from my parents' house made sense, but I couldn't seem to silence my parents' disappointed and angry voices forcing their way into my head when I imagined them discovering the missing things.

"Where'd the fish tank come from?" I asked.

"Bought it today. Nice, eh? I'm gonna catch fish by the locks and fill it up with them. Make it real natural. Unique."

"Cool." I walked over to grab the lighter, pausing to take a better look at the tank. I'd never had a fish tank before. My boyfriend had talked of having many over his life and often mentioned his desire to get another. "I thought you couldn't afford it yet?"

He raised one eyebrow, flashing me a devious grin. "Could after today."

Excited, I ran back over to him and plopped myself back on the couch. "Why? What happened today?" I assumed he must have received a large deposit from a client.

"I already told you. Your parents chipped in what they owe me for taking you off their hands."

My mouth fell open. "You stole money from them?"

He laughed. "Of course not, silly." He bent over and kissed me on the cheek.

I pulled my face back a few inches. "Then what do you mean?"

"I just pawned some stuff, is all."

"Like what? We just took my stuff."

"Anything I could." He let out a chuckle. "Real slim pickings, though. We went back after we dropped you off at your placement and dropped your shit off here."

My parents made good money but never indulged in material or superficial things. They had used their hard-earned money to pay off our house mortgage as quickly as possible and spent the remaining portion mainly on family trips. I accredited this to my father having grown up as poor as he had. For a while, his family of six had lived in a tent while his father had spent all his spare time building a garage for his family to move into, and then he'd built a house for them.

"Obviously, you stole that candle," I said, glancing at it. "But what'd you sell?"

"Your dad had a huge stash of stuff in the bunkroom in the basement. What's that all about, anyway?"

My dad wanted to be prepared in case there was ever an apocalypse or something of the sort. I didn't want my boyfriend making fun of my dad's left-field belief system, though.

I lit my cigarette and blew the smoke from my first drag in his direction. "Yeah, so that explains the food and the candle, but not what you sold."

"What the hell does it matter, eh? You wanted out, I got you out, and you repay me by questioning me like I'm the asshole here? I can't believe this." He ripped my cigarette out of my hand, burning the inside of my middle finger with its hot cherry. He took a shallow drag and continued speaking before blowing out the smoke. "A few thousand dollars is nothing in comparison to what they'll save in costs from not having to support a third child that they don't even want anymore."

Guilt sunk my stomach. He was right. Of course, he was right. They hated me, didn't want me. He was my savior, my hero, my knight in shining armour.

There was a knock at the door. My boyfriend got up and answered it. I could just barely make out a young guy. His face had clearly gone a few days without a shave, his clothing a few wears without a wash. I couldn't hear any of their conversation, but I saw my boyfriend reach into his pocket and hand the kid something as the kid handed him money in return. My boyfriend shut the door and returned to the couch.

"What was that about?" I asked.

"That, little girl, was about investing and multiplying money to make enough to last until you finish grade school and can contribute financially."

"Drugs? You're selling drugs?" I felt disgusted, enraged.

"How else am I supposed to support a fourth child, Katee?"

Confusion overtook my face.

"You heard me," he said as he walked over to an open box and pulled out three framed pictures. He held up the first one. "He's my youngest, just a baby, stolen by my cunt ex-wife." He held up the second one. "This is my little buddy, he's five years old and stashed away somewhere." He exchanged it for the last picture frame. "And she's my eldest by my high school sweetheart who ran away with her years ago. She'd be nine now."

I didn't know what shocked me more—these bastard children or the fact that my boyfriend's only daughter was closer in age to me than I was to him. Eight years between his eldest and me. Fourteen years between me and him. Almost double the difference.

"I didn't know you had children."

"Had? Wow. Way to rub it in."

"That's not what I—"

"And now, instead of saving up my money to get them back, I'm spending everything I make to support you, a kid who's not even mine. So, don't you dare judge me for doing whatever necessary to provide for you. You're just lucky my kids have mothers who take care of them. Since you don't, I have no choice but to put you first—ahead of my own children and me."

The next day, he left me a letter.

Dear Cutie,

After everything you and I have experienced together in such a short time, both good and bad, I've learned a lot about myself and my feelings. You're so mature most of the time that I forget you're still inexperienced in this thing called life. Your priorities are still all mixed up. But that's not your fault. You'll get it as you grow up more. And I'll help you.

I've tried before to succeed at relationships, hoping they would last forever, but I fucked things up every time. Then when I met you, right after my wife and I split, you showed me that I could move on and love again. The first thing I thought about after I realized how fast and strong I fell in love with you was, how could I marry a girl I didn't love even half as much as I did this new beautiful, sexy Katee? After only a short while with you, I knew we were different together than anyone else. You feel it, too, I know you do. I don't want anyone else; you know that. Love me, not your family who hates you. I understand you, they don't. Sure, we've gone through a lot to get to this point, but I'm not giving up. It's all or nothing, Katee. Forget them. I love you. They don't. I'll make you happy. They won't.

We didn't have a landline at our new place, and only my boyfriend had a cell phone, so leaving me letters became the way he communicated with me when he disappeared for hours, sometimes days, on end—a habit of his I was quick to learn.

Everything changed drastically in our first month of living together. It didn't take long until my boyfriend was my entire world. The few in-town friends I'd made over the past couple years didn't condone our fourteen-year age difference. Allison and Arleen said the gap was cringy and questioned why things with him were moving so fast. They swore my boyfriend was bad news, so they started pulling away. I hadn't even told them he'd robbed my parents, so they didn't know moving back home wasn't an option.

By mid-November, I felt increasingly alone. The day after I first expressed my unhappiness, my boyfriend brought home a kitten. I'd mentioned I'd always wanted my very own, one I didn't have to share with my siblings, one that loved me best. My boyfriend said it would keep me company and give me household responsibilities. Caring for the pets—his dog Harley, the fish, and this new kitten—would be fully on me. I happily agreed and named the beautiful long-haired tortoiseshell Ambrihl.

No sooner had he brought her home than he used her as an excuse to keep me housebound to look after her. He said I needed to watch her every move to know when she needed to be taken to her litter box. I assured him that one of the perks of cats was they came fully trained, but he would have none of my "back talk." He demanded I stay home until he believed Ambrihl could be trusted in our home alone. Since he didn't like me having people over, staying home further isolated me. Sometimes, he'd send people to check in on me when he was gone. And one night, at the end of November, my boyfriend's drug dealer showed up. The next day, I worked up the courage to hint to my favourite high school teacher that I needed help.

Chapter 13

Alex

As Yoshi rummaged around looking for the perfect spot to unload behind my house, I noticed through the little garage window that the overhead door was fully open. I jogged over from the backyard and entered the detached two-car garage.

I'd parked on the street the previous night because I'd had to pee so badly by the time I'd gotten home that I hadn't been able to risk the extra few minutes or the bumpy back alley to get into my garage before still needing to cross my backyard to get inside my house. So, my vehicle wasn't in the garage, but I looked around to investigate if anything else had been taken. Bike—there. Skis—there. Lawn mower—there. Christmas decoration bins—there. Thankfully, everything seemed to be in its rightful place.

I pressed the button on the wall to close the overhead door and exited the garage. Yoshi stood at the house backdoor, nose to glass, waiting to be let in. I pondered the possibilities. How on earth could the overhead door have opened? I was overly meticulous about locking up. My best friend Jack made fun of me, saying I obsessively locked up like I was an American. It'd taken me years of intentional practice to stop locking the bathroom door even when I was home alone. Some habits died hard.

What if last night had been the one night I had somehow forgotten to lock my back door after letting out Yoshi for her final business trip, and someone had not only gotten into my garage but also into my home? Chills bubbled up in my body like fizz in a glass of champagne. How had my garage door opened, anyway?

"Okay, baby Yosh. Today you're needed as home security instead of school support pup."

Yoshi couldn't give a flying frisbee. She waddled to the couch and climbed her doggy stairs to put herself to bed in her little nest.

I kissed the top of her head. "Another day, another dollar. And more dollars for me means more treats for you."

Yoshi cocked her head, and her pupils dilated for extreme cuteness.

"Oh? You require payment in advance of your shift?"

Yoshi perked her ears.

I kissed her head again before grabbing sliced cucumber and a baby carrot from the fridge for my virtuous, wannabe-vegan dog. As I made my way to the front door, I sang to her, and Yoshi howled along. "Bye, baby. Have a good day," I said as I closed and locked the front door behind me.

When I got to my car, the state of its insides shocked me. Everything was everywhere, as though the car had flipped upside down then right side up again. The middle console was open and empty; its contents littered the entire vehicle. The glove box door lay open; its contents were dumped on the floor below. I caught a glimpse of a picture of me—correction, dozens of pictures of Yoshi and me. Christmas cards I'd created far in advance of the upcoming holiday season had been scattered like snow throughout the vehicle. A break-in blizzard. And the break-in bastard had my mugshot instead of the other way around. Now he knew what I drove, what I looked like, and where I lived.

I began tugging at my eyebrow hairs. The garage. I searched the mess for the garage door opener, terrified a criminal had stolen easy access to me and my belongings. Maybe they'd scoped out my garage and decided to come back later with a truck to take the stuff. I found the clicker. Nope. But, wait—how had the robber gotten into my car in the first place? No window had been broken. I absolutely could not believe I had left my car unlocked.

I started rubbing my eyelashes between my middle finger and

thumb. I pulled out a few. Then I dug my phone out of my purse and called the police.

"Oh, for Pete's sake," my mom said. "What the hell is wrong with Jim? You need protection, Alex. What if the robber comes back?"

I had just finished explaining to my mother that it was highly unlikely my most recent ex of three years would be able to stay with me for a few nights while I calmed my nerves. Jim's online gaming addiction had played a huge factor in why I'd broken up with him in the first place. When he had multiplayer quests and combats scheduled, he was unable to do anything else, even work. These meet-ups occurred daily at random times depending on the time zone of the teammate arranging it. Most days, he'd stay up to the dead of night or wake up in the wee hours of the morning to play. Jim claimed he couldn't let down his teammates and that "his people depended on him." He didn't expect me to understand. He'd been a part of something, something that had trumped a true partnership with me. Clearly, the irony had been lost on him—he'd been blindly loyal to people roleplaying a game in a fantasy world but unable—unwilling—to show up for his team in the real world. So, no, Jim was not going to stop pretending to be a courageous, tough guy online to go to his ex-girlfriend's place, be an actual warrior, and protect her from the rogues in the real world.

"Wow."

I laughed at my mother's inadvertent use of Jim's favourite game's acronym. "You can say that again."

"Such a man-child," my mother continued, "thank God you finally kicked him to the curb. But what are you going to do? I do not want you in the house alone, Alex."

"I know, Mom. But the cops assured me I'm safe. I guess this kind of thing happens all the time. The fact that they didn't take anything suggests they were only looking for change. And they must have just unknowingly hit the garage door clicker. I'm shocked it works from so far away."

"Please call a friend to spend at least tonight with you."

"Already did. Jack is coming over later. But I've got to let you go now, Mom. Just pulling up to the school."

"Call me when you get home tonight, please. Before you enter your house."

"I will," I said.

"Oh, and two more letters came here. I posted them to you earlier this week."

Holy shit. What if the break-in had been *him*? Was *he* out? I had to call the jail.

"Alex? Still there?"

"Sorry. Yup. Gotta go, though. Thanks for forwarding them on. Love you."

"Love you more, Magoo."

"Love you most, and that's the end of that," I said, quickly ending the call to win the doting debate.

Chapter 14

Katee

Student: Katee
Assignment: Greek Mythology
Teacher: Miss Templeton
Submission date: November 29th

Persephone

They came into my home—five young men from the city. My boyfriend owed them drug money. It was strange. He was gone; they knew he was gone; they were still coming. What was stranger? They were coming; he knew they were coming; and he was still gone.

My heart sounded as if transmitting Morse code. SOS. I immediately searched for an out. I picked up the dog leash. "I'm going to walk Harley."

The leader stood out from the rest. His presence demanded attention and obedience. It was difficult to tell the true colour of his skin, as his scrawny body was entirely covered in black ink. He didn't just make eye contact, he seized it. He only barked orders; never asked questions. Although they were all much bigger than him, his gang stood by like eager dogs waiting for their next command. He invaded my personal space. My entire body tensed up. I felt the moisture from his words land on my face as he firmly stated, "I'll come along." I knew not to argue. My boyfriend had taught me that.

Desperate to lose him, I hurried ahead, pretending not to hear his intent to accompany me. Hometown advantage: I knew the shortcuts and secret paths. This town being unfamiliar territory to this unwanted visitor was my only chance to get away from him. But the crunching of the cold snow beneath my feet was an absolute—although inadvertent—betrayal.

"She's here," it tattled. Game over.

His breath was warm on my neck; a contradiction to the cold pistol he held to my breast. As my nylons were ripped open, I dropped the leash. My body stayed motionless as it was forcefully taken over. But my soul escaped and ran free with the dog.

"So that's why we're reading stories about the gods, goddesses, heroes, and rituals of Ancient Greeks," Miss Templeton said.

The bell rang.

They may not have been enthusiastic about diving deep into Greek mythology, but the Grade 12 students were certainly eager to get out of their seats and out the door for lunch as fast as possible.

"And don't forget to submit your short stories. Remember, the question is: would you rather sacrifice your daughter to win a war and save your comrades, or not sacrifice your daughter and lose the war?"

The young teacher was met with grunts and groans.

"Katee?"

From the back of the classroom, I looked up. My courage had been consumed and replaced with regret.

"Can you stay back for a few minutes, please?"

I felt my face flush as I sheepishly looked around at my gawking peers.

One whispered, "Jail-Baitee Katee strikes again," as she intentionally bumped past me.

Miss Templeton pushed her glasses back up on her nose and crossed her arms while she watched the last of the students exit the classroom.

I waited in my seat.

Once we were alone, Miss Templeton shut the classroom door. She was wearing my favourite dress. Bubblegum pink. It looked like a uniform of sorts: short sleeves, high neckline, below the knee. It reminded me of my beloved childhood hair barrettes. When I was young, I'd always asked my mom to put them in my hair for Sunday school before begging for a squirt of her white musk perfume. I'd made a point of always complimenting Miss Templeton when she wore that dress—for the nostalgia, sure, but I also found it adorable. Miss Templeton had a thick, muscular build like that of a linebacker. She also seemed like a real tomboy. So, a dress, especially one as solid pink as this, was cute.

"I love your dress," I said playfully, as though it was the first time Miss Templeton had worn it and the first time I had admired it.

Miss Templeton cracked a tiny smile. "Well, I hoped it would earn me some brownie points with you today."

I took a deep breath. This didn't sound good. "Oh?" I asked, sounding a little too fake. I knew exactly what this was about. I regretted the bold choice I'd made the previous day.

Miss Templeton awkwardly crammed herself into a neighbouring tablet desk. We both chuckled.

"I'm worried about you," Miss Templeton said.

I shifted in my seat. "I'm fine."

"Are you?"

"Promise," I lied.

Miss Templeton looked down and pressed her lips together.

I watched my teacher's shoulders rise and fall. I knew what was coming next.

Pushing her glasses back up her nose, Miss Templeton tried again. "You handed your assignment in early," she paused, "and I had a chance to read it."

I tried to swallow. My hands and feet went cold. I did not break eye contact. Didn't even blink.

"That question was referring to Iphigeneia. I'm curious as to why you titled your short story, 'Persephone'?"

"You didn't specify that, though. And Iphigeneia wasn't the only one sacrificed by a man she loved and trusted. Not the only one given up for the 'greater good.'" I made air quotes with my fingers. "And is there a difference between being killed and being kept prisoner in Hell?"

Miss Templeton looked up and seemingly questioned the ceiling.

"Did anyone actually love her, miss her, search for her?"

"Persephone?"

I shrugged.

"Katee, is this story about you? Did someone hurt you?"

"It's just an assignment," I scoffed. "You gave it to us." I smiled at my teacher, attempting to lighten the mood.

"Your mother must want you back," her teacher half pleaded.

I wished. I huffed and rolled my eyes before they leaked and gave me away. My armpits got damp. "It's not so literal. Perhaps it's a war between the boyfriend and the gang leader, not the mother and Hades. Genders and roles could be reversed. Maybe the father is the mother, and the boyfriend is the father. Who knows? Is the gang leader god of the Underworld or just a minion to him? I guess it's left up to the reader."

"Well, as the reader, it's left me worried. About you. About what's happening at home."

"I don't live at home anymore."

"Not that home."

"I'm fine. I promise. It's just a story."

"Do you have a lunch today?"

"I'm going to go to the store to get something." I knew my teacher wouldn't follow me any farther than my locker to check.

Miss Templeton reached behind her and grabbed my assignment. Paperclipped to the top of it was a Subway gift card.

I reminisced about Subway being a special family treat on the long drives to and from our cottage.

"Have a few lunches on me at the only store within walking distance of the school," she said. She placed the card in my hand and squeezed my hand closed around it.

"You don't—"

"I want to. I'm here if you want to talk."

I thanked my teacher and got up to leave.

When I reached the door, Miss Templeton called out, "Oh. You never actually took a position."

Without turning around or stopping, I said, "Doesn't the greater good always win?" Then I quickly disappeared.

I peeked through the glass window of the guidance counsellor's slightly ajar door. I saw a middle-aged lady with a ballerina-perfect bun typing at a desk. The lady stopped and glanced up. I ducked back and took a few breaths to gather myself. When I heard the typing resume, I gave one of those not-quite knocks that didn't have the courage to be fully heard. A sigh came from within the office. The rolling sound of an office chair was followed by approaching high-heeled footsteps like those of a Clydesdale. The door was yanked open, and in it stood the most prim-and-proper, stuck-up-looking lady I had ever seen.

I wilted, burrowing my head into my shoulders and focusing my eyes on the floor. I was very aware of my skin-and-bone, far-from-up-to-par appearance. The saying "look what the cat dragged in" came to mind.

"Katee?"

The lady's flat tone threw me off. I didn't respond.

The lady asked more firmly, "Are you Katee?"

I looked up at the lady's face. "Yes," I said, making eye contact for the first time. "The secretary said you wanted to see me?"

The lady stepped aside, gesturing for me to come in. I hesitated and broke eye contact. "Is it okay if I go back to class?"

"It'll be quick," the lady said.

I did not want to stay but gave in. The lady gestured to the couches.

I slid past her then stopped. "Which couch?"

She pointed. "That one."

I sat on it sideways and kept watch of the door.

"My name is Ms. Sande. I'm one of the two guidance counsellors here. Would you like me to leave the door open? Or shut it for privacy?"

From anyone else, the question would likely have gotten a quick response. But I couldn't help but hear the *Jeopardy* theme song. My eyes scanned the room, surveying my surroundings.

Door.
Phone.
Window.
Three framed university degrees.

My gaze paused on Ms. Sande's feet before I lifted it, and our eyes met again.

Ms. Sande looked at her watch. "We'll leave it open, then."

Every muscle in my body relaxed. A small breath escaped. My shoulders lowered. "Am I in trouble for something?"

"No. Should you be?"

"Then why am I here?"

Ms. Sande sat down diagonally from me and crossed her arms. "Your teacher, Miss Templeton, is worried about you. Do you have any idea why that might be?"

"'Cause of my assignment?" I asked.

"Did that actually happen to you?"

I knew this silk-blouse-tight-pencil-skirt-four-inch-stiletto-wearing Ivy Leaguer wouldn't have the slightest clue how to begin helping me. She needed an attitude adjustment.

"If you were raped, Katee, I'm required by law to report that to your parents."

"You can't. I'm emancipated."

"Well, the police, then."

I glared at her. "It was just a freaking story. Miss Templeton knows that."

Ms. Sande pulled her glasses down from the top of her head and glared right back. "Watch your language and tone, young lady."

"She follows me around between classes. She probably thinks I'm anorexic."

"Are you?"

My mouth twitched. "I could out-eat my golden lab, Shasta," I said.

Ms. Sande hummed. "There are exceptions to confidentiality, Katee. I don't need your permission to report any concerns I might have about your wellbeing, much less your safety. Do you understand?"

"Yes. But I'm not anorexic."

"Fine. So, how do you explain your appearance? What about

your appalling attendance? Or your plummeting grades? There is much concern about you from many people. Your parents want you home."

I wished that was true. "That's a lie."

"It's not. Your mother calls here all the time."

To maintain her perfect parental image, not out of actual concern. I opened my mouth to interject, but Ms. Sande held up her hand, silencing me.

"Your emancipation may stop us from sharing information with your parents, but it doesn't stop them from being able to share any with us."

I stiffened. "So, what exactly do you think you know about my situation?"

"I know you've run away from home—again. I know that things have recently started going off the rails again rather quickly. And your mother has informed us she believes it's due to a negative male influence."

I glared at the ceiling so intently my face started to quiver. Angry tears escaped my squinted eyes. What a judgmental bitch.

"Where are you living now?"

"With my family," I said.

"I was under the impression you're living with your boyfriend."

"Yeah. He's my only family now."

"Are you safe?"

I looked down at my feet and wrestled with the raw, fleeting feeling that my boyfriend was somehow connected to the rape.

Ms. Sande reached over and grabbed a clipboard.

I flinched.

"Are you safe, Katee?" Ms. Sande repeated.

Still refusing to make eye contact, I said, "Yeah. I'm safe, so you can't tell my parents anything. I don't consent to them knowing anything about me or my schooling. Not even if they call here." I reached my trembling hand to my chest and rubbed my skin. My mind drifted.

Would my parents take me back? Could they ever understand?

After a few seconds of silence, I got up and bolted for the door. On my way out, I said, "Please just leave me alone, Ms. Sande."

Getting raped at gunpoint by the leader of a gang while my boyfriend was out of town was the first really bad thing that happened to me. My boyfriend had owed them drug money, and when he came home the night after the rape, he no longer did. I struggled to tell him what had happened. Not only could I not find the words, but I worried he'd confront the guy and get himself killed.

But a few days after the rape, I blurted it out on our drive over to James's apartment—the same escape route I'd taken three nights earlier. My ears felt like they had been lit on fire. My eyes flooded with tears. I could smell the gang leader's overpowering mixture of cheap cologne, skunked beer breath, and stale cigarette aroma seeped deep into his clothing. My body crawled as it relived the pain of his sharp, dirty fingernails ripping off my clothing, scraping my delicate skin, mauling my frozen shell.

It came out like projectile vomit. "Joe raped me." I started to vibrate and sob.

My boyfriend wasn't sad; he wasn't angry. He showed no emotion at all. "I don't hate you." With a smile and a wink, he said, "Fix your face before we get to James's. No one else needs to know what you've done."

I couldn't catch my breath. Had he known? My head spun. Had he set up the whole thing? My stomach's contents curdled. Had he knowingly put me in danger? My body wanted to jump out of the car. My heart wanted to stay and pretend things would be okay. I pinched just above my knee so hard my nails pierced my skin. Not a dream. My shaky hand pulled down the visor, and I looked at myself in its mirror. I was being ridiculous. He would never. His reaction was simply mature; this was the way an adult handled life's hardships. I felt childish for being so distraught, so dramatic over something that clearly didn't upset my boyfriend in the least. I figured this must have been what people meant when they said there was a maturity gap between a seventeen-year-old and a thirty-one-year-old. I guessed I still had a lot of growing up to do.

Was I to blame for what had happened? Guilt surged through my body like an electric shock. The soft pads of my middle fingers wiped away my tears and the last of my innocence.

Chapter 15

Gabbi

"A secret?" Bryanne's voice crackles over the Bluetooth connection.

I take a deep breath, unsure of my readiness to disclose the truth. But this moment is perfect, as my destination arrival provides an out. I'm not ready for an in-depth conversation, and my sister prefers to stay surface-level anyway. "Yeah. And you're the first person I'm telling," I say. I flick my indicator light before turning into the parking lot. I'm meeting friends for karaoke at our favourite dive bar.

"Oooh," Bryanne says. "Why me?"

"Honestly? I feel bad. You're the most private person in our family, yet cancer forces you to share so much. So, I thought I'd share some malignancy living within me."

"Do tell."

Before now, I'd only ever mentioned that my past relationship had been bad, kind of abusive. No one in my family had asked for any details or for my definition of abuse. I Coles-Notes confide in my little sister.

"He wasn't just . . ." I stop and second guess sharing my secret, but I know the significance of this moment for my healing. "He wasn't only controlling and verbally abusive."

"Okay," Bryanne says, patient with my pause.

"He also hurt me physically," I say, freeing that part of me. My misplaced shame is finally silenced from speaking my truth.

I hear a soft gasp. "Oh, Gabbi. I'm so sorry."

I tell her I'm not quite ready to share any specifics but I am halfway through writing a book detailing my experience. I thank her for being my catalyst.

"Me?" she says. "How so?"

"Hang on a sec," I say. "I've gotta park."

I loop around and wait for a car reversing from its spot. Once parked, I kill the engine.

"Still there?" I ask.

"Yup."

"Well, it's something I've wanted to tell you guys, explain to you for decades now. I just never found the words. Or the guts, I guess. When you got sick, I knew it was now or never. It's not like Mom and Dad are spring chickens."

We laugh. Nothing is funny. Certainly not us pretending the deadline of my book is the threat of my parents' old age as opposed to my little sister's impending death.

"Heavy stuff. And you've already written half a novel? Holy. When did you start?" Bryanne asks.

"Five months ago. Literally the morning after we got home from our family trip out West."

"Wait, does that have something to do with what you wanted to show me so badly?"

12009.

My heart drops. Anxiety overwhelms me. I grab my purse and get out of my car, quickly slamming the door as if attempting to escape *his* essence and trap it in the car. "Yeah," I say. "It does."

Bryanne waits, always comfortable sitting in silence and proficient in patience.

"Um . . ." I hurry toward the pub entrance and shiver away my fluster. The air is uncharacteristically cold, even for March. "I wanted to show you where I lived with him all those years ago," I say.

12009.

"Oh. Why?"

"I don't know. I thought being back there, with you, and being older, stronger, wiser, would somehow empower me. Stupid, I know."

"It's not stupid."

"The address kept taunting me. It sounds crazy, but I swear it was, and I just wanted it to stop. I thought going there, facing it, would put an end to it. A little exposure therapy with myself, for a change."

"For a change?"

"I just mean instead of with my private practice clients."

"Ah. So, what's the address?"

12009.

I swallow it down, knowing damn well it needs to come up, needs to get out. I promised myself I'd find a way to reclaim it. But how do you reclaim a number?

I reach the entrance of Captain Bob's and pause beside the door to finish up with my sister before entering the boisterous bar. Leaning against the wall, I brace myself to brave saying it out loud.

"Twelve thousand and nine," I say. I watch my breath disperse into the chilly air, taking the numbers away with it, breaking them down into minuscule droplets of water that create a fleeting misty cloud.

"See? Easy."

I scoff.

"Gabbi, I'm in awe of you. I've always looked up to you as my big sister. But this? This is huge. I can't wait to read your story."

The weight of her words suffocate me.

Chapter 16

Alex

The doorbell rang. My heart beat glitched. Yoshi went ballistic, barking incessantly. As we made our way to the door, one of us much faster than the other, I reminded myself that robbers didn't politely announce their presence.

"Ladies," Jack greeted.

I jumped up to hug my six-foot-six-inch best guy friend before he could get through the doorway. Never one for affection—physical or verbal—I clung on tight to prove the embrace needed and necessary.

Jack appeased me but kept it cool by resorting to his typical sarcasm. "Geez, Alex, let me greet the woman I'm here to see first, will ya?"

I released my reserved bodyguard, and he bent down to love on Yosh. "Beauty before age, right, girl?"

I slapped his shoulder then gave him space to come in.

I busied myself slaving over the stove to prepare the most guest-worthy meal I could muster—spaghetti—while my overnight protector reprogrammed my garage door opener, cleared every room in my house like the cop he wasn't, and promised to install a home security system like the owner he was—of ISS: Integrated Security Systems. I'd been in awe of Jack, three and a half years my senior, since the day we'd met almost a decade before. At just twenty-three years young, he'd owned a Pita Pit franchise. In the years that followed, he'd started his own security company and worked his ass off, becoming a self-made millionaire.

"Hungry?" I asked, as Jack and his helper joined me in the kitchen.

"We both know you don't cook," he said.

"Wrong," I rebutted. "I've perfected the art of boiling water."

He laughed. Then the smoke alarm started wailing. Yoshi barked like the guard dog she knew she needed to be now. I'd forgotten my attempt to make garlic bread.

"Hopefully your water doesn't taste as burnt as it sounds and smells," Jack teased.

With the near disaster deterred, we sat down to eat. I desperately wanted to tell him about my ex making contact, but what was the point? Until I got brave enough to tell him everything that had happened in that relationship, he wouldn't understand the scary significance of the letters or the creepy coincidence of the break-in. Jack never shied away from stating his strong feelings of disapproval for the men I dated. I couldn't bear his disappointment if he learned of all I'd put up with—all I'd stayed through in that specific relationship. The last thing I wanted was for my most judgmental friend to have a reason to judge me instead of the men I dated.

My cell rang.

"It's my sister. Mind? We need to sort out a few trip details."

He shook his head. "I'll clean up."

"I'm so glad you're coming for Christmas," said my sister over the phone.

"Of course, Trolley. I wouldn't let you spend your first one away from home alone," I said. "Plus . . . Australia," I joked.

"I didn't think being so far away would be so hard. Summer was the worst. Not only did I miss being with you guys up at the cottage, but it's bloody winter here then."

I couldn't begin to imagine how homesick my sister must have been this past summer. For our entire lives, we'd spent as much time as we could at our cottage in the summers. As kids, since our mom had been a teacher, we'd moved up to our cottage every July and

August. Our dad drove back and forth to join us on the weekends but worked in the city during the week.

It hadn't been just our immediate family up there. Our uncle had a cottage beside ours, our Grandma Kathy had a cottage five down from his, and our aunt's cottage was beside hers. Our aunt was a teacher, too, so she and our three girl cousins—the same age as us—also spent the entire two months on Shabomeka Lake. Their dad made the same commute back and forth as ours did, making our summers mostly ladies'-only. We filled our days with swimming in the cool lake; salamander hunting and fort building in the immeasurable acres of the provincial park forest; fishing; burning dirty dogs and marshmallows over the campfire on sing-along nights; playing card games and cribbage and backgammon on our sunny screened-in porch; and holding singing competitions while we washed, rinsed, and dried the daily dishes. Although we lacked the luxury of a dishwasher at the cottage, the nightly experience bonded us—after we'd fight over responsibilities.

Christmases were a close second to our summers, so I refused to let my sister spend her first Christmas in Australia without at least one of us. It was a bonus that I'd be leaving Canada's winter weather for a selfish second summer.

"Mom told me about your car. Scary stuff. You okay?"

"Ya. Jack is here now." In the kitchen, I saw the dishes were done and drying on the rack. "He's spending the night." I turned to see Yoshi and Jack snuggled up on the couch.

"I'll let you go, then. I'm excited to see you so soon."

"Sounds good. Love you, Trolley." I hung up and joined my besties in the living room.

Yoshi stumbled over to my side of the sectional and greeted me.

"Why'd you call her Charlie?"

I laughed. "Trolley," I corrected. "When we were little, I couldn't enunciate her name. My garbled attempt sounded like Trolley, and it just stuck."

"Your mom is such a weirdo," Jack said to my doting dog. "And an idiot," he said to me. "I still can't believe you almost called your crazy friend to come tonight instead of me."

I tossed a pillow at him. "Don't be mean." I rarely saw Tiffany anymore. Truth be told, she had a diagnosed personality disorder, but she meant well. And I held a soft spot for her. If people knew all she had survived in her childhood, they'd give her grace.

Also true was my intentional distancing from her over the years. When we'd met as teenagers, her behaviour had seemed developmentally appropriate. But as I'd matured and grown and become a professional, she'd struggled to do the same, and it'd strained our friendship.

Jack had always been my most dependable friend. The man had proven time and time again he would do anything for me. But Tiffany remained the most non-judgmental person I knew. This made me think perhaps I could confide in my friend from my past about my relationship from the past.

Chapter 17

Katee

Everything felt different leading up to Christmas. People still rushed around like the world would otherwise leave them behind, but instead of some obligatory duty or a necessary-yet-dreaded mundane routine driving them, during the holiday season, people seemed to rush willingly, in anticipation and excitement, toward something magnificent. Christmas time captivated me.

But this year, the season had me homesick for my family, especially my mom.

Growing up, my mother always pointed out that stores put out their Christmas stock and displays earlier and earlier each year. I remembered once, in the first few days of November, walking into the mall while my mother shook her head and sighed loudly. As the three of us girls shuffled along behind her and into Sears, Mom said, "Can't they let us take down our Halloween decorations before they shove Christmas in our faces?" I loved Christmas so much, I didn't mind at all. But as the eldest, I was to know better than my little sisters, so, by the time I turned double digits, I'd shake my head and sigh in disgust, too. "It's just the most ridiculous thing ever. I mean, really. What is this world coming to?" I said that day, picking up my pace until my mother and I marched side by side in the store, leaving my kid sisters trailing behind.

But once Mom thought the time appropriate, she always outdid herself. She perfected Christmas. Our hands-down favourite Christmas Eve experience was us girls camping out on the floors of our parents' closets. Sure, it freed up our beds for our out-of-town family, but just like everything else, Mom turned it into an epic adventure. Unrolling foam mats, digging out our parents' old, stinky sleeping bags, and watching my little sisters fight over who got to double up and sleep with me became the memory to beat.

Unpacking our old Christmas tree decorations excited us girls even more than unwrapping our presents on Christmas Day. We searched for our favourite ornaments and loved rediscovering the ones we had forgotten about. I vividly remembered one year because of my youngest sister's heart-melting smile.

When I was eleven years old, I carefully reached into a cardboard box and removed the tissue protecting a long-lost treasure. "Oh my gosh, Leigh. Remember this one?" I cradled in my hand one of our all-time favourites: a tiny mailbox made from clear plastic mesh. Brown and red yarn, most likely hand-stitched, alternated in and out of each tiny mesh hole. The door opened, and each year, us girls filled the mailbox with top-secret mail from mystery senders. Once we found unopened mail from the previous year, patiently waiting to be read, hoping for a response.

Beth squealed with excitement. She proudly swung the ornament of a tiny porcelain baby bear in a swing back and forth between our faces. In unison, Leigh and I grunted in defeat.

Yearly, we competed to see who could find their "Baby's First Christmas" ornament the quickest. Hands down, Beth could win any contest for cutest kid ever born on earth—or any other planet, for that matter. With platinum blonde hair, almost translucent skin, and beautiful blue eyes the size of saucers, she looked like an adorable, friendly alien—the kind that couldn't frighten a soul and that everyone wanted to take home and keep. On this particular Christmas, she also sported an orthodontic metal contraption called a "twin block." Picture silver metal twice the size of her mouth—in her mouth. It looked painful and magically impossible. It contorted her face and skewed her still-developing speech, making her look and talk like a robot. Leigh and I used it against her whenever need be, but truthfully, it made her even more adorable and endearing. Of course, we never told her that.

Beth giggled and shoved her ornament closer to our faces. "See? Told you. I won."

Leigh and I looked at one another before Leigh glared at Beth. "Ya, 'cause we let you. We have to let you win sometimes."

Beth's proud, ridiculous metal grin didn't waver, and for once, we backed off. She could have this one, it being Christmas and all.

At seventeen years old, I experienced two bittersweet firsts: my first Christmas without my family and my first Christmas with my boyfriend. Noticing my nagging nostalgia, my boyfriend tried distracting me by spoiling me rotten during our first holiday season together.

The first weekend of December, I came home from work to find him sitting on the couch with a cheesy, ear-to-ear grin consuming most of his handsome face.

"Come, come, come," he said, as he patted the vacant spot beside him. I examined the room while I kicked off my boots and walked over. No clues. I plopped down on the couch and, with a raised eyebrow, looked up at him through my lashes. He leaned forward, pushed open the doors of our dark brown secondhand coffee table, and pulled out a stack of colourful construction paper. "For your chain-link Christmas countdown."

When I was a child, every year as the holiday season approached, my sisters and I counted the number of days remaining until Christmas on the calendar that hung beside the kitchen phone. We'd cut long strips of paper, one to represent each day that remained. I never had to put my name on my advent chain since my chain differed greatly from my sisters'. I used a pencil and ruler to make it easy to cut each strip straight and ensure each strip's width measured the same number of millimeters. Of course, I erased all the pencil marks before bending each piece into a circle and stapling its ends together. My sisters cut outside of their crooked lines if they even drew any in the first place. My countdown chain also stood out from my sisters' because I only used Christmas colours, which I alternated in a pattern. Eventually, I learned my friends counted down the days until

Christmas with elaborate, store-bought advent calendars by pulling back little numbered flaps and uncovering a chocolate surprise each morning. I looked forward to tearing off one of my coloured construction paper links just as much.

"Cutie?" My boyfriend plopped the package of construction paper onto my lap. "Gonna show me how it's done?"

I nodded. Best boyfriend ever. Using my nails, I sliced through the package's thin plastic covering. "We're going to need a ruler and scissors."

A few days later, a familiar and comforting smell greeted me in the hallway of our building as I searched for my keys. I inhaled deeply to capture all that I could. The aroma swirled around my head, seducing me and stimulating a memory.

Mom and us three girls had invented the sharp, spicy Christmas aroma at our old house. I could see my mother laughing in our old kitchen, wearing her faded orange apron with the million tiny brown flowers covering it. I pictured her with beautiful, long, chestnut-coloured hair. I never got over her chopping it all off. My aunt used to ask her for the brand and box number of the hair dye she used. Mom had always gotten a chuckle out of that because even though Aunt Pat never believed it, us girls knew Mom had never dyed her hair once in her whole life. I recalled my little sisters sitting on either side of me at our white table with the brown and gold speckles. A bowl of fresh oranges sat in the centre. We echoed Mom's laugh—Leigh with her right eye squeezed shut, as it had been shot with the orange acid. We squirmed in our chairs and squealed with excitement as we stabbed the fragrant fruit with dozens of sharp, brown, delicious-smelling cloves and juice squirted out of it. We named this tradition making Christmas perfume.

Now, the smell intoxicated me, lured me toward its source. In a dreamlike daze, I unlocked our apartment door.

"Surprise," yelled my boyfriend from our bright apartment kitchen. He yanked his hands behind his back, hiding what they held. "Smell it?" His smile made my own smile grow so big my cheeks ached.

I dropped my bags and ran to him, tracking snow from my boots across the carpet. I jumped on him and heard a *plop* on the floor as he dropped the contents of his hands to catch me. He wrapped his arms around my hips to support my weight.

I squeezed my legs tightly around his waist and looked into his mesmerizing blue eyes. "You're the best, babe." Ruining the moment, our kitten Ambrihl pounced from God knows where and attacked an orange rolling across the floor. After stopping it, she leaned in to sniff the brown specs on it before instantly pulling her head and ears back. She squinted her eyes and dropped her jaw. Laughing, I nudged my boyfriend. "Look. She's doing her stink face." He glanced at her, laughed, and then spun me around and around.

My boyfriend had gone out of his way to ensure Christmas didn't fall short for me. As I reminisced about my family's traditions, he added them to our list. We strung popcorn and cranberries onto fishing line; he managed to find a copy of *Jingle Cats* to listen to while we wrapped presents and a copy of my favourite holiday movie, *One Magic Christmas*, to watch while we drank eggnog. We bought pumpernickel bread and spinach dip, a shrimp ring, clementines, and pumpkin pie.

My boyfriend spoiled me rotten, but in the end, I couldn't help myself from acting like a spoiled rotten brat. The ghost of Christmas past continued to taunt me with a never-ending reel of nostalgic memories. No visions of sugar plums danced in my head. My visions were more like snippets of old family movies: counting the holiday cards we received from family and friends; making the long drive to and from my grandparents' house with the five of us, our overnight bags, and all the presents packed into the car "like a can of sardines," as Mom always said; waking up Christmas morning to find what little remained of the bread cubes Mom had cut up, left out to dry, and scattered across the floor—apparently, our black cat Nibs loved stuffing, too; finding our fake Christmas tree destroyed after Shasta dragged it around to the back of our house then spent a few hours chewing and pulling off most of its branches.

But this year, no cards came in the mail, we had no family to visit, and even though Ambrihl assumed the role of the family pet providing comic relief, it still didn't feel like Christmas.

Sitting with my boyfriend on the couch wrapping presents, I dropped the see-through bag of colourful bows. "Oh my God." I stared at the bare spot in the middle of our living room wall in between our Christmas tree and entertainment shelf. I elbowed my boyfriend and pointed to the anti-holiday hole. "It still doesn't feel like Christmas 'cause we don't have a fireplace to hang stockings on."

I didn't intend to sound so ungrateful. I fought to hold back my selfish, childish tears. I didn't know what was wrong with me. My boyfriend had listened to every memory I'd shared and done everything in his power to recreate each one for me. But it had been to little avail.

A few days later, the biggest surprise yet shocked me as I plopped down on the couch to relax after getting home from work. "No way. Oh my goodness, babe. I can't believe you did it."

There stood my boyfriend with a wand. "I am your Hairy Godfather," he said. "I am here to grant you your wish." He pointed the wand at what used to be the anti-holiday hole and said, "Bibbidi-bobbidi-boo."

In its place stood a Christmas miracle: the most perfect fireplace I'd ever seen.

My boyfriend curtsied like a cheeseball. "I only needed the right-sized boxes covered with the perfect wrapping paper, a proper shelf for the mantel, and, of course, a 1950s electric wood-imitation fireplace insert."

"Some girls want glass slippers, others want fireplaces," I said, barely able to contain myself.

"Well, cutie, if you keep believing in me, the dreams that you wish for will come true."

I leaned back to admire our complete Christmas scene. Beside the new homemade fireplace stood our handpicked Christmas tree covered in classic, elegant, and grown-up ornaments. All brand new. All matching. None came with a story. Nothing unique. No one-of-a-kinds. We had successfully created my dream tree. Growing up, I'd consistently felt unsatisfied each year once we'd finished our tree. Sure, I loved rediscovering our old ornaments, but I hated that our tree always turned out the same: mismatched, asymmetrical, and tacky. No matter how much time and precision we put into decorating our tree year after year, somehow the result looked amateurish, childish, and cheap.

Now, taking a closer look at the tree my boyfriend and I had decorated, I smiled at its catalogue-perfect beauty. An entire set of three-different-sized-but-otherwise-matching red velvet bows demanded attention; each one had been placed an equal distance apart. Another full set of much smaller but identical red-and-gold-patterned bows filled the remaining spots. Somehow, my boyfriend had found old-style string lights—the ones that glowed softer, more like candlelight, but with alternating red, orange, green, and blue bulbs. Not only did we have more than enough lights to evenly hug our entire tree, but every bulb worked. No duds. The garland looked professionally placed, and the tinsel hung just so. The excessive amount of impeccably positioned presents belonged to only two people, so for the first time ever, I felt truly spoiled. It had always irked me that my parents used the same two or three rolls of wrapping paper on all their gifts, so this year, my boyfriend had bought an unreasonable variety. He'd surprised me with a dozen festive prints and remembered to only get traditional Christmas colours that complimented one another. Each present stood out from the next. Expensive, thick, wired ribbon was perfectly bent around the edges of each parcel and topped each one with a beautiful bow. Our presents looked so aesthetically pleasing, someone might have confused them for props.

And yet, somehow, still, my seemingly perfect, dream-come-true tree fell short. I'd finally gotten what I thought I'd always wanted, but its beautiful shell lacked substance, memories, and meaning. It lacked any remnants of my family. It was them I'd been missing. I felt an overpowering urge to close my eyes, click my heels together, and scream out, *There's no place like home!* I so desperately wished to open my eyes and find myself standing in front of my once-upon-a-time-embarrassing childhood tree. I silently promised God I'd see it with much more appreciative eyes if He would just grant my wish to return home.

Something trampled across my foot.

"Ambrihl, leave it!"

Our kitten held the end of a piece of garland in her mouth. As she ran, dragging the garland across the carpet, it caught on a red velvet bow tied to the tree. The resistance jerked Ambrihl back. With wild spaz-cat eyes and contorted ears, she lunged forward again. The garland plucked the bow off the tree and bungeed it across the room. It landed in front of Ambrihl. She dropped the garland and pounced on the bow then tossed it up in the air and fiercely caught it before taking it down for the kill.

I grabbed the garland before she could come after it again. "Frig. Think she's gonna keep doing that?"

A strange bird-like chirp came out of Ambrihl. She crouched down and flattened her ears as her body vibrated from side to side. I reached down to try and scoop her up, but my sudden movement only set her off. She sprinted forward, hurdling a present and jumping into the tree. Pine needles sprinkled to the ground like snow as the tree rustled and shook. As she climbed higher, the tree teetered to the left.

I stomped my foot and yelled, "She's going to destroy everything."

Startled, she fell out of the tree, barely landing on her feet.

I sighed. As I exhaled, my Christmas spirit deflated with my lungs until the lack of oxygen snuffed it out completely. The colourful lights on the tree blurred together as tears drowned my eyes along with my naïve belief that we could somehow recreate my previous sixteen Christmases without the key ingredient: my family. I forced myself to remember the time Shasta had eaten our fake tree; we retold that story more often than we reread *T'was the Night Before Christmas*. It always made people laugh, and because of it, Shasta would forever be a part of our Christmas memories. I looked at Ambrihl. Though rambunctious and annoying, as a member of my new family, any role she played in Christmas, regardless of how destructive, was an important one.

"Cutie, relax." My boyfriend pulled me into him. "Who takes care of his girl, huh?" He swept my hair off my face. "I brought your childhood Christmas to life. Being as this is technically your last Christmas as a kid."

I scowled at him, hating when he teased me about my age.

"Well?" he said. "It's true. Next year you'll be eighteen—a real, true adult. So, enjoy this. Moving forward, we need to make our own memories. 'Cause I'm your only family now."

Chapter 18

Katee

"Va-va-voom! You're a vision, my vixen," my boyfriend said as he entered the guest bedroom we had previously rented at Patrick's house. Patrick was hosting a New Year's Eve party, and we were sleeping over, though I wouldn't be bringing in the New Year here. My boyfriend had surprisingly agreed to let me celebrate with Allison and Arleen at the community hall party.

Feeling my cheeks blush, I smiled at my boyfriend before turning away to admire myself in the mirror. Never had I felt so elegant or looked so grown-up, classy.

"You look like a real-life princess, cutie."

A floor-length red satin gown hugged my body. A tiny tiara crowned my head. Blood-red tint glossed my lips.

Blood. "My period!" I blurted out. "Jesus. What if my Aunt Flow shows up to ring in and ruin my new year?"

"Looking like that," my boyfriend looked me up and down, "if anyone other than me is showing up for you at the stroke of midnight, it's your fairy godmother to tell you it's time to get your sweet ass back here to me."

I giggled. "Ha ha, funny man. But, seriously. I've been spotting on and off since getting that shot a few months ago."

"That stupid thing is supposed to stop you from getting your period, not make you bleed even more often."

"I'll have to use a tampon. I can't wear underwear under this slip of a dress due to panty lines, much less attach a pad to them."

"Don't want an accident when you're all dolled up and tipsy on the bevvies your girlfriends will be sneaking you all night, my bad girl."

Patrick's doorbell rang.

"Katee," someone called from down the hall.

"The girls must be here," I said.

My boyfriend grabbed me and pulled me into him. "Don't you be kissing anyone at midnight, little miss."

I touched my nose to his. "I wouldn't think of it."

He kissed me on the forehead. "You'll have to wait till you're back for your proper New Year's Eve kiss."

"I wouldn't miss it for the world."

I stumbled into Patrick's around 2:30 a.m., but the house party seemed as lively as though the night was still young. Upon spotting me, my boyfriend whisked me off to the guest bedroom and ravished me like a vampire with seconds left to feast before the sun rose and burned him alive.

When I woke up the next afternoon, every part of me hurt. Hangover headache, body aches, tender tits, and pain that pulsed throughout my entire vaginal vicinity—I was a full mess express. But the evening had been so fun, so worth it. I heard chatter coming from the kitchen and stopped at the washroom before joining the leftover crowd.

It stung to pee, and something smelled kind of off. It hurt to wipe. Oh, the cost of great sex.

I washed up, fixed my face, and headed toward the kitchen commotion.

"I still can't believe the dumb bitch actually got herself life insurance."

The room roared, and everyone shared their collective disbelief.

"Morning," I interrupted.

"Katee!" everyone greeted me.

"You mean 'good late afternoon,' my sleeping beauty," my boyfriend said. "Thanks for a great late night." He winked at me, causing the others to whistle and bark him on.

Truth be told, I didn't remember much of what had happened when I'd gotten back from the community hall, but I remembered having the time of my life.

As late afternoon turned to evening, I started to feel increasingly unwell. The earlier symptoms of a much-deserved hangover morphed into flu-like ones. In addition to the headache I'd woken with, I felt unreasonably cold, exhausted, and overall sick. My whole body ached, and I started to feel nauseous. By the next afternoon, I felt feverish, and every time I used the washroom, I wiped up varying colours of discharge: brown, yellowish-green, grey. It stank more and more until I was certain something must have died up there.

"Oh my God!" The precautionary tampon. Rammed in then covered in semen and left to rot for—how long had it been? Over thirty-six hours, almost forty-eight.

"Babe," I said, ushering my boyfriend into Patrick's guest room, where we'd stayed another night, and shutting the door behind us. "I think I need to go to the hospital," I whispered. I felt my face flush, and I teared up.

"Why?"

"I think I might have a tampon stuck in me."

My boyfriend burst into laughter.

I prayed the shame would swallow me whole.

"You can't be serious, Katee," he said, still chuckling. "What do ya mean, *might*? How might you not know?"

"I can't feel it to know for certain, but I don't remember taking it out. And there are signs."

"Like what?"

"Let's just go to the hospital, please. I think that's what's made me so sick."

My boyfriend scoffed. "Not a chance."

"Huh?"

"I wouldn't be caught dead with an airhead who somehow managed to lose a tampon up herself. I won't be humiliated alongside you. Sorry, clumsy. You're on your own for this one." Chuckling, he left the room, hollering down the hallway, "You guys will never believe this."

The only good thing about still being at Patrick's house was it was much closer to the hospital than ours. After the truest walk of shame imaginable, I struggled to explain my idiocy to a triage nurse then another nurse who performed a medical screening examination to determine my condition and the level of care I needed. Each new person I had to explain my stupidity to told me not to feel awkward because they saw this type of situation all the time. I didn't believe this for a second, but I appreciated them trying to make me feel like less of the airhead my boyfriend was convinced I was.

When I finally saw the doctor, he explained he would need to look inside me using a speculum then remove the tampon using large forceps. He expressed concern for my symptoms and said something about toxic shock syndrome and a possible staph or strep infection. He took blood and urine samples and swabbed inside my vagina and cervix.

When the doctor returned from testing my samples, he looked puzzled.

"So, Katee, the results of the other tests we did aren't back yet. It could be an hour or two, but it could take longer. So, I'll send you home with a prescription for a common antibiotic just in case. But I need to consider the safest option for you."

"Okay."

The doctor seemed to be asking me a question with his expression.

Confused, I matched his look of inquiry.

"The nurse asked you if you were pregnant, and you said no, correct?"

I nodded.

"Well, Katee, your urine tells a different story."

I fainted at the shock of the news. Like, I legit passed out. The second the doctor's words hit my ears, I hit the floor. I couldn't believe it. I never thought it would happen to me. My mother would be so ashamed. Since there was no way I'd be telling her, I internalized enough shame for both of us. I'd become a teen pregnancy statistic. It was far from my proudest day—easily my most dishonorable accomplishment to date. But at least I'd managed to live up to the latest updated expectations placed on me by the jury of my parents and teachers. I didn't understand how I'd gotten pregnant while on birth control. I'd even switched from the pill to the shot so I'd never forget a dose. Could I really have been the anomaly? The one of six out of a hundred that managed to get pregnant on birth control?

I knew my boyfriend would be over the moon for the opportunity to be the father his exes had never allowed him to be. I started warming up to the idea. The thought of holding a key to his happiness, of gifting him a first—even with all the life he'd lived and all the firsts he'd had before me, without me—and of knowing I had something so special to give him overjoyed me. Besides, I could figure it out. Women, even young girls, became mothers all the time. And I wouldn't be doing it alone. I had him. We'd be a real family. I had so much love to give, I'd excel at motherhood. A euphoric feeling snuffed the shame, and I couldn't wait to share and celebrate my secret.

That night while preparing dinner, I asked my boyfriend to pass me the jar of pickles from the fridge. I loudly crunched on them as I finished steaming the vegetables to accompany the chicken. After I'd prepared his plate, my boyfriend watched with a curious expression as I filled mine with pickles in the place of regular veggies. When we finished our main course, I took our dishes to the kitchen and brought dessert back with me to the living room. I rejoined my boyfriend on the couch and handed him his bowl. He glanced at mine and noticed the huge pickle in the place of a spoon. Finally getting my hints, he said, "Geez, cutie. You've polished off an entire jar of pickles like you're pregnant."

I beamed until he noticed my glow. His eyes grew wide. My smile grew big. He glanced down at my stomach then back up at my face. I nodded then made a heart with my hands and placed it over my belly. I wondered how long it would take to grow, to show.

My boyfriend started to cry and mutter nonsensical gratitudes. He got off the couch, dropped to his knees, put his head in my lap, and worshipped me. "Thank you so much, Katee. You have no idea how much this means to me. You've given me the best gift ever. You've made me the happiest man in the world."

While he rambled through tears of joy, I thought about how this was the missing piece of our puzzle, all we needed to truly thrive. I had known he'd be happy, but this was next level. Seeing him glow warmed my heart. Knowing I'd caused it felt fantastic.

"See? You being an overachiever and me having super sperm makes us such a power couple," he gloated.

That he'd already had three children with three different women wasn't lost on me. Neither was the fact that he wasn't involved in any capacity in any of their lives. But he distracted me by thanking me endlessly and profusely for giving him the best possible gift—the chance to finally be an active father. It was something all his exes had denied him. He'd claimed they'd all used him to guarantee they'd have beautiful and intelligent babies and discarded him once they'd had what they wanted. I hadn't believed this when he'd first mentioned having kids, but seeing him so excited that I was pregnant made me feel bad that I'd doubted him.

His elation was contagious and won me over. He loudly and proudly announced my pregnancy to everyone, even strangers on the street. I felt like the first woman in the world to carry another life inside me. He treated me like a goddess and catered to my every need. I couldn't get enough. I basked in his addictive adoration.

A week later at Patrick's house, I'd finished using the bathroom and just unlocked the bathroom door when I heard Patrick holler from the other side of it, "The dumb bitch is dead!"

Ovations ensued.

I hated when the guys called women names.

Wait, dead? Confusion dizzied me. Who? Why were they cheering? It must have been someone on TV. I started to turn the bathroom doorknob.

"How'd he off her?" someone asked.

Panic pricked at me, and I quietly re-locked the door and put my ear to it. *How'd he off her?* What the—?

"She OD'd," Patrick said.

"Called it," I heard my boyfriend say.

Called what?

The chatter on the other side of the door became difficult to differentiate, but I was able to make out that Patrick had just received news that his brother's brand-new wife had died of a drug overdose.

We had just met her. Mere days ago. Could she really be dead?

I felt faint. The bathroom light seemed to get brighter before dark spots provided cloud-like shade. I needed to sit down.

I sat on the floor and put my clammy head against the cool bathtub.

No one in my life had died before. Even my grandparents were still alive. Patrick's brother's wife probably hadn't been as old as my mom.

I replayed the conversations from the other night when she'd been here.

Oh my God. She'd been here. Jesus, a dead woman had been here. She'd used this very washroom. I wanted out.

I pulled myself up and resumed listening at the door. No one on the other side of it sounded phased in the least. All I heard was laughter as they joked around about a dead woman we'd all just met. I went to the sink and splashed water on my face. I looked at my pale complexion in the mirror and slapped both my cheeks to force their colour back.

As I cautiously exited the bathroom, not wanting to be seen, I heard Patrick say, "So, my brother'll get her life insurance payout."

"Genius," said my boyfriend. "Making her get a policy before he married her."

A lump grew in my throat as I remembered the snippet of conversation I'd overheard on New Year's Day. *I still can't believe the dumb bitch actually got herself life insurance.*

Now, I heard Patrick laugh. "That beaut didn't know she was

nothing more than a quick-'n'-easy payday. Cheers to my brother, the brainy brute."

I heard the clanking of glasses and beer bottles before my boyfriend giggled and said, "And an even bigger payout and so much easier to pull off than robbing a bank."

I felt ill from terror. But I had no reason to be scared. My boyfriend would never hurt me. They couldn't be serious. But how could they joke about the death of a woman? How could they be so insensitive? Just to maintain macho energy around one another? How toxic. Revolting. I wanted no part of it and decided to leave.

Not wanting them to know I'd overheard such distasteful dark humour, I tiptoed up the stairs and grabbed my coat and purse before intentionally stomping back to the top of the stairs and yelling, "Bye, guys. I'm heading home now. See you later, babe."

The icy air burned my throat as I picked up my pace to get out of the cold and into the warmth of my home as quickly as possible. Something caught my eye in the distance. A fast blur. I waited to witness more movement. When nothing happened, I turned back and continued on. I was four minutes into a twenty-two-minute walk. A block and a half down, seven and a half to go. I heard someone running behind me. Someone, not something. I spun around. But again, whatever—*whoever*—it was outran my vision. Nervous, I scanned my surroundings. Nothing notable: parked cars in driveways and on the road, a few couplings of children playing on the lawns. The sound of someone running behind me must have been the kids.

I couldn't trust the corners of my hypervigilant eyes. They registered every little thing, motion, and movement as a potential threat. Distant car: level-one threat. Garbage bag blowing across the street: level-two threat. Someone exiting their home: code-blue-level threat. Why the sudden sense of panic?

Just when I'd talked myself down, I heard a jingle. Maybe even a giggle. Then I swore I heard my name. A fuzzy figure passed my peripherals. Even the cold air hadn't chilled me as deeply as this sight. My alarm levels peaked. The wider I stretched my eyes and the quicker they scanned my surroundings, the better my odds of identifying the danger I felt. My core got hot from stealing the little remaining heat from my extremities. I felt ready to run. Ready to fight.

Footsteps. I stopped and whipped my head around to investigate. Photopsia but no person. Nothing but stars.

A few more steps into my escape, I heard both the jingle and approaching footsteps again.

"Katee," whispered a voice like a fingernail running from the tips of my toes to the top of my scalp, awakening goosebumps over my skin.

I spun around and scanned the parked cars lining the residential road. Then I saw it—out of the corner of my eye, something dashed near the ground behind the closest vehicle. A person? I bent down to see under the truck. Shoes. My boyfriend's brand-new white-as-his-smile sneakers. I crouched lower and saw him and his Guy Smiley grin. He waved his fingers flirtatiously.

"What are you doing?" I demanded.

My boyfriend stood up from his kneeling position, blinked at me for what felt like an eternity, then began retreating slowly. Eventually, he turned around and jogged away.

The face of the dead woman who'd OD'd appeared in my mind like a warning. Could my man hurt me? I gnawed on the thought and the inside of my cheek. Jesus. No. Stop being so dramatic. He was playing around. I just didn't like it. I was overreacting. He'd probably say he was showing me how good he'd be at playing peekaboo with our baby.

Our paths crossed twice more before I made it home. Both times were like the first. He snuck up as close as he could get until I sensed him, eventually showed himself, then took off again.

Hours after I got home, I heard his key unlock the front door. I looked up from my book.

He entered the room. "Ready or not, here I am."

Chapter 19

Alex

The school bell rang to release the beasts for their much-needed recess break. That meant I had fifteen minutes until I had to present Stranger Danger to the kindergarten class. I heard the rustle of paper being shoved under my office door. The start of recess proved a popular time for students to drop off appointment request slips.

I waited a beat before getting up to retrieve it. I didn't want the kiddo on the other side of the door to hear me; I didn't have time for an impromptu session. I picked up the folded piece of lined paper.

> *Hanson is mad at me. Will Hanson kill me and Rosslynn? Yes or no? Will Hanson try to kill my mom? Will you keep us safe? Pick yes or no.*

Kristen and Rosslynn. The young sisters in Grade 2 and Grade 1 whom I'd met a few weeks back. I had known something wasn't right. I'd sensed both the girls and their mother had been withholding worrying information. Though their mother hadn't given me consent to take on her daughters as clients, the Child, Youth and Family Enhancement Act required anyone who believed a child was at risk to report their concern to the authorities. Now that I had something tangible, I immediately called child services to share my concerns and name Hanson.

Seated in the back corner of the kindergarten classroom's carpet-time area, I heard the hallway come alive with the rush-hour-traffic roar of children. Hollers and shrieks and whining closed in. A bunch of kinders burst through the classroom doorway, each claiming they'd beaten the others and gotten there first.

"I win! Me!"

"Was not! Teacher? Teacher! Livy's lying!"

"Am not, Tattle Snake!

"You budded! And I'm telling the teacher on you!"

"Liar, liar on fire!"

I felt like a zoo patron observing the 10:55 a.m. show. "Lying and tattling and brags, oh my!" I said, announcing my presence and inspiring instant silence and a standstill.

More kids piled in, nearly domino-ing their gawking peers before discovering the shiny new person in their room. The growing group resembled little zombies slowly but steadily approaching me with outstretched arms, gaping mouths, and unblinking laser-focused eyes. When the pack reached me, they ate me up.

"You're so pretty," said one of them.

"You have long hair like me," said another, as she reached out and pet my side braid.

The rest chimed in:

"Why you here?"

"Are you a big kid?"

"I like your face."

"Look what I can do," said a little red-haired boy as he yanked the bottom of his shirt up and over his head, exposing his entire belly.

"Put your shirt back down, you nudie bandoodie," I said, in my silliest high-pitched voice.

The crowd went wild with giggles and snorts and squeals.

"Nudie bandoodie. Nudie bandoodie," the kinders chanted.

A little brown-eyed girl used the classroom chaos as an opportunity to get some individual attention from me.

"Hi," she said, batting her tiny eyelashes. "I like you." She climbed onto my lap. "You're my favourite lady."

This bold movement caught the attention of the others, and the focus returned to me.

"I like your high heels, and I know how to walk in them cause my mom has lots and lots and she lets me try them on. Can I try yours on?"

"I want to try them on!"

"Can me, too?"

A little boy grabbed my hand. "She's my friend," he said. "She knows my sister, and my sister loves her."

The rest seagulled in:

"She's mine, too!"

"And mine!"

"I love her, too!"

"By golly, kinders," interjected the young and sweet Miss Silk. "Please take a seat on the carpet."

In a silent game of musical squares, the carpet spots closest to me became prime real estate. Multiple kiddos plopped their bums down and fought for squatter's rights.

"I was here first."

"Not true!"

"Yes, true!"

"Geez Louise," said Miss Silk. "Where on earth are your manners? You know the rules: only one person per square, hands and feet to yourselves, and crisscross-applesauce or mermaid."

One by one, the children spread out as stubbornly as thick, chunky, all-natural peanut butter on fresh, warm bread. Most of the boys sat with their legs crossed in front of them. Most of the girls had theirs tucked to the side.

"Olivia?"

Wearing a purple and pink Disney princess dress overtop grass-stained blue jeans, light-up shoes on the wrong feet, and a home-made-looking wool monkey sock hat, the girl still snuggled on my lap looked up at her teacher. She seemed to have lost a finger up her nose on the search for promised treasure.

I gagged.

The girl gave me a hug before leaving my lap to join her peers on the carpet.

"Thank you, boys and girls," said Miss Silk. She nodded at me.

Even though all parents drilled the public safety alert into their kids' heads from the time they could comprehend the words "stranger" and "danger," it remained scarily evident that kindergarteners lacked the nuanced understanding of the concept, and thus it remained cause for concern and continued practice. I loved teaching the snuggly little lovebugs not to instantly trust, obsess over, and crawl on every kind-looking smiling face they saw in their environments. It proved a hoot year after year. The kids practically presented the information themselves. They regurgitated and parroted everything they'd been taught by their well-meaning parents. Theatric yet serious. Eyes wide, voices low, tones matter of fact. Confidently certain they knew it all. You could hear and see their internalized parents in the matching mini-me packages.

Yet every year, every single one of them fell into my trap.

"What do you girls and boys know about strangers?" I asked.

Uproar ensued.

Strangers were bad! Strangers were scary. Strangers were men.

"But not always men!"

Strangers hurt kids. Strangers had knives. Strangers were danger!

On and on they went educating me on all things "strangers."

Then I asked the boys and girls if anyone knew my name.

All of them said yes and shouted out various incorrect guesses.

Next, I asked the girls and boys if anyone knew why I was at the school.

All of them said yes and shouted out more guesses.

"You're the principal."

Heads nodded.

"You're a big kid in a big grade in the big kid side of school."

A debate broke out.

"I think my mom knows you."

"Mine, too," echoed three or four others.

"No, she's Alyssa's bus driver."

Alyssa vehemently disagreed.

"Nope," I said. "You don't know my name or why I'm here because I'm . . ."

Their eyes, the silence, and the tension grew like invisible balloons ready to pop.

". . . a stranger!" I said in my most playfully malevolent voice.

Utter pandemonium broke out at this claim. The boys and girls adamantly objected. They knew I wasn't a stranger. I couldn't be. I was pretty. I was young. I was nice.

"And strangers aren't allowed in schools, silly."

They continued educating me on all the reasons I couldn't possibly be a stranger.

I loved demonstrating the complexities of human interaction and connection, discussing the importance of building rapport with people but highlighting the essentiality of trusting one's own instincts first and foremost around strangers—and also those who weren't strangers. Children were far more likely to be in danger in their homes and environments by persons known to them.

"Until someone you know and trust introduces you to someone, they're a stranger," I said. "And even when someone is no longer a stranger, you still need to be careful as you get to know them."

The last of the kinders headed back to their classroom after concluding the world's shortest field trip—my counselling office was maybe a dozen steps away from their room. It was directly across the hall and at the bottom of the stairs, but they needed to see it.

Afterward, looking forward to some quiet and personal space, I closed my office door. My cheeks hurt from grinning nonstop throughout the thirty-minute kinder comedy show. Kids really did say the darndest things.

My desk on the other side of the room caught my attention—and my breath. It had been cleared. My organized disorder had been shoved to my desk's edges, and in the clearing sat a white envelope.

My heart dropped. I cautiously approached my desk, trying to make out the messy penmanship from a distance. As if that distance would keep me safe. I could see the letter was addressed to me in pencil. My body braced. Like *his* letters last week. Was this another one? I couldn't tell. I took a step closer, equal parts of me wanting and not wanting to know. My heart ran. My feet inched. My eyes blinked. Blinked away the possibility. Blinked away the tears.

No stamp. Thank God. I released my breath.

But what if that meant *he'd* hand delivered it? I sucked the breath back in. What if *he* was out? What if *he* was here?

I took a few more steps closer, more quickly now. I snatched the envelope from the desk. Fu—

"GOTCHYA!"

I screamed. The kinder's gut giggles and grin turned to whimpers on the verge of tears. Every hair on my body was ready to fight, and every muscle in his body was ready to flee; our combined fear blocked either of our exit routes.

"What's the matter?" asked a voice from the doorway.

I wasn't sure.

"I'm sorry," said the cowering kinder in front of me.

"Alex?" said the doorway voice.

"I—" I blinked at the child and turned to the doorway to see Jessica, and a moment later, Miss Silk appearing beside her.

"Hi, Jessica," said Miss Silk before looking at me. "Alex, is Adam still here with you?"

"Teacher!" Adam pushed passed me and ran straight into Miss Silk, nearly knocking her over.

"I think this young man gave Alex quite the fright," said Jessica, as she ruffled the boy's white-blonde hair.

"Yup, I did," said Adam, a big smile back on his face.

They all laughed. I slowly joined in. The crowd dispersed.

Jesus Christ. That little bugger had popped out from right under my desk as I'd reached for—

Oh. Right. The envelope.

I retrieved it from where it had fallen to the ground.

Dear Miss Alex,

I exhaled, granting my body permission to relax. Not from *him*. Relishing in the relief, I peeked ahead to the bottom of the second page and saw it was signed by a student who'd graduated the previous spring. I took a seat, allowed a smile, and continued reading. I stopped when I got to the line that soured the whole sweet letter: *You will NEVER be replaceable.*

My ex's exact words shivered through my body, covering even my scalp in goosebumps. I swallowed and pushed past the eerie coincidence.

When I finished the letter, I felt both touched by my past student's complimentary words and taunted by my ex's threatening ones. *His* power was omnipotent, inescapable. *He* held the key to unravel me. Only *he* could taint such soul-warming words of affirmation. Only *he* could piss on something so positive, so flattering.

The time had come to call my therapist and book a session. I hadn't needed to see her in years, but I had an ethical obligation for self-care.

"Sorry to have missed your call, as today was my last day in office. I will be away for two weeks, during which time I will not be responding to voicemails or emails. If this is an emergency, hang up and dial 911 or go to—"

I hung up. I knew the spiel. At least I'd made the first call. The next would be easier.

With three hours left in my workday but zero hours left in me to give, I packed up. My nerves begged for an Ativan and a glass—or three—of wine.

Chapter 20

Gabbi

I enter Captain Bob's karaoke bar and scan for my friends. I spot them sitting at a long table in the back. One of my besties, Maria, sees me and waves. I smile and make my way over.

The seven of them greet me simultaneously, "Gabbi!"

I smile and say my hellos.

"Where's Vince?" asks Maria.

I look around and notice he has yet to arrive.

Before I can answer, Maria hollers, "Vince!" and everyone turns and welcomes my handsome hubby as he struts through the crowd toward us.

He waves his signature "V" from one end of the ten-person table to the other. Then he collects me in an embrace and a kiss, and we set up camp at the far-right end where three counter-height chairs remain unclaimed. He sits at the head of the table and begins stroking his beard as he silently surveys our company. I laugh to myself because he looks like our Viking ruler, and us, his peasant patrons.

A playlist of songs later, the karaoke host announces the first singer rotation is complete. Having yet to be called up myself, I turn to face the little stage in the corner. I'll be up any minute now.

Then I see *him*.

My mouth dries. It can't be. But those are my ex's eyes. My skin cools. But that's not *his* body. I blink. How would I know what *his* body looks like twenty-one years later? I release my breath but not my stare. I gawk at the man. Same-ish height. Same eyes. Fully tattooed. I close my mouth. He walks toward me. Bile lurches to my throat. My heart pounds. This can't be real. I look around and wiggle my body, trying to ground myself, to ensure I'm awake while praying I'm asleep and hoping this is a nightmare.

He heads straight for me. I jerk my head back to follow him as he rounds our table. He gets closer and approaches the only empty chair, the one directly across from me. I shift in my seat. He hasn't made eye contact, hasn't looked at me. It can't be *him*. Plus, this guy's hair is silver. But *his* would be, too, wouldn't it? My ex would be fifty-four now. If *he's* still alive. What if *he's* still alive? What if—

"Guys, this is Eric," says our friend Isabella. She kisses the guy on the cheek.

He blushes, nods, and looks down.

Different name. And far from the life-of-the-party, loudmouth, centre-of-attention guy I once dated. It's not *him*. Or maybe the stark personality difference is because *he's* changed drastically from the booze and drugs eating away at *his* brain? Maybe life beat *him* down, and *he* lost *his* spit and vinegar, and that's why *he* hasn't been on social media for the past two years?

Maybe *he's* not dead.

"We're finally official," Isabella says. She beams. In the six years I've known her, I've never seen her glow like this.

I can't shake the feeling that it could be my ex-partner. But it can't be. Jesus, it's not. For one, this guy smells different. I laugh at my own naivety. People do change their cologne. But, oh my God, he looks just like what my ex could look like now. *His* eyes. The exact blue. I'd know them anywhere. But these aren't *his*. This is not *him*. I need to snap out of it. This is lunacy. I realize Isabella is staring at me with a look of . . . guilt? Shame?

"Yeah, so there's a seventeen-year age difference," she says to me.

"What?" I say. "I wasn't—"

"It's okay. It's a shock for people at first."

"No, that's not it. It's not that. I'm just . . ." I trail off. I have no words. I need to get away.

I excuse myself and go to the washroom. I exit the washroom

and take a lap around the bar. I hear my name called for karaoke but ignore it and head outside for fresh air. I need to pull it together; I can't even breathe. Outside, I see Maria having a cigarette, thankfully alone.

"You okay, sugar?" she asks.

"Course," I say.

Maria distracts me with the story of Isabella and Eric. Definitely not my ex. I'm not in danger.

Once back inside, I struggle to stop staring at this eerily familiar stranger sitting across from me. Though I know this isn't my ex, seeing someone who emulates *him* so closely yet looks so unthreatening gives me the creeps. Writing about the abuse I survived more than two decades ago has brought it all bubbling back up to the surface, shaping and distorting my current reality, mixing past and present. My thought process over the past five months has been far from normal, and it'll probably get worse before it gets better. It's like my ex somehow knows—even if from the grave—that I'm finally speaking the truth and outing *him*. *His* ghost haunts me, tries to detour me, unravel me. But I need to tolerate the triggers while finishing my novel, while reliving it to record and recount it. I'm writing it to rest, once and for all.

Chapter 21

Katee

On March 27, a sharp stabbing pain raised me from a dead sleep. I yelped as I climbed over my boyfriend to get out of bed.

"Shut up, Katee," he said under his breath as he helped me over and off him.

I lost my balance and fell to the floor.

"Ah!" I cried but quickly forced my shout to a whimper. Pain shot out from my pelvis, and I struggled to catch my breath. I tried curling into myself to hug it away, but that movement alerted me to another problem: a wet feeling in my crotch. I touched it. Sticky and warm. Keeping my hand there, I braced myself to stand, but the push off the ground forced something out of me—a hot blob. I felt some of it spill over my cupped hand. I dropped back to my knees and crawled to the washroom.

The general pain remained constant, but escalating waves of stabbing spasms on both sides of my lower abdomen and pelvic region winded me. I couldn't pull myself from my knees onto the toilet. I hung over the cold bathtub and tried to use the edge of it to get up. My whimpers were no longer containable, and I began to shriek.

"Baby!"

"Christ, Katee! I'm trying to sleep here," my boyfriend yelled from the bedroom.

"Help!"

Angry grumbling and curses came from the other room. The sound of Harley's nails gave away her quick escape.

The bathroom light blinded me.

"Jesus. What did you do?"

"I need to go to the hospital."

He argued with me for what felt like an eternity. Called it spotting. Claimed it sometimes happened. Tried to convince me I was overreacting and that if I thought this was bad, I had a rude awakening come labour time. Eventually, he came around and agreed a hospital trip was a good idea. Just to be safe. I begged him to call me an ambulance. He asked if I thought he was made of money. It was only a thirty-minute walk. And the walking would help the cramps. I asked about the bleeding. He went to my closet and brought back three pairs of winter tights. Told me to triple up. He steadied me while I lifted my leg into the baby pink pair. A blood clot splattered on the bathroom floor.

I wailed—first in horror then in pain.

My boyfriend handed me wads of balled-up toilet paper. "Stuff this in there," he said.

"What about a tampon?" I asked before screaming through another unsufferable stab.

He rummaged around under the sink and tossed a maxi pad and tampon at me. He left while I finished sorting myself and returned with a roll of paper towels. "For the road," he said.

I looked down and saw blood leaking through my triplicate tights. "I'll never make it walking all that way. It's over a kilometer and a half. Please call nine-one-one."

"The walk'll do the cramps good. Exercise releases feel-good hormones."

Maybe exercise could be helpful on a light menstrual day—I didn't know; I'd never had period cramps—but for a fourteen-week fetus in crisis?

It took me almost an hour—double the normal time—to stumble and struggle my way to the hospital uptown. Once I arrived, I was whisked immediately into an examination room. I felt weak and faint from the severe, unrelenting cramping. The triage nurse commented on my pale yellowish tone and something about my blood pressure. My shortness of breath made answering any of her questions close to impossible, and she told me to just focus on breathing.

A nurse took me to an operating room and told me to remove my clothes and lie down on the surgical table. She handed me a hospital gown and, after seeing me shaking, promised she'd bring me heated blankets.

I held onto the counter while I peeled down my pants. A blood-drenched mass hit the floor. I stared in shock at the sickening sight. Through my tears, I saw a red tampon string, red wads of saturated padding and paper, and a shiny dark red sac of tissue and blood clots. My whimpers turned to wails. I tried to see my baby. I tried to make her out. But she just looked like the leftover mess my family cat would leave on our doorstep. Nothing more than a slimy sac of discarded organs. I bawled and blubbered until the nurse came back. She wrapped me up in a warm blanket resembling a hug. I don't remember much more. Something about a surgical procedure and sleeping for a while under general anesthesia. I wanted to sleep forever.

Once I woke up, the doctor told me I might have vaginal bleeding and cramping for a few days but that it should not be severe or heavy. If so, or if I developed symptoms of infection, he told me to come back to the hospital. He advised I avoid tampons and sexual intercourse for one to two weeks.

When the time came to release me, they sent me home in a cab because no one was there to take me home.

I arrived home to find my boyfriend sitting on the couch in the dark.

"The smell of your blood, Katee." He looked away and shuddered.

I smelled my old cast-iron piggy bank.

"I just couldn't handle it. I'm . . . I'm so, so sorry." Silent tears licked down his face.

I couldn't handle the sight of him. Couldn't stand to be in the same room as him. I walked over to my desk in our kitchen and shoveled his shit off the desk chair so I could sit.

"The smell of my—?" I gulped. My words beat my bile. "Jesus. Never mind that. What the hell was wrong with you? I needed you! I've never needed anyone more in my entire life."

I sobbed. Shock and confusion fogged my brain. The silence from the usually noisy street outside and apartment above screamed in my ears.

I had no clue what my boyfriend was staring at so intently, but it certainly wasn't me. It wasn't at anything I could see. His dog took a few slow, stretching steps toward the door then flopped over to lie down. She looked dead.

My boyfriend's mouth opened then closed before it reopened. "I couldn't clean it up again," his words were like a whimper, "I just couldn't."

I looked around, questioning the stability of my reality, looking for a witness or two to pinch me or snap him out of his trance. Instead, I saw two of the three ceiling light bulbs burnt out, the dark mystery stain on our living room carpet reminding me of last night's blood, and week-old cat barf in the corner between the couch and the fireplace. I glared at him for proper answers.

"Again?" I asked. "What do you mean, clean it up *again*?"

I couldn't help but wonder who'd cleaned up my bloody mess at the hospital. I wished that same person would've spared me cleaning up the beginnings of it in our home. I closed my eyes to allow the nausea to pass through me as I inhaled deeply. I tried to exhale away the disturbing images from the previous night.

I asked more firmly, "Clean what up again, huh?"

No part of him moved but his lips. "The blood," he said, slowly turning to look right through me. If sad was a colour, his eyes were the exact shade of it. He sighed. "Have you ever smelled that much blood before?" His words were like hungry moths attacking my heart as it tried to beat them off.

I'd tasted it more than I'd smelled it that night. Did a lot of blood smell stronger than a little blood? I suppose one penny had a weaker smell than the handful of pennies from my old cast-iron piggy bank. The metallic stench that'd seemed impossible to get off my hands as a kid after playing with the pennies probably smelled even stronger.

Last night, there'd been a lot of blood. I'd never seen so much. And it hadn't just been blood; it'd been chunky blood. Clots. A dozen variations of red, some whiter, some blacker. What blood had been mine? What had been hers?

Oh, God. What if I smelled like blood forever?

"Katee."

I startled.

"I need to tell you about the last time I saw my dad."

Tears formed in my eyes, and I blinked them out, wanting him to see my pain. "You've got to be kidding me. I just lost our baby—alone, I might add—and you're held up on your dad?" My stomach cramps doubled me over in my chair. I yelped in pain. The knees of my jeans soaked up my tears, and I faced him again.

With downcast, vacant eyes, he continued his monologue, "I came home from school to find my dad's brains blown all over our walls."

The clock on our wall stuttered as it always did when it hit the eleventh hour.

"What?" I started to heave but stopped myself, swallowing mouthfuls of saliva as fast as I could stomach it. I couldn't picture my boyfriend's dad's brains all over the walls; it just reminded me that my mess—in our bed, our bathroom, my pants, the hospital floor—hadn't been a mess at all. It had been our beautiful baby girl.

Had the whitish-red parts been her little brain? Maybe I'd seen brain matter, too.

Ambrihl jumped onto my lap, offering purrs for pets. I stroked her soft hair until it felt surreal. Looking at my boyfriend, I realized that not only were we sitting in separate rooms but separate worlds. Past him, I watched the tranquilizing rain. Day three of it. April's showers had arrived a week early to help me mourn the death of my daughter. Spring was meant to bring life, not end it. But not everything survived spring. Certainly not the worms forced out of their flooded holes to struggle to cross the sidewalks without being squished by traffic or swooped up by birds. And, sadly, not for my baby bird, my little Robin. Guilt pressed down heavily on my shoulders. I sighed, lifting it briefly.

Ambrihl bit me and jumped off my lap. I'd been stroking her hair the wrong way. To break our separate dissociative states, I stood and walked over to the couch to sit on my boyfriend's lap.

He placed his right hand on my sore stomach. "Katee, I feel like I'm in the ocean all alone in a shitty boat I made in Grade Nine shop class. Sometimes it's smooth, most of the time it's rocky, and when I least expect it, a tidal wave smashes me in the face."

I'd thought only my heart could be this broken. How selfish. "I won't let you drown, babe." I placed my hands on the sides of his face, wiping away his tears with the pads of my thumbs. "I'm sorry for getting so upset. I didn't know that about your dad." I gently massaged his earlobe between my thumb and forefinger. I knew how to soothe him. He'd told me I was the only one who ever had.

His movements seemed exaggeratedly slow as he leaned back and placed his head on the back of the couch. He looked up at the ceiling, reminding me of a heroin addict after injecting in a movie. The neighbour's kid wailed above us.

"My mom took off the night before, after he'd beat her good. He'd been sitting on her stomach and just wailing on her. Even though only twelve years old then, when his fist smashed into her already bloody face for the fourth or fifth time, I became a beast and attacked him as my mom ran out of the house. Later that night, from my bedroom where I was just waiting for my turn—that for once didn't come—I heard my dad stumble out as he left, too. With my brother sleeping over at a friend's and my parents both fuck-knows-where, I woke up the next morning alone and got myself off to school. When I got home, I found my dad's body in the middle of thick plastic sheets spread out all over the floor and taped up the wall. He . . . or I guess just his face . . . was unrecognizable. It was fucking everywhere." My boyfriend started sobbing. He struggled to get me off his lap, replacing me with his elbows on his knees and burrowing his face in his hands. Through his snivels, he said, "The note he left was for me. It said, 'Since you think you're the man of this house, clean me up before your mother and brother come home.'"

The next afternoon, I woke up to find a letter from my boyfriend.

Dear Cutie,

I'm just writing down my thoughts. I'm going to burst if I don't get them out of my head. I need you to understand where I was coming from.

I can remember being as young as two or three years old. They were never around, my fucking parents. Never. My brother and I raised ourselves. Raised each other. We couldn't depend on anyone. We were little shits too. So, lots of times we didn't even trust one another. We'd get into these huge fights because we'd try to parent one another. We didn't really get a childhood. We were little scavengers. Hunting and gathering food and shelter. But you know how it is. To not be loved by your own goddamn parents. I mean, what's a person supposed to think of themselves? That you're just a piece of shit people step around? Something they can't even be bothered to pick up? They just ignore it and hope it magically goes away? So, I guess that's what we did. We fucked off. Stayed clear. We ran the streets all hours of the day and night. When we were home, we were expected to take care of our mom. She was fucking useless. Couldn't so much as get herself out of bed most days. And when she did, it was only to drag herself to the couch. Our dad beat his expectations into us. Whenever he decided to grant his presence, we were not to be seen or heard. And since with every beer he drank he got scarier, we just fucked off. There were nights we didn't even come home. And you think either of those two fucks came to look for us? Nope. When he wasn't around, which was often, he made it painfully clear that our jobs were to check on her. Make her food. Every time we saw him, he told us it was our fault she was so depressed and useless. Our fault he drank. Our fault he beat her. We were forced to take our dad's side in his abuse against her. You couldn't really call them fights. She never fought back. She was pathetic. Needy. Just a walking corpse. Constantly muttering quietly about how we were too much to handle. For days after each time he beat her, she'd rant under her breath about it being our fault. He had to take out his hatred and disgust on someone, and we should be thankful that she ensured it was on her and not us. And him? He told us we took after her, weak and pathetic. Just a waste of skin. He was a total sadist. He beat us and humiliated us all the time. He even made us beat one another for his own entertainment. "My little WWF boys," he used to say. He played us off each other a lot. Whoever he decided had won whatever sick game he forced us to play would feel special. Feel a sense of power, if only for a minute before he changed the rules and left us feeling humiliated and used. Like, this one time, he screamed at us to get naked. We looked at each other confused. He came over and with a hand on the outside of each of our heads, smashed them together. He laughed at us for crying as he ripped down our pants. Then he went back and sat down on the couch. The sick fuck compared our dick sizes. Started laughing at my brother cause his was smaller. Even though I didn't think it was, I started feeling pretty good about my own, you know?

And our mom? She used to tell us she'd leave him all the time. We stopped believing her. By the time we were seven or so, she used to say she was going to leave all three of us. All she ever wanted, she used to say, was two good boys. Two good boys who did good in school. Loved their mama. Played sports. But look what she got? Two little versions of the man she hated most in the world. She used to tell us that she thought we would save her one day. Save her from him, from her life, from herself. But no. We couldn't even do that.

We were exposed to a lot of violence. Not just between them, and him with us, but also in the shitty neighbourhood we lived in with them— and then in and out of foster homes over the years. I had some fucked up foster home parents too. We could never let our guard down—could never trust anyone. If we wanted something done, we had to do it ourselves.

I'll never let anything like that ever happen to me again. In life you're either a leader or a loser, and I'm no loser. I worked hard to become someone people look up to. I built up my business and made everyone want to know me, want to date the girls I date. Want to be me. I have hundreds of acquaintances—but I don't consider any of them friends. I'll never let my guard down. I'll never let anyone in. No one but you. I don't need anybody—but you. And that's scary as fuck, Katee. Thinking about you ever leaving me? It would kill me. You can't tell anyone any of this. Ever. No one can know this stuff about me. I want so badly to trust you. To depend on you. But I'm not sure I can. Trusting others is a good way to get used and betrayed.

I've been thinking about you and her so much while you've been sleeping it off. The thought of losing her is driving me crazy. I don't blame you for her death. And I don't blame you for being pissed. But I don't know what I could've done. I didn't realize you actually needed to go to the hospital. I thought it'd take care of itself like they usually do when these things happen, and you were just too young to know any better. I thought you were being overdramatic. Sorry. And I had to leave you at the hospital to go get my own head straight. It really messed me up and got me thinking about a lot. I've been through a couple miscarriages before, but they didn't affect me quite like losing our baby girl is affecting me. I've honestly never hurt this bad *in my life or been this emotional. I didn't tell you about my piece of shit dad to get your sympathy. I just needed you to understand why I couldn't be there for you. You don't even know how much I really do love you and want a family with you. You're it. You're the one. We've already lost our baby, and now I'm scared I'll lose you too. I've lost all direction, because when I found out we were pregnant, all I focused on was our future as a family. Now I'm a broken man. I'm nothing. Not worth your time. A loser. I don't deserve you.*

I heard keys in the door lock and looked up as my boyfriend entered our apartment.

"You're finally awake," he said.

His letter had shaken me awake with concern and questions. I nodded. I didn't know what to think or believe. Was it all true? And if embellished, which parts?

He stood his ground as though waiting for something. He glanced down at his letter in my hand and extended his arms. "Katee, I've never needed a hug more in my whole life than I do right now. Could you give me one already?"

I set the letter on the desk and walked over to him. The spicy aroma of his cologne drew me in. We embraced. When I pulled away, he pulled my head back and kissed me deeply. I tasted cinnamon from his mouth spray. His freshly shaven face was soft against mine. Realizing how badly I had unknowingly needed one, too, I hugged him again, squeezing him tightly this time.

He guided me to the couch, and we sat down. "We're at a crossroad, Katee. But we get to decide whether it's a crisis or an opportunity. Everything finished, or a new beginning."

I barely knew which way was up after the events of the last twenty-four hours, much less what he was talking about now.

"I have a new plan, and I need you to just go with it, okay?"

I twirled my hair mindlessly around my finger and chewed on my cheek, still a little groggy from my early morning nap and getting groggier from the prescription-strength pain meds I'd swallowed as soon as I'd woken.

"I've thought a lot about it and decided we have to move to BC."

These words made me more alert than the contents of his letter had. "British Columbia? Why?"

"We could do it. I just know if we stay here, it'll be the biggest mistake of our lives."

Harley appeared from around the corner and walked over to Ambrihl, poking her to play. I didn't want to move to BC, to be so far away from everyone I knew. I already felt lonely here. Ambrihl flattened her ears. Harley taunted her with another jab. Ambrihl hissed.

"Well? If you'll still be mine, I'll put every heartbeat I have into our relationship. I'll do it right this time, forever. I'll feed your ego by telling you this—I could never get over you, I will never fall in love with anyone else. I hope you can forgive me and understand that I'm just no good at the sappy supportive shit. But I'll try to get better at it if you come with me. Promise."

Was he saying we'd be over if I didn't agree to move? I reached for his hands and intertwined our fingers. "I love you. But I don't want to move to BC."

"I can't stay in Ontario any longer, Katee. I'll fuckin' snap. But I'd totally fall apart emotionally if I don't have you to help me through this crappy life. If we leave, we can start over. We don't have to wait. We can go right away."

"How? There's still three months of school."

"Forget about school, Katee. I make a hundred dollars an hour, and I didn't finish high school. And I've got a buddy moving out there, he's taking his girl, too. He has an affiliate who's setting them up in a grow house. Free rent in exchange for guarding the plants. He offered to connect us with the guy in charge out there."

I imagined getting caught and how terrifying prison would be, surrounded by cold-blooded murderers. And I always ran cold; I'd freeze amidst all that cold concrete and rusting metal.

The reminiscence of the cast-iron smell of blood from the night before engulfed my nostrils and threatened to choke me. I realized the only people I'd ever heard use the word "affiliate" were the questionable crew who hung around with Patrick's brother, the brainy brute with the dead bride. There wasn't a world in which I would move out to BC, especially to work in a grow house. But how could I explain that without sounding like a goody two-shoes?

"And all our stuff?"

"Already solved. My buddy rented a U-Haul for their things and said they'll save a little room for our essentials."

Moving to BC wouldn't solve any of our problems, much less be a good idea. But breaking up would certainly cause more problems for me. I couldn't go home now. And I had nowhere else to go. Besides, I'd seen a whole new side of my boyfriend last night. A vulnerability I hadn't known was possible. I couldn't throw in the towel yet. I had to stall his plan.

"I don't want to move to BC, babe. Not right now, anyway."

"If you love me and want to try again for real, tell me and never stop telling me."

"I love you and want to try again for real. I promise."

"Thanks, cutie. Now think about BC."

"I already did. I'm not ready to move across the country. My answer is no."

Chapter 22

Katee

"Can you believe I used to hate this stuff?" I held up my spoonful of cottage cheese for context. Ambrihl and I sat snuggled up together at the end of the couch, my little miss Muffet hoping to catch a dropped dollop of curds and whey.

"Such a slut," said my boyfriend. He lay sprawled out on the opposite side of the couch. His foot began twitching, signaling his escalating irritation. The movement shook me, as his foot brushed my thigh.

Licking the spoon clean, I glanced over at him. Engrossed in our new favourite show, *Temptation Island*, he must have been referencing one of the reality show's contestants. The show followed multiple couples at crossroads in their relationships who stupidly agreed to be separated from their partners and live on an exotic island filled with eligible sexy singles. As much as we enjoyed watching the drama unfold, we often found ourselves taking different sides of the same couple.

I shoveled another scoop of cottage cheese into my mouth.

"You just can't get enough of it, can you?" he said, peeling his pissed-off eyes from the TV to look at me.

I grinned and vehemently shook my cheese-filled chipmunk cheeks.

My boyfriend's face softened, and he smiled. "You look like my little buddy when he first tasted applesauce. He wouldn't try anything new unless he saw me try it first," he said.

I hated when he compared me to a child, much less a baby. But our stories were too similar not to share. "That's pretty much how I became obsessed with it, actually."

"This fucking slut is obsessed with creamy goo, too."

His distasteful comment soured me, further curdling the milk product in my stomach. As much as I loved this show, I hated watching it with him. Especially once I'd lost track of the number of beers he'd consumed.

"I used to hate cottage cheese with a passion," I interjected, trying to steal the spotlight back from the young woman on TV about to cross the line of no return. "My grandparents always filled a small glass bowl with it and placed it on the table to accompany every meal."

The memory saddened me. I missed my grandparents so much. Our family made the nearly two-hour-long drive to our grandparents' house at least every other weekend. And before we'd moved, the drive had taken half that time, so we'd seen them even more often. Now, I hadn't seen my grandparents, or even talked to them, for six months. I wondered what they knew about me, about my living situation—what my mother had told them.

Guilt squeezed my heart. Grief swelled in my eyes. I quietly cheersed a spoonful of cottage cheese to them against the side of my own little glass bowl and cracked a smile. *Miss you guys.* I sighed.

"Just like the tramp I knew you were all along."

"Anyway," I re-collected my boyfriend's attention, "the sight of it repulsed me. Chunky, snot-like, pigeon shit-barf, or whatever. And since we were vegan till I was seven, I wasn't allowed to try it for so long that by the time I could, my mind had been long made up about the lumpy gross goop."

My boyfriend walked to the kitchen and came back with another beer. He sneered at the girl on TV before clanking his bottle down on the coffee table and himself back on the couch.

"When I was, like, nine, a neighbour's teenage son babysat us while our parents and grandparents were out somewhere. He raided the fridge, found the huge tub of cottage cheese, grabbed a spoon, and standing right in the middle of the kitchen, ate it right out of the container."

My boyfriend turned to look at me.

"I couldn't believe it," I laughed. "He devoured it like it was a pint of ice cream. When he asked if I wanted some, I agreed to impress him 'cause I'd always had a crush on—"

When I came to, I was in an awkward position on the floor and covered in a white, sticky mess of spilt cottage cheese. I started to cry. As my tears hit the cottage cheese, it began to pink before darkening to red. I touched my face. Blood dripped from my nose.

A blow to the side of my face. I hadn't sensed much less seen it coming. My first physical punishment. For what, I wasn't sure. Something seemingly insignificant to me had set my boyfriend off. Had the cause of the hit slipped my mind? Or was the completely unexpected blow to my temple playing a part in my obliviousness?

Ambrihl helped clean me off; my boyfriend was nowhere to be found. In his place sat my first "apology" letter.

Dear Katee,

I can't forgive myself for doing that to you.

I'm lonely, scared, depressed, sick. I love you more than everything in the world. I need you. You're the only person who can save me.

I know I fucked up big time. I've never regretted anything more.

You're my entire life, my cutie, Katee.

Forever yours . . .

My boyfriend came home a few hours later. I'd already cleaned up all traces of what I wished so badly could have been nothing more than a nightmare. When he joined me back at the scene of the crime on the couch and reached for me, I flinched.

"Katee!" His eyes grew bigger and bluer in disbelief. "I would never hurt you."

But he had hurt me. Tears welled up in my eyes as I searched his for the truth.

"Never on purpose. But you drive me mad sometimes. I can't see the real you through it."

The real me? Who was the real him?

"Come here," he said, as he patted the empty space between us.

Ambrihl jumped up to occupy it instead.

My boyfriend looked on the verge of tears himself. "You said you'd do anything for me. Well? This is it. Forgive me." He outstretched his hand again, slowly this time.

Ambrihl began purring loudly and kneading the maroon throw she perched on like a throne. I closed my eyes to press the tears loose, and my boyfriend gently cupped my face. His warm hand smelled of satsuma. It felt leathery against my sore cheek.

"If you can forgive me, I will marry you, I promise."

My heart screamed no. My head nodded yes.

He swiveled my chin back and forth in examination. "There's not a mark on this pretty little face of mine," he said. Tenderly, he kissed my nose. As the pressure from his lips released, I felt a tug of separation from the remnants of dried blood inside my nostril.

I controlled what I could. I stopped eating cottage cheese and refused to watch *Temptation Island*. In our eight months together, my boyfriend had never shown an ounce of jealousy, not even when his friend had raped me. He seemed to get off on flaunting me in front of other men. In the wee hours of a morning in mid-April, he came into our bedroom while I slept on my stomach and pulled down my pants and underwear. Excitement stirred in me, as I anticipated a middle-of-the-night seduction. I pretended his quiet and careful attempt to surprise me hadn't woken me.

"Isn't that just the finest piece of ass you've ever seen?" I heard him say. "Now tell me what you'd do to it if I let you have it."

We weren't alone. My body tensed, and I prayed it didn't give away that I was awake. My heart pounded so loudly I feared my boyfriend and whoever was with him could hear it, too. The sheets beneath me dampened from my sweat.

"Go on; tell me."

Another male voice mumbled and stuttered. He sounded as uncomfortable as I felt.

My boyfriend laughed. "Jesus. You're such a pussy, man."

I didn't recognize the other voice. Probably some guy my boyfriend had just met at the bar and invited back for a drink after last call. Possibly a client he'd just finished doing a piece on. I kept my eyes closed and my body braced.

My pervert and his peeping Tom left the bedroom, quietly clicking the door shut behind them. I breathed in deeply to the count of ten before getting up to add a layer of extra-tight tights between my underwear and pajama pants. I returned to bed but thought better of it. I got out again and climbed the metal ladder to the safety of the top bunk.

A few times that month, my boyfriend used a bobby pin to unlock the bathroom door while I showered. He guided male acquaintances in and ripped open the curtain to give them a show. Hearing me shriek and seeing my eyes swell and my makeup-less face turn red while my desperate hands covered my bee-sting breasts wiped the excitement off their faces. My boyfriend always stood around a little longer than his entourage then left the bathroom without closing the curtain or the door.

After the first time that happened, I stayed in the bathroom until I heard his company say their farewells and leave. I hadn't brought my clothes into the bathroom with me, though this was something I planned to start doing moving forward. And I sure as hell wasn't walking out in nothing but a girlie-pink towel. Once positive the coast was clear of my boyfriend's voyeur visitors, I came out of hiding to find him frying an egg in the kitchen. The smell of turkey bacon tried taming me.

"What the hell?" I demanded.

He turned and faced me, his eyebrow raised in question.

"How degrading! What were you thinking? Why would you do that?"

He turned back to the stove and flipped his egg. It sizzled. "Katee, you have no reason to be so insecure." Two pieces of toast popped up, announcing their readiness.

"I'm not insecure." But I was deeply insecure. I tugged my towel tighter.

"It's for your own good, baby. I'm helping boost your confidence to where it should be." He grabbed a plate and built a BLT before topping his masterpiece with the egg.

He consistently made his attraction to my body clear. He went on and on about it. Although twisted, perhaps this would somehow make me feel more comfortable in it, too.

He took his first bite and wiped mayo from his cheek with the back of his hand. "If I get you enough validation, you'll eventually start seeing what everyone else does."

I supposed that might be true, albeit icky. How else did one grow self-esteem and body positivity?

"Besides," he said, eyeing me up and down, "I'm just so damn proud you're mine." He approached me and spun me around slowly, taking all of me in. "I can't help but brag about your hot little body to all the poor pathetic suckers who will never have what I do."

I took a step back and readjusted my towel before tightening it again. "I guess telling them is fine. But don't show them. Please. I don't like it." I turned to get dressed.

"I won't," he said, slapping my ass.

He did.

The brisk walk home from school the following day felt refreshing. I loved the smell of the changing temperature of the air, the fresh

budding tulips, and the recently thawed river. I loved the sidewalks full of loose gravel left after the winter melted off the roads.

Once home, I grabbed a snack and sat on the linoleum floor in our quaint kitchen to resume the project I'd started the previous night: scrapbooking old pictures of my sisters and me. I desperately wanted to make things right with them and my parents. But I didn't know how to. After finishing a few pages, I had an idea. I tidied up my crafting mess and gathered my courage.

My boyfriend sat at my desk cutting tattoo transfer paper.

I cleared my throat. "I think I'm going to try talking to my sisters at school. Test the waters."

The snipping from his scissors ceased. Nothing set him off faster than me mentioning missing my family.

I held my breath as tension thickened the air. "I don't wanna move home," I said. "Just want a relationship with them."

He resumed his work.

I released my breath.

Curtly, he said, "It's me or them."

"Why?" I asked.

"Can't live in both worlds, Katee. So, choose."

"Why, though?"

He pushed off the desk, and the chair rolled back a foot or so. "Still a greedy little girl." He spun himself to face me. "Nothing's ever enough for you," he sneered. He narrowed his eyes as their colour cooled. "You're just a selfish, self-centered brat." He dropped the scissors to the ground. "Now I get it. Your parents' resentment toward you. Contempt for you. They didn't want you then, and I don't want you now. Let's go."

"Go where?"

"Get up."

Shock stilled me.

Bending down, he grabbed my arm so tightly I yelped.

"Tomorrow's garbage day. Perfect timing for your epiphany." He started pulling me up, and when I resisted, he yanked me so hard I lost my balance and fell forward, and he began dragging me. "I'll put you out on the curb like the trash whore you are."

My bare knees clung to the carpet and burned from the friction.

"Prostitutes fuck men for money. You're no different. You just fuck me for food and shelter. Even more pathetic."

"I'm sorry! I won't talk to them at school. I promise."

We'd reached the door. He stopped then dropped my arm.

"No more school for you."

"But I—"

He raised his fist, and I shut my mouth.

The fight over my family—and me making it up to him—lasted all through the night and into the early morning. It was a nerve-wracking and exhausting game of chance in which he loaded a bunch of mixed feelings into a figurative revolver, spun the cylinder, placed the muzzle against my head, and pulled the trigger. I never knew what feeling would fire: rage, sorrow, or passionate desire. Sometime in the calm of the chaos, my boyfriend turned off my alarm clock, making me late once again for my co-op placement.

Chapter 23

Alex

While Yoshi dug at and pulled her blankets this way and that to perfect her nest on the couch, I poured myself a glass of wine. I swallowed a large mouthful of the liquid courage before heading to the front door to check the mailbox. As promised, more mail from my mom. A chill shivered through me. My hairs prickled to stand guard.

Yoshi cooed to me from the couch, low-pitched grumbles and moans and snorts.

"I'm coming, Yosh."

Yoshi rolled on her back, exposing her bald tummy. She pawed at the air, beckoning for my full attention.

"You're a mini pit," I said, as I second-guessed myself and double-checked that I'd deadbolted the front door.

Yoshi howled softly.

Letter in hand, I grabbed my wine glass and approached my pup. "Yes, you are."

A muffled bark.

I set the glass on the coffee table, tossed the letter to the couch, and jumped knees first beside Yoshi. I grabbed her front paws. "Yes, you're my mini pit with stinky pits," I said, as I lowered my nose into her armpits and took an exaggerated sniff. "Eww! P-U!"

Yoshi curled her lips, wrinkled her nose, and sneezed.

I covered Yoshi's bare belly in kisses until the pup righted herself, fulfilled.

You will NEVER be replaceable.

I hoped other inmates were teaching *him* some of the "lessons" he'd taught me.

I couldn't continue functioning if these intrusive thoughts of *him* kept up. Should I respond to keep *him* at bay? To placate *him*? Would *he* give up if I ignored *him*? I doubted it.

Needing to figure out what I was truly dealing with, I ripped open the letter and found two more envelopes from *him* inside.

Bitter Sweetheart,

I'm still thinking about you. I just woke up, it's about 4 am. My dreams about you are so real and so far away. You're still driving me crazy. Wish I could make it stop. I miss you and I don't understand why you're not writing me back. Is someone stopping you? Seems like everyone in my life decided all at once to stab me in the back, you, Rich, my mom, even my brother. The only one I can forgive is you, but you still won't let me. It's been years. Get over it already and forgive me. Someday you will feel those feelings again, I hope. When you're done fooling around and actually realize what you've done to me. What are you trying to do to me? Get back at me? You did it, girl! When I get outta this mess soon, I'll come find you. I'll keep writing you and give you my new phone number and address. Each time my address or number changes I'll let you know, in hopes that someday you'll love me again and want to be with me. We could have that special relationship that only you and I could have.

Miss ya, babe.

Within you, without you.

Xoxoxoxo

I hoped the second letter would give me some clues as to how long I might have to figure out a plan.

Bitter Sweetheart,

I don't get it. What you're putting me through. I could have done more than just fuck a few pigs. At least I told you. You're a real cunt and a selfish bitch, only thinking of yourself and only how you feel. I need you right now dammit! Write me back and come visit me. I think about you every day, morning and night, and it's not all good! I know I love you more than you'll ever believe, but I'm trying hard to forget you. You are driving me nuts. If you someday figure out that you really love me and want to spend the rest of your life with me, let me know, and I might tell you to fuck off!!! Go fuck some guy with AIDs or go lick a cunt! Unless you want me. I don't have much more time to do in here and I'm getting pissed off more every day. I can't believe that I've spent over a year in jail already. I work out to focus my anger and all I think about is how everyone fucked me over real bad. I'm going to want to blow up at a lot of people for what they've done to me. My brother won't take my calls. What a fucking goof he is. My mom said her loser husband gets mad at her for taking my calls. Wait till I see that piece of shit face to face again! You won't even answer my letters much less come and see me. I said I'm sorry and you did what I never thought you would do. Ignore me. Fuck you! I'm fucked right up about this whole mess. It's my own fault, I know. If only I didn't hurt you, right? Can't change the past. Unless you're wearing my ring and want to spend the rest of your life with me, fuck you! You got me back real good messing me up like this and rubbing it in by not even writing me back. When I get *out, I need to see you. You are all I'm looking forward to. I just hope you're there. Am I wasting my time writing to you like this? Is this all for nothing on my part? Are you still there? Can you forgive me? Do you love me? Do you want me? Where are you?*

P.S.

I hate loving you! At times . . . I love hating you. I miss you. I'm lonely, afraid, and sorry. I know you feel the same. Someday you'll forgive me and . . . well . . . I'm not sure what happens then . . .

I was in trouble.

The next day, as I drove to work, I called my mother. The two most recent letters from my ex sat on the passenger seat beside me. All she knew about that relationship was that it had been bad, very bad. She had called it from the very beginning; the guy was bad news. But she had never asked for details, and I had never offered any.

"Yes, Mom, they're from him," I said.

"No, I saw them. They're from your old work."

"They're from Hamilton-Wentworth Detention Centre, not Hamilton-Wentworth District School Board. And all three are covered in cutesy romantic drawings in pencil. That didn't seem a little odd to you?"

"Well, I guess I didn't really think too much about it, Alex. Just saw they were for you, and the return address listed your old work. Or so I thought. I guessed maybe they were from a bored colleague-friend or something?"

My mother never wanted to talk about *him*. In fairness, I never wanted to, either. But I did wish my mother could have just magically known somehow that it had been much worse than just bad. My mother had never liked *him*, which at the time had made me dig in my heels, stand my ground, and defend *him* even more. Useless hindsight. Mothers always do know best. I could admit that now. My mistakes, my stubbornness. I could admit just how wrong I had been. But what I still couldn't do—what I would maybe never be able to do—was admit out loud to anyone that that relationship had been downright abusive.

"Mom, I'm approaching the valley. Will lose reception any second."

"Okay, hun. Have a great day at work. Talk—"

The call dropped. Bluetooth disconnected. The satellite radio resumed.

I could not believe my ears. I loathed this song. Son of a bitch. *He* had this supernatural way of infiltrating my life—the other week with Sandra Bullock's home intrusion and now this song taunting all its praying-to-God glory. Unbelievable. I couldn't help but wonder whether these were coincidences coming from within myself or synchronicity coming from outside myself—or whether they were truly warnings or threats. Did *he* have the power to make things happen to me from a distance? Either way, I hated this memory-lane torture.

I smashed in the volume button so hard I apologized out loud to it. Another upsetting memory. For years I found myself apologizing to inanimate objects. Furniture, pens, uneven ground—so embarrassing, so pathetic. Here I was, alone in my car, doing it again. *He* never apologized. Not once.

And that song? *He* went out of *his* way to taunt and hurt me with it—*he* would put it on repeat every time we fought, get all mopey and silent, and act like a man in mourning. I had loved the song when it'd first come out long before I'd met *him*, before *he'd* ruined it for me. Not anymore.

I pressed the volume button again, turning the song back on. I turned it up—way up. I belted out the lyrics. As I sang, I recalled *him* sharing the song's significance; *he'd* told me about it after our very first fight, after playing the song on repeat for over an hour until I'd turned it off. In that moment, *he'd* told me it had been *his* wedding song and that our fight had made *him* really miss *his* ex-wife. The nerve. The manipulation. I'd immediately seen through *his* pathetic performance, the fake grieving, because I'd known the toxicity of *his* and *his* ex's short-lived, short-on-love relationship. *He* despised *his* ex. In those moments, *he'd* wanted me to think *he* despised me even more than *his* ex. Callous cocksucker. The song had been a spiteful strategy to try and make me jealous. But it hadn't worked. Not that first time and not any of the countless times we'd fought over the next couple of years when *he'd* repeated that torture tactic. It'd only made me bitter.

Bitter Sweetheart.

I no longer loved *him*. Not anymore. Not for a long time now. But I couldn't help but wonder about the next girl—there'd likely been multiple girls by now. Had *he* used that same cruel tactic on them? Had *he* weaponized our song and tortured *his* new girlfriends with it? Absolutely. It was impossible I was the anomaly. No. *He* was patterned.

The song faded into the background. The highway faded into the scenery. I faded into oblivion. Highway hypnosis took the wheel. I mindlessly stroked and smoothed the raised scar on my left wrist with my right thumb. When I arrived at work, I had no recollection of getting there.

Chapter 24

Katee

The jingling of Harley's collar woke me. My stomach crept up into my throat, making it hard to breathe as I pushed the covers down to free myself. I sat up, careful not to hit my head on the top bunk. The shadowy window suggested some time before dawn. A beam of light peered through the crack of the door just before my eyes fully adjusted to the dark. My boyfriend had finally come home after three days. The first day, I had been worried. The second, angry. Now, I just felt relief. I wanted his muscular arms to embrace me.

I stood to greet him, but as he marched into the room toward me, his glossy eyes and unnerving sneer warned me to brace myself. He staggered toward me, the stench of sour beer seeping out his pores and stale cigarette smoke clinging to his clothes. He jerked his clenched jaw side to side. His face appeared shiny and slightly puffy. He glared at me without blinking. His blue eyes looked more alive than ever, but the soul behind them had checked out. This wasn't my extremely handsome boyfriend; it was his alcoholic alter.

I lowered my gaze and sat back down on the bed. After an endless, suffocating silence, I glanced back up at him. His ink-covered arms swung out, barely missing my face. I flinched. Snickering, he grabbed the railing above my head, caging me in. The confinement felt demeaning, but tolerating it felt like the safest choice. His unsettling smirk and raised eyebrow dared me to make a move. Trying to escape would be viewed as accepting his invitation. If I started it, I was asking for it.

His thin lips parted and rose into a smile. "Hi, whore."

My body temperature dropped. My heart pounded irregularly.

"Wanna know where I was, cunt?"

My forehead and eyebrows tensed. "I'm just glad you're finally—"

"In Oshawa." He paused and widened his eyes. I racked my brain, trying to make the connection between Oshawa and his current mood.

"Okay. Did you have fun?"

"Does it fucking look like I had fun? Think it's fun being publicly humiliated by my dirty slut of a girlfriend? I'll tell you what was fun, though. Beating your little fuck friend to a pulp, breaking his jaw. That was fun. Finding out my girlfriend is fucking some total loser behind my back? No. Not fun at all."

It was difficult to see him through my tears. "I don't know what you're talking about." In the nine months we'd been together, I'd never cheated on him.

"Can't lie to me, bitch. I know the real you: a useless, unlovable child. Don't know why I put up with you when your own parents don't even want you. Get out."

My heart tensed. My body stiffened. My face got clammy and cold.

His eyes narrowed, and a grin grew on his face. "You're white as a ghost. Funny, since that's all you are to your family. Now get the fuck out."

"I never cheated on you. I don't know what you're—"

"Shut the fuck up, and get out."

I stood, keeping my knees bent to make myself shorter to show I knew he was in control and I would comply. He thrust his clammy forehead into mine. It took all my strength to resist the pressure. Terrified for my safety, I ducked under his arm and rushed to the bedroom door. I grabbed the handle but couldn't pull it open.

He stood beside me with all his weight against the door. "I'm putting you on the street where whores belong." He removed his hands from the door, and I reached for it again.

As I pulled, he pushed.

"As we left the bar, some asshole called after me. He said your first and last name and asked if you were my girlfriend. Then the big shot laughed and bragged about how he'd fucked you and how great you were."

I couldn't fathom why someone would claim that. "Babe, I swear on everything, whoever said that lied! I've never cheated on you! I love you. You're my everything."

"Exactly. I am your everything. But you were stupid enough to throw it away. Now you have nothing, no one. Wes doesn't even want a slut like you."

I frantically searched my memory as if it were a rolodex. I couldn't think clearly. I doubt I could've remembered my grandmother's first name under such pressure. I gulped. "I don't even know anyone named Wes."

"Liar." He grabbed me, pulled me over his outstretched foot, and let go. I fell onto the bed.

I cried hysterically. I couldn't control my shallow breathing. Feeling like I might have a heart attack, I worried I could die right there. I started to hyperventilate. He grabbed my feet and dragged me down to the floor. My head hit the bed frame. I yelped in pain. Everything spun. Dizziness swirled. When it stopped, I grabbed my throbbing head in agony and curled up in the fetal position.

He stared at me for a few seconds then scrunched his face and moved a little closer. "Are you really hurt?"

I was.

His jaw dropped. "Baby?"

I didn't answer.

He bent down and put his face right up to mine. "You okay?"

I wished we didn't live on the main floor of a house with a useless crackhead for a neighbour upstairs. She was probably so high she didn't hear our commotion. It probably wouldn't have made an ounce of difference if she had.

I pulled my hand away from my head and examined it. "I think I'm bleeding."

"Shit. I didn't mean to hurt you. I just love you so damn much. You do this to me! You make me go crazy. It kills me thinking about you with someone else. I'd die if I lost you."

He gently put one arm under my neck and the other under my

knees, lifting me up and onto his lap. I felt comforted. With his chin tucked in and his baby blue eyes looking up and deeply into mine, I sighed, releasing some of my fear.

He kissed my lips. At first, I was hesitant. My gut told me it wasn't over, but my heart wanted so badly to believe it was. I kissed him back. I loved molding our full, soft lips together. I always gently bit his bottom lip and held onto it a little longer; it drove him wild. Tears still soaked my face.

Then I felt a hardness; he ground his pelvis into my upper thigh. His zipper hurt. I felt him grow. He was turned on. I was still shaking. There wasn't time to analyze. I had to do whatever it took to stay safe. It didn't feel right, but what did I know about serious adult relationships? Nothing. So, I complied.

The man I had fallen in love with was back. His eyes had calmed, and through them, I could see his soul again. I felt a sense of familiarity, of belonging. He made slow and passionate love to me. We christened the rebirth of our relationship with happy tears. It was raw, beautiful, and true.

His voice cracked. "I love you, baby. You're my everything. You're mine forever."

My heart fluttered. Forever. So romantic. The moment was like a scene from a famous love story. My endorphins soothed the pain in my head, causing me to forget his earlier rage. My mind filled with girlish dreams of the future. "I was so worried when you didn't come home. I had terrible nightmares of bad things happening to you. I'm so relieved you're back."

"I'll never leave you again, promise. You need me."

"You promise?"

"I do."

I envisioned us standing at the altar. Till death do us part.

The sweat dripped off his face onto mine. A salty bead landed in my eye, causing it to burn. Our wet bodies slid up and down. My breathing kept time with his rhythm. In . . . out . . . in . . . out . . .

His eyes rolled back. "I'm gonna cum."

I smiled. "Okay." I was ecstatic to still excite him, to still please him so easily.

He pulled out and ejaculated. It marked my breasts, claimed my face, and soiled the bedsheet around me. He'd never done that before.

I felt dirty, used, and owned. I looked away, hoping he wouldn't see my tears of humiliation.

"What? You don't like that, slut? You're a filthy whore for other guys but can't play the part with me?"

Nausea trumped my pleasure. I had no idea what had just happened. Maybe I had a concussion from bumping my head so hard. Maybe I was coming in and out of reality. Either that, or I was truly going crazy.

"Well, thanks for nothing. My left hand could've done a better job. What a waste of good sperm. I'll save it for a real woman. Now, get the fuck out."

What had I done wrong? I didn't understand how he could turn his emotions on and off and up and down so easily. But I did suddenly remember who Wes was.

"Wes Scott!"

"Huh?"

"That's who you're talking about."

"I knew you'd finally admit it. Nothing a good fuck can't get out of you, eh?"

"That's Allison's brother. And I did sleep with him but before I met you."

"Bullshit! *Wes?*" he mimicked. "*I don't even know anyone named Wes.*"

My eyes overflowed with tears. "I swear!"

He didn't want to believe me. His smirks and laughter proved he enjoyed this charade, this twisted game.

I had a moment of clarity. "You said he called after you? Bragged about sleeping with me? Wes would never do that. He's far too shy. There's no way."

"Shy now that his big mouth is broken. I doubt he'll wake up from his coma."

"I don't believe you," I said through a clenched jaw. Rage at him and his lies readied me.

He laughed; a smirk lingered on his face. A proud alpha male. His body straightened, and he sighed, sounding satisfied.

I took a long, deep breath and looked him right in the eye. "I didn't do anything wrong. It was a one-night stand before I even met you." Secretly scared but desperate to hide it, I braced myself to be brave. I stood up and marched to my wardrobe to grab something to put on so I could leave. I'd come back another day for my stuff with a few of my guy friends. Perhaps I'd arrange for a police escort.

I felt his hands around my ankles, but before I could process it, they were yanked out from under me, and my face hit the ground.

"Oh, so sassy. How dare you talk to me like that, you crazy cunt? Do you know who I am? Do you know my connections? I'll make you a slut, alright. I'll invite every guy in town to line up and take a turn. You'll only fuck other men if I make them fuck you."

Fear demanded control of my body. Naked and in pain, I frantically started crawling to the door. No sooner had I reached it than he grabbed the toes on my left foot and jerked them backward. He cuffed my right ankle and pulled me toward him; my knees and chin scraped the rough industrial-grade carpet. I dug my fingers into it. One of my brittle nails flipped back. He crawled on top of me, pinning me down. I kicked and screamed. He silenced me by covering my mouth and nose with both of his hands. I couldn't breathe. The more I squirmed, the harder he squeezed my face.

Finally, he let go and shoved my head into the floor. "Shut up! Shut the hell up!"

Too petrified to move, I tried controlling my rapid breathing and silencing my sobs. While I was still on my stomach, face down, he entered me again. Far from slow and gentle, every time he penetrated me, he ground my scratched knees and chin deeper into the coarse carpet.

"I love you so much, baby."

I couldn't say anything. I felt like I was in a foreign place, unable to speak its native language.

He started crying. "I forgive you. You're mine now, mine forever. The past doesn't matter 'cause you'll never do it again."

Out of the corner of my eye, I noticed the sun starting to rise. I wondered if it would be another cool and windy day. I wondered if I had anything to pack for lunch or whether I'd need to stop and pick something up at the gas station on my way to school. I wondered if my family would go to my grandparents' the coming weekend or whether, it being the long May weekend, they'd go up to open the cottage.

"You'll never do it again, right?"

"Never."
"Say you're mine forever."
"I'm yours forever and a day."

He penetrated me again, faster and faster. I could hear his voice, but it sounded muffled, distant. I wondered how many minutes of sleep I'd get before my alarm went off. I wondered if I'd incurred any bruises and brainstormed possible ways to cover them. I wondered what I could do to ensure this would never happen again.

I felt him pull out. "I'm taking Harley out for a piss, then I'll sleep on the couch with her. Dogs are loyal, and I'm still too hurt to lie beside you." With that, he stepped over my cold body and left the bedroom.

I didn't have the energy to crawl up onto the bed much less to stay awake to ensure my boyfriend wouldn't sabotage my going to school by shutting off the alarm.

Agony burst my eyes open as he forced himself into me again. I must have passed out. I was dry, and it stung like sandpaper as he scratched in and out of me. He didn't seem to notice, or he didn't care. My head ached, my knees burned, and my vagina throbbed. Still on my stomach on the floor, I glanced up at the clock on the side table. I'd only been asleep for an hour; my alarm would go off in three minutes.

"I need to get ready for placement," I croaked.

"You're not going. We need to make up."

Teachers expected me there on time and with my homework, which he always claimed my "dumb cat" must have eaten. With only one month of school remaining, my co-op supervisor had warned me about any additional absences. Already impossibly behind in my placement hours, I needed to somehow make them up if I wanted to graduate high school.

I pulled my body away from my boyfriend and tried to balance myself as I stood up.

He laughed. "You look like a baby giraffe that doesn't know how to use its legs. You couldn't even be a stripper. No one would pay to see your awkwardness." He laughed so hard I started to cry again.

If only I had the talent of a dancer, maybe that would be enough to keep him out of the strip clubs and home with me. But I wasn't nearly enough.

I stumbled out of the bedroom and into the bathroom. He stood directly behind me. "What are you doing?"

"I need to get ready for work placement. I can't miss any more days; I have to go."

He grabbed my arm and yanked it so hard I heard it pop. "I said you're not going anywhere. I need you here. You have a lot of explaining to do." He squeezed my arm so tightly I felt it going numb. He steered me back to the bedroom and, once there, pushed my shoulders, causing me to fall onto the bed. I knew I wasn't going to win. Trying was pointless.

"Fine. Please at least let me go to the payphone and call in sick." We didn't have a landline; he wouldn't allow it. His cell phone was off-limits to me.

"You're not leaving this house. They'll figure it out."

He climbed on top of me to finish what he'd started.

Just over eight hours after he came home, the game came to an end. His liver had broken down the alcohol-induced craziness; the scary entity that had taken over his body had left; and, most importantly, he'd convinced me I had the power to make sure this never happened again.

With an eerie smirk, he said, "I found your list."

"What?"

"Your fuck list."

In an instant, it all made sense. A group of my girlfriends and I had made lists of every boy we'd ever done anything with, from holding hands to having sex, to keep a record.

Wes had been a one-night stand. In fact, he'd been my only one-night stand. Where the confusion came in was the written order of these encounters. I'd kissed several boys, so, naturally, most of them appeared first. Of course, my current boyfriend was at the end of the list, as I was already with him at the time I made it. My five-minute encounter with Wes, my best friend's brother, had happened while I was exceptionally under the influence. He was older than us, and I rarely ever saw him at Allison's house. Months after we'd had sex, when I came out of her upstairs bathroom, Wes and I shared an awkward glimpse of one another. My memory scrapped up a visual snippet of that one drunken evening when we'd found ourselves alone at the end of the night. Once I got home, I naively added his name to the only place it would fit on the list: the bottom.

Naturally, when my boyfriend found the list, he assumed I had slept with Wes since being with him since Wes's name came after his own. No wonder my boyfriend, fourteen years my senior, was so disgusted with me. This was entirely my fault.

I started to explain, but he interrupted me with a loud sarcastic laugh. "How juvenile. If you wanna keep a man like me, you're gonna have to grow up. Fast."

My mouth hung open in awe. "I knew you didn't see Wes in Oshawa."

He laughed through his nose. "Clearly didn't have to."

Dear Katee,

You're very erotic, my cutie, you teach me more about sexuality than any other woman I have ever known intimately. There is no coyness or false modesty about you. I've come to understand your needs and desires, since you make it clear what pleases you the most. Also, in a curious way you teach me about my own body and make it come alive as it never had before you. You love my body and tell me so; you take all the pleasure you want from it and from the fulfillment I give you. You please me in return, as no woman ever has. When we make love, it is with no restraint and there is ecstasy between us.

Lilacs laced the air with their floral perfume. Finding their sweet scent sentimental, I breathed in deeply. Similar lavender-coloured bushes had lined the perimeter of my family's old house in the city. On May mornings, my sisters and I would pick bunches for our bus driver. I looked down at the pack of cigarettes I had just bought from the Mac's convenience store two blocks from our apartment. In that moment, I decided to quit smoking.

I noticed my boyfriend's rusty old car, parked in front of our house, displayed a new boastful bumper sticker: *This delinquent is fucking your honour student.* That had been his claim to fame, but it was no longer accurate. Smoking wasn't the only thing I quit that month. I had so much potential, but I threw it all away one month before high school graduation. A passive-not-planned high-school dropout.

I couldn't keep disappointing people. I couldn't bear it anymore. I no longer had my mother much less my lifelong-approval-seeking determination to keep up with her unattainable academic pressure. School was the only thing my mom had ever seemed to care about, the only thing I was ever truly good at, and I couldn't even bring myself to do it anymore. I never returned to my co-op placement. I couldn't even face my supervisor to quit. My abundance of absences and tardiness aside, now visible cuts and bruises marked me and showed off my shame. How could I begin to explain the situation I'd somehow gotten myself into? The "told you so's" from my friends and family and the fear my boyfriend instilled in me kept me silent.

My school didn't have my current address, and I didn't have a phone number. No one could search for me if they ever realized I was missing.

Chapter 25

Katee

While everyone I knew went to school or work during the day, I found myself housebound with nothing to do for the entire month of June. My boyfriend left frequently and for increasing periods of time—most often for countless hours, many times for days. He never told me when he was leaving much less where he was going and when he'd be home. Not knowing felt like an extra dreadful type of torture. In the beginning when I asked, he simply said it wasn't my concern. Eventually, he taught me not to question him at all. About anything. Ever. And as our relationship disintegrated, I became grateful for the time without him.

The odd time he finally came home after an excessively long stretch, typically after our worst fights, he brought me jewelry. At first, I thought it nothing more than guilt gifts, his way of apologizing. But a growing part of me realized there was more to it than that. The gifts were never wrapped, never accompanied by a card. He ensured I never took off a few of the pieces: a platinum, antique ring with five small diamonds that was far too big for any finger but my thumb and a silver necklace and bracelet set with different-coloured precious gems. These three pieces seemed peculiarly important to him, and although he didn't explain why or where they had come from, he made sure they became important to me, too. I guessed they were stolen from the houses I think he robbed; I hoped they weren't trophies from the tarts I think he fucked.

Our upstairs neighbour claimed my boyfriend had slept with one of my in-town friends. At first, I didn't believe my friend would do that. I trusted her more than I trusted him. But when she disappeared from my life immediately following the allegation, I started stressing about his female friend bar stars with whom he spent most evenings. Since I was still underage, I only ever saw them when they came to our house to pick him up. Each time, they deliberately dismissed me, acting like I wasn't there. After he left with them, I'd spend the entire evening and sometimes part of the next day or two until he finally returned wondering and worrying about what might be occurring between them.

My female friends scurried away, but my guy friend, James, became increasingly concerned and protective. I didn't dare share with him, or anyone, that anything was less than perfect in my relationship, but James knew something wasn't right. On the eve of the Canada Day long weekend, my boyfriend came home livid.

"James needs to mind his own fucking business," he ranted, "and mind his own fucking bitch."

I worried he'd accuse James of having a crush on me, or worse, the other way around.

Instead, he said, "I invited that goddamn goof on the road trip. I'll off him in the middle of nowhere and leave his body in a ditch."

I didn't believe he would, or could, kill James, but when my boyfriend returned at the end of the long weekend, alone, without James or Harley, I panicked. I couldn't help but question him and demand answers.

"Get off my fucking back, Katee. Harley ran away to a better place, and James followed her, okay?"

Terror immobilized me for three days until James finally made his way back. Word on the street said my boyfriend had pulled over somewhere way out of town, taken James's shoes, made him get out of the car, then left him. James never crossed paths with me again. Word on the street also said my boyfriend had gotten rid of Harley because pets weren't permitted on the Greyhound bus, which we'd be taking for our news-to-me four-day commute to BC.

I continued feeling unbearably lonesome for my family. Although my boyfriend tried keeping me convinced of their hatred for me, I began challenging that notion. One day, when I mentioned trying to reconnect with them, my boyfriend upped the ante and used something against me that I'd made the mistake of telling him early in our relationship.

"Remember your twisted-as-fuck fantasy about hiring someone for a fake home invasion? Well, if you've truly forgotten how your family feels, you'll leave me no choice but to prove that not only does your mother love Leigh more, but she'd be willing to let you die to save your sisters," he threatened. "And I'll conduct this very real attack on your entire family myself, at gunpoint."

I welcomed the wicked heat wave we endured at the end of July. I'd always preferred the weather as hot as possible, and it gifted me the excuse to spend the sweltering afternoons solo soaking up the sun on the edge of the river that ran through town. I cooled off, as needed, by dipping my toes in the refreshing water.

One day, after I'd basked in all the sunny solitude I could justify, I made my way back to our apartment. I noticed a familiar truck parked out front. I slowed my pace; a sick feeling began to overwhelm my stomach.

Flapping a big stack of cash in his hand, my boyfriend saw me walk in. "Hey, cutie."

Unsure how to address the wad of money he was holding, I smiled and raised my brows. His smile stretched from one end of his handsome face to the other. His baby blues flickered with enthusiasm. My boyfriend's dealer, also the owner of the truck outside, stood with arms crossed on the other side of our living room, a goofy look consuming his tan, weathered face.

I looked back and forth between them, my brows still raised. "What on earth are the two of you up to?"

"Tell me who takes care of his girl," my boyfriend said.

"You do."

"That's right. So, I sold all our stuff to get enough money to move out to BC."

I turned my gaze away to inspect the rest of the house. My desk was no longer under the window in the dining area of our kitchen. Hairballs, dust bunnies, and other debris sat in its place. My body warmed with anger. Five years ago, I'd sold enough cheese to constipate an entire village. The money had been meant to go toward the cost of my Grade 8 graduation trip to Ottawa. The morning of my class's departure, I started my first menstrual cycle. Distressed and embarrassed, I refused to go. Luckily, the money I'd earned selling cheese was returned to me, and with it, I'd bought my first big purchase—my desk.

I glared at my boyfriend before heading to our bedroom. Just before reaching the entrance, I gasped. "My wardrobe!" My seven-foot-tall, six-foot-wide, mirrored-front wardrobe was gone. It'd consisted of three panels; the middle panel had been anchored, and the two outer thirds had sat on wheels that'd pulled in toward one another, creating a 270-degree view that'd allowed me to create the most fabulous hairstyles. The middle section had housed my hung clothing, and the outer sides had consisted of seven shelves each. My wardrobe had been the most practical and coolest thing I'd ever seen, used, or owned. My parents had bought it for me because my new bedroom hadn't had a closet.

I crossed the threshold of our room. Seeing nothing out of the corner of my eye, my heart deflated. I wanted to pinch myself to ensure the completely bare room before me wasn't a nightmare.

"Jay and Betty have a twin bed we can borrow," said my boyfriend from behind me. He put his hand on my sunken shoulder, and I shuddered at his touch. Tears of futility spoiled my face. My bunkbed was gone, too. Nothing of "ours" had been sold. Everything had been mine.

I turned around. "How could you?" I said in the helpless voice of a child.

His eyes narrowed, creating goosebumps on my scalp. A cough from the living room softened his face, and he spun around to rejoin his company.

I watched my boyfriend hand his dealer the huge wad of cash. I couldn't make out what they said, but hearty chuckles filled the room as they left our apartment. I ran to the front window to catch a glimpse of their interaction. Standing beside his truck, the dealer hastily looked around before underhandedly passing something to my boyfriend. I retreated into the kitchen to avoid getting caught spying.

A minute later, our front door flew open. My boyfriend whipped something at me. "See what I do to support you?"

It clipped my ear before hitting the floor. Ambrihl ran to it, thinking we were playing a game. I watched as she batted the unknown object across the floor. I heard the front door slam but couldn't pry my eyes from the plastic baggie. I took a few steps toward it and shooed Ambrihl away.

I bent down and picked it up. A clear sandwich bag cradled a ball the size of a clementine. The bag had been tied tight, and the excess plastic had been cut off precisely at its knot. Unable to untie it, I retrieved scissors to cut it open. Inside were sixteen bags, four of them slightly smaller than the rest. They contained little yellowish-white stones. My boyfriend selling pot and pills for extra cash already scared me shitless. Now, he'd sold all my belongings to buy crack cocaine.

Chapter 26

Gabbi

I clear my work schedule for a two-week visit to take my little sister to and from her increasingly frequent medical appointments: never-ending blood tests, CT scans, and chemo infusions alongside all the new appointments in downtown Toronto for the experimental study she was just accepted into. Bryanne's getting sicker and sicker, and I'm getting more and more anxious I won't finish my book in time for her to read it. She's so invested in my writing process. Every time I ask her for health updates, she asks me for novel updates. Tit for tat.

I'm in the backseat of Bryanne's car. She and Johnny picked me up from the airport, and we're driving to their place.

"Did you hear about the Queen of Canada?" Johnny asks.

Bryanne scoffs. "If she survives her ninety-sixth birthday next month, I can sure as heck survive stage four's five-year relative survival rate of thirteen percent."

"No," Johnny says, "not Queen Elizabeth the Second, the whackjob cult leader calling herself the Queen of Canada."

I chill hearing *cult leader*.

"Oh," says Bryanne. "No. What kind of cult?"

"Some QAnon bullshit and absurd sovereign citizen crap," he

says. "She lived in BC until this year, but she just moved twenty kilometers from your mom and dad's place."

I swallow vomit down the back of my throat. She just moved to *his* place of birth.

"Oooh. So, what's a sovereign citizen?" asks Bryanne.

Johnny starts explaining the pseudo-legal concepts derived from the sovereign citizen movement conspiracy theory, and I unlock my phone and Google "Queen of Canada." Could my ex be connected to this woman? I click on the Wikipedia link and scroll through her page. It claims she's one of the most prominent figures of the QAnon movement in Canada. She gained popularity during the pandemic when she founded and led the non-registered Canada First Party. Until this year, she lived in British Columbia, but thanks to significant donations to fund her tour, she began traveling to various parts of Canada with a group of her supporters. This timeline means she still lived in BC last fall when we went there on our family trip. She lived in the same place my ex was last seen alive. And *he*, too, received donations from *his* supporters. They've both solicited donations through social media.

I choose to tell Bryanne and Johnny about the eerie coincidence of Johnny bringing this up. I choose to break my cycle of Googling and Facebook searching in silent shame and instead share why this topic is triggering me and speak the truth about my crazy ex and the uncanny commonalities between *him* and this self-proclaimed Queen of Canada.

I take a deep breath to brace myself. "He's into all that outrageous sovereignty bs," I say, my voice shaky.

"Who?" asks Johnny.

"No way," says Bryanne. She knows exactly who I mean.

I pull back up the Wikipedia page and read it to her. "'According to those who traveled with her, she exhibits authoritarian and abusive behaviour toward members of her team, with experts warning this fits some of the signifiers of cult-like behaviour. Some volunteers who quit, or simply displeased her, were threatened with execution. Several of her former followers organized into a group that monitors her activities, warning communities to which she travels.'"

Holy shit. My ex has someone who monitors *his* activities and locations, too: Burnaby Blogger.

"Cult-like? Are they connected?" Bryanne asks.

I unblock my ex and search *his* Facebook friend list for this woman's name. She's not there. "Don't look to be," I say. "Just one more thing suggesting he's likely dead. Maybe I should use whatever money's left over to hire a private investigator to ensure he's dead before publishing my book."

"Leftover money?" asks Bryanne.

"Oh, I forgot to tell you," I say.

"What?" asks Bryanne.

"Remember twelve thousand and nine?"

"Sure do."

"Well, I decided to 'reclaim' it by spending twelve thousand and nine dollars on publishing my book."

"Why would it cost so much?" Johnny asks.

"Many things go into the final product: professional editing, book design, production, distribution, and promotion. But, if I get it done for less, I'll donate anything remaining to a domestic violence prevention organization."

"Wow," says Bryanne. "Way to make the memory meaningful."

"Yup. A meaningful memorial. I'll make it count for something consequential."

"I'm so proud of you, Gabbi. Can't wait to read it."

No. She can't. I need to stop letting *him* distract me and focus on getting it done.

The next morning, I notice Bryanne is struggling to breathe. It's so bad it looks like she's faking it. She's not. Their basement suite is tiny, yet she can't even get to the bathroom and back without stopping for a break to catch her breath each way. Thankfully, she has a hospital appointment with her new experimental trial doctor this afternoon. But when it takes her ten minutes to get up the stairs to leave the house, I worry they might admit her.

Bryanne asks me to stop at the mall on our way out of town. She wants to make a return at Sephora. Her breathing is so bad it takes forever to get her from the car and into the mall, so I make her wait at the first bench I see while I handle the refund.

When I exit Sephora, I scan the busy crowd and spot Bryanne sitting across the hallway outside of a little café. As I approach her, I call out, "Done." I point behind me, "It's a zoo in there. Sorry it took so long."

Then I hear it. The song playing over the speakers. The lyrics shiver through me: "*I gave you all the love I got; I gave you more than I could give.*"

He's back.

Bryanne moves her purse and pats the bench for me to sit. "You know what I just realized?"

I gulp down my nerves and shake my head.

"I never asked the title of your book." My little sister offers me puppy-apologetic eyes.

Joining her, I sit down and shrug. "I'm not sure yet," I say.

Liar. My ex calls me out. The song playing over the mall speakers right now *is* the title.

Not a lie; I'm just not sure how exactly I'll reclaim and reframe the song's meaning.

Never one to pry, Bryanne returns the shrug and leaves the topic be.

But *he* doesn't. *He* ensures I hear the lyrics of our song playing quietly overhead: "*I keep crying, I keep trying for you. There's nothing like you and I, baby.*"

Over it, I grab my purse and root around for my earbud case. A love like that won't last. Time to override that memory by creating a new one—drown out one with another. I find my earbuds and turn to my sister. "I have a gift for you."

"Oh?" Her widening eyes search for the invisible present.

I hand her the left earbud and nod for her to put it in. I secure the right one in my ear. I plug the cord into my phone and unlock it. I click on my music app and search for the title. "I made a song for you."

"You did not," she says.

I find it and press play. "I did."

Bryanne takes my hand and intertwines her fingers in mine. I give her hand a squeeze. She squeezes back twice. After the first two verses, I glance at her. She smiles as big as her closed mouth will allow. I face forward as the tears come to my eyes. Holding them back traps my breath in my throat. My sister and I simultaneously squeeze our joined hands again, holding tight for the length of the verse. Then the chorus begins. We exhale. Tears fall.

The next verse mentions one of our favourite childhood pastimes: our post-bedtime singing competitions, singing "Somewhere Out There" late at night when we were supposed to be sleeping. We both chuckle and turn to look at one another, nodding a few times and giggling, reliving a precious moment that bonded us so many years ago. I'm too late hiding my tears this time. They aren't subtle or quiet or pretty. But neither are hers. We sit side by side in raw emotion. We allow the ugly cry to take over.

True, no ordinary love.

When we arrive at the hospital for Bryanne's appointment, they admit her immediately and inform her she's no longer able to take part in the experimental treatment. Her cancer has progressed too far, too fast. She requires constant oxygen. Our family moves into the hospital waiting room for the duration of Bryanne's two-week stay. The stress eats away at us as Bryanne gets sicker and sicker in a shockingly short period of time. When it's not my turn to be with her, I spend my time racing the clock by trying to type more than sixty words per minute to its sixty second-hand tics. When Bryanne asks about my progress, I offer to let her read some of it, but she refuses, promising she'll beat this and read the completed masterpiece with everyone else. Besides, she says cheating and reading bits and pieces ahead of time would be to accept defeat and death. As astonished as I am with my book's evolution, I fear it isn't coming together fast enough to be complete in time.

When the day comes for me to fly home, I don't feel bad leaving because Bryanne's been told she'll be discharged any day now. The hospital is just waiting for her home oxygen to be set up.

"I'll be back in eighteen days for Easter," I assure her as we embrace.

Tara, our parents, Warren, and Johnny all excuse themselves, promising Bryanne they'll come right back after they see me off. We head to the elevators and walk out to the front of the hospital. The men wrap up their sendoffs in record time and load my luggage into the waiting taxi. We ladies camouflage into the hustle and bustle of the comings and goings of the crowd.

My mom pulls me close and hugs me tight. "Thank you for taking so much time off work to come home every month."

"Of course. We can't get this time back," I say, as I give her an extra squeeze.

Tara hugs me. "It's less than three weeks till you're back," she reminds me.

"I know. But every moment together counts. I just wish I didn't have to work," I say. "Be grateful you guys all live in the same province. When I say goodbye, it's for weeks, not days."

"Hey, now. Bryanne made us promise no goodbyes," Mom says. "Only see-you-laters."

We all force smiles to seal empty promises.

I get into the cab, and they all wave me off as I'm driven away, leaving my heart behind.

Chapter 27

Alex

I entered my office to find an unfamiliar man poking around behind my desk. "Excuse me? Can I help you with something?" The heavy, windowless door locked shut behind me.

The man turned to face me, his nostrils flared. "Who the hell do you think you are, huh?"

"I beg your pardon?" Everything in me urged for me to prop open my office door, but my desire to come off as confident, competent, and professional outpulled the tug-of-war with my fear. Attempting to steady my hand, I gestured to the couches.

Slowly and steadily, the man stalked toward me. "I didn't give consent for you to talk to my girls, lady," he said, exaggerating the word *lady*. "And how old are you, anyway? Don't look old enough to be out of high school, much less the shrink at one."

I looked much closer in age to the graduating class than to my colleagues who were also in their late twenties. I got comments like this all the time, but I'd never been confronted in my own office with such aggression. I remained on edge.

"I'm sorry, who are your—"

"Take a seat," the man said, using his body posture and the shrinking distance between us to back me into the couch—keeping my back to the closed door.

To avoid physical contact, I gave in to the pressure to sit. With only a sliver of personal space remaining between us—he'd trapped me at eye level with his groin—his legs blocked me in like the posts on a baby gate. He took a step back, momentarily gifting me a foot or so of breathing room. Still standing over me, he bent down and leaned in until the sour smell of alcoholic body odour mixed with sticky sweet spearmint, and the spice of nicotine invaded my nostrils. The stench almost choked me. I could taste his rancid breath.

"Stay the hell away from Rosslynn and Kristin, or I'll fucking report you to whatever body governs your young, sweet ass."

I broke eye contact, turning to sneak a tiny gasp of sober air. I remembered the little note I'd found shoved under my door the previous week.

Hanson is mad at me. Will Hanson kill me and Rosslynn? Yes or no? Will Hanson try to kill my mom? Will you keep us safe? Pick yes or no.

"Understood, sugar tits?" he said, as his eyes molested my body, and his tongue massaged his smoke-stained teeth.

I fought back fear. "Please leave my office."

Pointing a dirty finger at my face, he said, "You'll leave my name outta your mouth if you know what's good for you."

The man left.

I exhaled both breath and tears. Shakily, I staggered to the door and rested my face against it, requesting it console me. I tried to hear through it for proof he'd left or that others were near, but it was solidly soundproof. I took my cell phone out of my back pocket and called the main office.

"Good morning, Port—"

"Doris, it's Alex. Why was I not informed Hanson Collins was waiting for me in my office?" I opened my door and kicked the rubber stop underneath it. I peered out the doorway and looked both ways. The goon was gone.

"Who?"

"Kristen and Ross—"

"Oh, their mom's latest boyfriend, right, well, actually, I didn't know he came. Hang on a sec . . . Maribel?" Doris called to the other secretary. "Did you take Mr. Collins down to Alex's office?"

While I waited, I studied the configuration of my office furniture. It wasn't set up for safety. Although from inside my office, a clear line of sight to the exit was visible, people outside were unable to see the back half of the rectangular room. This was problematic for potentially nefarious ongoings that might require immediate intervention.

"Nope. She didn't either. Strange. Let me look at the . . ."

I decided my couches and table and chairs needed to be switched up, so, at least with the door open, visitors would be visible and hollers for help would be audible.

"His name's not on the sign-in sheet. I don't know who let him in. Anyway, what can I help you with?"

Security. Building security. Fucking school security, for Pete's sake. I would start with my own office safety. Move the loveseat I sat on from the middle of the long room to directly in front of the door, facing it. And the guest loveseat would sit opposite it with its back to the door. That way, everyone walking by could clearly see all who occupied the office, and most importantly, my facial expressions.

"From now on, I won't see anyone without a preexisting appointment. No exceptions. Also, I'll come to the main office to collect all attendees. I don't want anyone just sent to me, not even if you call me first. And, depending on the parent, I might require either an admin's presence or use of one of their fishbowl offices so you or Maribel can keep watch."

"Oh, my. What happened, Alex?" Doris asked, sounding concerned.

"Alex?"

I shrieked and dropped my cell. "Jesus, Jessica!" I bent down to grab and inspect my phone for a crack.

"Jumpy," said Jessica, who'd appeared abruptly in my doorway, with a chuckle. "Did handsome Hanson already leave?" She puckered her lips and fluttered her false lashes.

"You!" I blamed.

Jessica's face dropped the cutesy kissing charade.

"What the hell, Jessica? You damn well know better than to just leave some stranger unattended in my office without even so much as a heads-up to me. That's both a confidentiality breach and a safety concern."

"Take a chill pill, will ya? Geez. First, he's not a stranger, he's a parent. A hot parent. Second—"

"First, he's not a parent, he's a partner of a parent. He does not have any biological children attending our school nor does he have any legal rights to his girlfriend's children who happen to be students of ours. Second, he absolutely is a stranger to me, and third, no member of that family is on my caseload. But what's most important, Jessica, due to the nature of my job, is that seeing me is by appointment only. Capisce?"

As she rolled her eyes, she raised her hands and waved them like white flags. "Holy moly, Alex. Sorrrrry—"

"Alex! Jessica? Are you okay? What's going on?" Doris and Maribel called out as they burst into my office.

"Alex is losing her damn mind," Jessica said.

Chapter 28

Katee

"What do you mean, we don't have a cat?" A growing balloon in my lungs hogged my air supply. What'd my boyfriend do with Ambrihl?

I scoured the six-by-six-foot bedroom. No litter box. Not a speck of litter on the floor. Not even a tuft of calico fur. I hunted under the single bed and in the closet. I searched my boyfriend's face last.

He lay on the bed looking totally content. Arms behind his head, fingers cradling his skull that I wanted so badly to crush.

Why did he play these games with me? Make me feel like I was crazy?

The most irritating smile spread, as thickly as peanut butter, across his smug face. Without taking his taunting eyes off me, he crossed his legs at the knee.

I'd just returned from my friend Arleen's house after spending the night there. She hadn't been home, but I'd spent the evening venting to her mom—a second mother to me ever since I'd met Arleen. The night before, my boyfriend and I had gotten into another fight about moving to BC.

"You're coming," he'd insisted.

"No. I'm not."

"It's not up for discussion, cutie. All our stuff is already there waiting for us." With that, he'd left me to go out to the bar. Feeling lonely and trapped, I'd called Arleen's to see if her mom was home.

"Marilyn?"

"Hey, kiddo. What's up? Arleen's not home."

I'd twisted the phone cord around my index finger instead of wrapping it around my neck. "Um . . . I actually—"

"Oh, love," she'd said then sighed. "Wanna come over?"

"Please." A tear had fallen over my lower lashes. "But I—"

"Just call a cab. I'll pay for it when you get here."

I'd tried to hold in my sobs. "Thanks."

No matter how many times I went to Marilyn and Arleen's, I still had a hard time believing so many rooms could fit into just a trailer. From the outside, it looked so tiny—like it might only be big enough for a small kitchen and a futon. On the inside, though, it seemed so spacious. A big living room with an attached dining room, a decent-sized kitchen, three bedrooms, and a bathroom. Plus, it had a basement, which Arleen claimed as her extra huge bedroom.

I really hadn't wanted to spend the night. I'd known that would totally piss off my boyfriend. I hadn't been allowed to spend the night anywhere else since being with him.

"Screw that asshole," Marilyn had said. "Serves him right. Take back ownership of yourself, kiddo. You staying here'll remind him he's not the boss of you."

So, I'd screwed that asshole and stayed.

"Where were you, slut?" My boyfriend sat up on the bed and swung his legs out to face me. His facetious smile disappeared, and in its place appeared a frown and an accusing glare.

"Don't talk to me like that. I'm sick of your shit."

His eyebrows rose in awe and seemed to consequently pull up the corners of his mouth into a haunting smile. He cracked his knuckles.

I remembered what Marilyn had said. *Kiddo, it's just stuff. We'll do everything we can to get it back for you, but at the end of the day, that stuff isn't worth your happiness.*

But it wasn't just stuff. I thought about the silver dollars my grandfather had given me. And his readers from elementary school.

I could picture his childlike handwritten name on the front covers. It seemed weird, almost impossible that he could ever have been in elementary school, that he could ever have been younger than me.

"Where the fuck were you that made you forget who you're talking to?" My boyfriend put his hands on his knees to brace himself as he leaned forward.

I replayed Marilyn's words. *What's the worst he can do? Has he ever hit you?*

I'd paused before responding to her. I'd started to feel like a silly little girl complaining about my relationship—like I hadn't expected it to have any problems at all.

I'd sighed. *No. Nothing like that,* I'd lied.

A pain in my throat brought me back. My boyfriend's pointer finger held my larynx hostage. "Hello? McFly?" he mocked.

Marilyn's words offered me strength. *What's the worst he can do?*

I took a few steps forward, pushing my boyfriend back toward our borrowed bed. Just before it felt like his finger would puncture a hole in my neck, he sat down, releasing me. I continued toward him until my knees grazed his. I felt so powerful in that moment, standing above him. Looking down at him.

He was pathetic. He'd always be pathetic.

He grabbed my wrists.

"Where's Ambrihl?" My voice came out a little shakily. A little weakly. Adrenaline exploded through my body. I took a slow, deep breath to steady my voice and released it with purpose. A little louder and a lot more firmly, I said, "Where's my cat?"

"Listen to me carefully, cutie." His eyebrows bunched up, and his eyes softened. "Come over here." He patted the bed beside him. "Sit with me."

"I'll stand."

He reached up to cup either side of my face with his warm hands. "Katee, you're freaking me out. First you leave and don't come home all night. Leave me worrying sick about you. Then you show up all crazy-like? Making accusations about some cat you're convinced we have?"

My body lunged forward. I heard a godawful sound. The animalistic howl had emanated from me. "You lying bastard!"

A smile grew on his face. "You need help, Katee." He chuckled. "Serious, professional help."

"Where is Ambrihl? Tell me!"

"I'm too hung over for this. I can't be around someone as crazy as you right now. Take a time out. Think about how insane you sound." He stood up. I didn't budge. He pushed past me then stopped to pat me on the head. "Poor baby. You wanted so badly to grow up and play house. But you cracked under the pressure of pretending to be an adult."

I spun around. "People know we have a cat."

"If they think so, it's only 'cause you told them that." He laughed. "Tell me this, psycho . . ." He got right in my face. I smelled the stale beer and cigarettes from the evening before. ". . . did any of the people you told actually see this supposed cat of ours?"

My brain overheated with thoughts, memories, and emotions. I couldn't think straight. People knew we had a cat. Didn't they? I tried remembering which of my friends had come to our house in the eight months we'd had Ambrihl.

As my boyfriend opened the door to leave, he said, "You think about it real hard. If you're still living in an imaginary world when I get back, I'll commit you to the looney bin."

I spent the next hour making "Lost Cat" posters to post around town. They seemed extra childish considering I didn't have a picture of her to use. When I finished putting up the posters, I had no idea what to do aside from pack my remaining belongings. I had an out. Marilyn had said she'd take me in. She'd reminded me of all the people who loved and cared about me, all the people my boyfriend had forced me to believe hated me and had forgotten about me. I'd be okay.

As I placed the last of my folded clothes into a plastic grocery bag, I wondered what he could have done with Ambrihl. She must have been so scared without me. What if he never told me where she was?

I heard the door open but refused to turn around. This was it. Time to tell him I was leaving him.

He pushed me to the side so hard I lost my balance, twisted my ankle, and fell to the floor. He started picking up the plastic bags full of my clothing and throwing them at my face. I didn't even raise my hands to block them. Every one that hit me triggered more anger, and I needed all I could get.

"Where do you think you're going?"

"You're going to tell me where to find my cat, and then I'm leaving you."

He laughed, looked at the plastic bags surrounding me, and laughed harder. "Don't you get it yet, you fucking idiot?" He crouched down and crawled toward me, never taking his eyes off mine. When his forehead reached mine, he headbutted me—cracked my head like a baseball off a bat. My head rebounded off the window behind me. I heard the glass break. My boyfriend grabbed my chin between his bent forefinger and thumb. He squeezed so tightly I yelped.

"If you ever leave me, I'll fucking kill you."

I took a deep breath. "You're a lot of things—"

"Yeah, bitch? Like what? You're a pretty ballsy idiot to talk to me like this when I'm seconds away from breaking your jaw."

"—but you're not a killer. And I'm not an idiot. I'm leaving you."

He released his grip and stood up. "You are an idiot. Now stand up." He didn't wait for me to respond—not that I had any intention of obeying him. He shoved his hand under my armpit and yanked me to my feet.

I didn't think much of it as he dragged me out of the room, out the front door, and to the end of the driveway. He'd done that before—put me out on the curb like a trash whore, as he'd said. But then we passed the curb and started crossing the road.

I wondered where he was taking me. Whether I should scream or try to get someone's attention. Fuck it. What was the worst he could do?

He stopped once we arrived at the abandoned railroad track that passed through town.

"Call for her," he mocked. "Come on. Let's hear it. Call for her. I'll let you leave if she comes."

"Like she's going to come to me if you put her outside. You're such an asshole. She's probably terrified."

"Get looking. You have five minutes."

She was probably long gone by now. He'd just watch me call after her like a moron.

The light breeze made the overgrown bushes on either side of the tracks play tricks on me. A movement here. A rustle there. I stopped caring about what my boyfriend thought and started searching for my cat.

"You might wanna get down on your hands and knees. Too much growth to see much of anything from where you're standin'."

Bile bubbled up and stung the back of my throat. "Shut the hell up!"

My boyfriend laughed, checked his watch, and shoved his hands in his pockets.

I turned back around and continued looking.

"If you get down on your hands and knees, I'll give you clues."

"You've got to be kidding me, you sick fuck!"

"Meow. Cold," he mocked.

Tears welled up in my eyes. This couldn't be happening. I got down on my hands and knees. Once I found Ambrihl, I'd be rid of him for good.

"Gonna stay cold unless you start movin' around. Meow." He watched me crawl like a puppet he controlled, guiding me with *cold, warmer,* and *warm* clues until I'd had enough and stopped. He kicked gravel at me. "Okay, okay. Close your eyes."

Lava-hot tears spilled over my lower lashes as I glared up at him. "Fuck you." I spat in his direction.

"I'm serious. Promise. Close your eyes, and I'll bring her to you."

I closed my eyes and prayed to God. I heard gravel scatter beneath his feet as he moved around behind me. How would I even get her to Marilyn's? I needed to find a box or something. Should I poke holes in it?

The sound of his footsteps warned me of his return. I felt my body tense. Saliva pooled in my mouth, but I found it difficult to swallow.

His hand smacked my face. "Ready, Freddy? Meow."

I heard a thud. Something soft grazed my leg. I reached out. "Ambrihl?" I touched her soft fur. "Baby!" I ran my hand down her body. Wet. Cold. Sticky. I opened my eyes. "Nooooo!"

My heart catapulted into my throat. I grabbed her. Gathered her mangled body in my arms and pulled her close. My surroundings circled rapidly around me. I screamed as I rocked Ambrihl back and forth. I glanced down at her and threw up all over myself, all over her bloody body.

A blow to the back of my head caused my face to hit the ground. I heard my boyfriend's wicked, high-pitched laugh. "I am a killer, you fucking idiot!" He kicked more gravel at me before kicking me in the back. "Do you get that now?"

"How could you?" I spun around to cut him with my glare. "How could you do this?"

"Pretty easily, actually." He grabbed a clump of Ambrihl's fur and ripped her from my grip. He shook her limp body in my face.

The metallic smell of blood offended my nose. I couldn't make out her head.

"You didn't come home. Needed to be taught a lesson you'd never forget."

It wasn't real. It couldn't be real. That couldn't be her. It had to be roadkill, a look-alike. This couldn't be happening.

"So, I brought your annoying cat over here, held her down, and smashed in her skull." He tossed her lifeless body into the brush and wiped his hands on his jeans. "And so help me, God, Katee, if you ever leave me—or threaten to again—I'll kill you. I'll kill your entire fucking family."

Bitter Sweetheart,

I've looked deeply, unforgivingly, at my own behaviour and have come to see it for what it is: unremitting cowardice. I've cried for the hate that filled my life, for the guilt and the jealousy that had been my companions, for the loneliness that I had brought on myself, for the contempt and disgust that I had directed towards you. I'm sorry. Forgive me. I pray you will.

Someday you'll forgive me and . . . and . . . well . . . I'm not sure what happens then. But for now, you need to get the fuck over it. We've both had to give up a lot. I had to get rid of Harley who was my dog for many years, you lost our baby—an actual human being—and now you're moping around about a stupid, annoying cat you had for mere months? Come on, Katee. Stop being such a child. Your immaturity is not becoming. Grow up. They're all in a better place. And soon we will be too. This move to BC promises goodness out of evil, hope out of despair, life out of death. It will bring our dreams into existence. Going to BC will put an end to our anguish and offer us the beginning of true joy. All our stuff is already there waiting for us. We are getting on that bus. I'll take you there kicking and screaming, if necessary. You'll thank me later.

Chapter 29

Alex

I thought back to the handful of texts my ex had sent me via Facebook messenger over the years since our breakup. I signed into my account to see how long ago the last communication had been. Just over two years ago. I scrolled up through *his* attempts to interact.

Call me sometime . . . I miss talkin to ya. Followed by a couple phone numbers with two different area codes.

Keep in touch more often, so I can see your smile, its soooo cute.

I scrolled past a few music videos *he'd* randomly sent of our old favourite songs. And, of course, *he'd* sent our song. There was no doubt in my mind *he'd* since weaponized it to hurt *his* more recent girlfriends.

Typically, I hadn't engaged. But I came across one time when I had. I remembered feeling both enraged and empowered after hearing some new-to-me song lyrics, and I had confronted *him*.

Have you heard the song 'Stupid Boy' by Keith Urban? You should listen to it.

All I'd ever wanted was an apology. I'd hoped *he'd* listen to the song, reflect on all *he'd* done to me, and finally offer me one.

He'd replied, *Yeah, I've heard the song. You're funny. Lol*

Even after all these years, it was clear I'd never get an apology from *him*.

One time a few years back, I'd gotten sloppy. I'd updated my profile picture to one taken when my sister and I had visited Montana's Glacier National Park and taken the scenic Going-to-the-Sun Road. I had climbed onto the roof of my car and spread my arms as wide as they could go to try and underline the stunning peaks of the Rocky Mountains. I had never felt so free.

Yet immediately after I'd posted it, *he'd* sent me a private message. *Back in the mountains I see.*

I'd felt tracked, hunted, found. I couldn't believe I'd slipped up so badly. What an idiot. I had immediately changed my profile picture back to a generic one with no dead giveaways. I'd been meticulous with what information I'd kept on and off the social media platform and what my public picture showed. My profile settings were as private as they could be, but *he* could still see my main profile picture. Unfortunately, we still shared a few mutual acquaintances, so I refused to list my current living location to even my friends list. I couldn't risk *him* collecting any clues as to my whereabouts.

I'd considered responding to *him* and rebutting *his* assumption, telling *him* I'd just gone on a vacation. Then I'd considered the benefit of letting *him* think I'd moved somewhere near the mountains to keep *him* the hell away from looking for me anywhere near my family's home. I had thought *he* might stop mailing letters for me to my parents' house if *he* had limited access to me through Facebook Messenger.

Looking back now, years later, and still receiving letters from *him*, I realized I had been wrong. I clicked on *his* open profile and went into *his* photo albums. Still there: pictures of me plastered proudly like prized possessions. Years ago, I had discovered a few new additions, pictures of me taken in the many years since our breakup. From their grainy quality, it looked like they might be pictures of my pictures. Stolen copies. At the time, I had gone back to *his* main page and clicked on "friends" then "mutual" and blocked all five of our acquaintances. Then I'd messaged *him*.

I noticed you have an awful lot of stolen pics of me under your 'family' album . . . what's that about?

He'd responded a few days later: *Just where they went when I made the album. Lol . . . and there are no awful pics of you.*

I couldn't stop rereading the message. *He'd* been playing with me. I hadn't said they were awful pics; I'd said *he* had an awful lot of stolen pics. *He'd* always excelled at twisting words.

I yelped as I realized I had been repeatedly scratching the same spot on my wrist. Blood oozed out from the edge of my tattoo that covered my scar. Adrenaline drew me in. A hunger, an urge, focused me. I massaged the blood around and around into my skin like sticky finger paint. I opened my desk drawer and pulled out my pack of colourful pens. I first reached for the red but on second thought grabbed the purple. I searched for the old, nearly invisible scissor-snip scars on my forearm. I circled them with hearts and filled them in with colour. I went back to the pen pack and took out the green. I wrote "SAFE" on my wrist, allowing the white scar to underline the word.

Years had passed since I had questioned my safety. Did I need to worry now? One thing I knew for sure was I had to play nice. Placate *him*. Pretend we were on good terms.

I felt like I might suffocate. "Let's go, Yosh."

The pup jerked, startled from a deep slumber.

I needed some crisp, cool fall air in my lungs. "Come on, lazy bones." I drummed the couch with my palms to rile Yoshi up. I stood and stomped as loudly as I could as I ran to the door, adding in an excitable squeal. Yoshi went ballistic and shuffled down her special couch steps to race toward me.

Yoshi's interest in and tolerance for the great outdoors rarely stretched more than a block or two, and this suited me perfectly. As the old pup pulled me back home instead of on another lap around the neighbourhood, I heard a jingle behind me. Nervous it was a loose dog, I glanced back, but didn't see anything aside from parked cars and a few rabbits racing around the lawns. I allowed Yoshi to resume pulling me home.

"Are you Mommy's little reindog? Yes, you—" I stopped again, giving poor Yoshi whiplash.

Footsteps.

I whipped my head around to investigate. No one. Nothing. I looked back at Yoshi, who appeared oblivious to any unexpected noises. Weird. Once again, I gave in to my dog's insistence to get the heck home already. But only a few more steps into our retreat, I heard both the jingle and approaching footsteps again. I spun around, nearly choking poor Yoshi. Slowly, I scanned the parked cars lining the residential road, acutely aware of all minor movements: leaves blowing, cars passing on the perpendicular street, feral rabbits.

Then I saw it—out of the corner of my eye, a dash of something near the ground behind one of the parked cars. A person? I began to bend down to check under the vehicle for feet, but Yoshi tugged me back. I pinched my wrist with my nails to get a grip. I couldn't brave looking under the cars. No thanks. *He* might be in jail, but the person who broke into my car was still out there somewhere. Fabulous time to remember that, too. More to worry about.

I yanked hard on Yoshi's leash. Too hard. "Let's go," I said, as I started a slow jog.

Once safe inside, and after checking multiple times that both doors and all windows were secure, I ran down to the furnace room and burrowed to the bottom of my Rubbermaid bins full of old treasures, tossing things from side to side and out onto the floor, until I found the one that contained the purple dollar-store shoebox filled with past pain. I dug around and pulled out the six-inch switchblade: a vintage 1980s Maxam MX 45 Seki Japan large fighting folding hunter lockback knife.

I thought back to when *he'd* given it to me. *He'd* said it was for my own protection. Just the thought of carrying it caused me anxiety. I imagined an attacker wrestling the knife off me and using it against me. And what if I used it in self-defense then ended up being the one charged? The knife itself was what made me feel unsafe. That, and my boyfriend suggesting I wasn't safe in the first place. I'd never felt unsafe before that.

And now? I wasn't sure. Maybe it was best for Yoshi and me to stick to the backyard from now on. Lazy Yoshi would be happier, and I could feel safer. I could carry the knife on my own property, right? Probably. Yes. That was what I'd do.

I shoved everything but the switchblade back into the bin and tucked it away. If I ever had to use it—and God help me that it wouldn't come to that—I would claim it was my letter-opening knife. The one I used to open all the lunatic's letters.

I pulled open the freezer drawer and removed the ice cube tray. Recognizing one of her favourite noises, Yoshi trotted over to beg for a frozen treat for her water bowl. I popped out a few cubes and plopped them into Yoshi's bowl so the pup could go bobbing for them. I cracked the tray to release two more ice cubes for myself and took them to the sink. I held one in each hand and made fists around them. Without taking my eyes off the switchblade sitting on the counter beside me, I lost myself in the sensations. I noticed the cool turn to cold, the sharp pain turn to heat, and the numb turn to drips, shrinking smaller and smaller and smaller. I held my hands up in front of my face and refocused my gaze to the melting, the dripping, as the cold water trickled down my wrists and soaked my sleeves. I watched the drips travel down, down, down. Like clear, cold blood. Blood barren of breath, heat, life. A damp chill broke through the numb and woke me from my trance. The trickle tickled me back. I released my grip and looked to see two tiny shards of ice remained. I flicked my wrists to free them, and the ice chips *tinked* as they hit the sink.

Chapter 30

Katee

Within days of killing Ambrihl, my boyfriend came home with two Greyhound tickets scheduled to depart August 12, the following day. At just two weeks shy of twelve months together, a four-day bus ride would relocate us to the other side of the country, physically isolating me from every single person I knew. At least that meant they'd all be safe from him.

When we arrived in British Columbia, the lack of humidity compared to Ontario's summers surprised me. We stayed for two weeks with his friends who left Ontario before us and brought our things with them in their U-Haul. They'd moved out West to live in and run a marijuana grow house. This opportunity had been extended to us, but my boyfriend and the contact person rubbed one another the wrong way, so the deal fell through, and we were forced to find alternative employment and accommodations.

Our limited money ran out by the time my period arrived. My boyfriend took me to the local welfare office and told me to explain our situation and ask for enough tampons or pads to get me through the week. I'd already found a job, but I didn't start for a few days, and even then, my first paycheque would be delayed two weeks. The woman I spoke with at social services practically snickered me out the door by schooling me on what welfare was and was not. And it most certainly was not a bank offering payday loans. Since she believed I had a family to whom I could return, and because I had a job lined up, my needs didn't fall within their mandate. So, using a ripped-up tank top and wads of toilet paper I'd scavenged from the park washroom facilities and squirreled away for the craft, I MacGyvered something to get me by.

My boyfriend walked me to the mall on the first day of my new job at GNC. On the way, he noticed a small apartment building across the street from the mall. A large window of a second-floor unit suggested it might be vacant. He said he'd check it out during my shift. When we arrived at GNC, he proudly chaperoned me through the entrance and right up to the counter and introduced himself to my three new male colleagues. An instant bromance, as usual. But the youngest guy, Sean, a good-looking ginger who was my age, became an instant friend for me. My boyfriend made sure to claim me by kissing me on the lips before slapping my ass and telling me he was off to the hair salon directly across the mall floor to chat up the ladies to see if they might consider adding a tattoo artist to their menu of services.

Ten minutes before my shift ended, my boyfriend returned to resume befriending my new boss and coworkers before collecting me. Everyone loved him. I loved this side of him, too.

On our warm walk home, my boyfriend boasted about his resourcefulness as he pulled me off the sidewalk and into the parking lot of the two-story apartment building across from the mall. We entered the building, and he guided me up the stairs and into a bright, beautiful, and completely empty one-bedroom, one-bathroom unit he'd claimed as our new home. He told me that aside from needing a new front door lock, it was move-in ready. He'd chatted with a tenant across the hall who'd told him that only three of the eight units remained occupied, and that the landlord hadn't collected rent for two months. My boyfriend had asked for the name and contact information of the owner, and the rest was history. We moved in, and my boyfriend assumed the role of property manager. He replaced each apartment's door lock as his first order of business.

The first Saturday in September, my boyfriend surprised me with two kittens as a belated one-year anniversary gift. I named them Oakley and Monkey. Of course, I worried after what had happened to Ambrihl. But now I knew what not to do: never spend the night anywhere other than our home, certainly never make plans without first checking with my boyfriend, and ideally keep any new friends I might make here at arm's length. I would focus on working as much as possible so I could finally contribute and have some money of my own to start secretly saving. And my boyfriend seemed so much better. Happier. I'd do whatever it took to keep him that way.

I got a second job in the same mall at a boutique children's clothing store called Popi. It came with a colleague two years my senior named Jill: a full-figured blonde bombshell who became another fast friend. Between working with Sean at GNC and Jill at Popi, I worked essentially seven days a week from 9 a.m. to 9 p.m. to save up enough money to move home. But within two months, my boyfriend caught on to my selfish plan and decided to take charge of our finances by confiscating my paycheques. He started giving me an allowance. I saved every bit of change I could get my hands on and deposited these meager savings daily when doing bank drops for the stores. Between working twelve hours almost seven days a week and sleeping, eating, and chores, I didn't have time for much else. My boyfriend spent a lot of time out with the middle-aged sisters from the hair salon he was tattooing out of. I considered all time away from him a blessing, so I didn't question it. It was clear one sister was infatuated with him, but I wasn't worried. It kept him away from me, and she was older than him and about twice his size, so, naively, I didn't feel threatened.

My boyfriend started encouraging me to hang out more and more with Sean and Jill. I took this new development as a sign that he was starting to lose interest in me and would hopefully let me go soon. Jill was a BC native, but Sean was from Ontario, too, and he, too, had just moved here and desperately wanted to move back home. We spent hours plotting our escape—Sean from his parents and me from my boyfriend—although Sean thought I just wanted to leave BC. Fairly soon after Sean and I met, as though my boyfriend had read our minds and uncovered our plan, my boyfriend offered Sean freedom in the form of a discounted rate on one of the four suites that remained vacant in our eight-unit apartment building. Sometimes I thought my boyfriend wanted to keep Sean close so he could keep a closer watch and hoped Sean's company and closeness might placate me enough to stay in BC. Other times, I wondered if my boyfriend was trying to set us up. I prayed the latter was true if it meant my boyfriend was preparing to discard me, though Sean and I were only ever purely platonic.

I knew I had to get out of my relationship but was biding my time until I was sure it was safe to do so. Finding a secret way to reconnect with my family proved an essential step of my preparation. But our phone bill was in my boyfriend's name, and he put a long-distance block on our line. He also bought a recording device that attached to our phone. He claimed it was just in case he had to record any controversial conversations with disgruntled tenants.

I started sneakily writing letters back and forth with my maternal grandma and my aunt Sue, two strong, brave, and brilliant women who always managed to gift me grace and whose love for me I never questioned. I hoped these letters would help pave the way for me to eventually rebuild a relationship with my mom. Since only my boyfriend had access to our mailbox, as he kept the only key, I used my work address with the permission of Jill and the guarantee of her sworn secrecy.

Chapter 31

Katee

In preparation for prospective new tenants taking possession on the first of the month, we cleared out and cleaned up the vacant units in our building. My boyfriend purchased three "For Rent" signs from the dollar store and put them in the windows of the remaining apartments. Our building was divided into two identical sides, each with their own entrances and separated by four individual garages. On the main levels were communal laundry rooms and one two-bedroom suite per side, and the second levels each had three suites per side. We lived on the second floor in unit five, which sat above two of the four garages below. Unit seven sat kitty-corner to ours and was occupied by a mother-daughter duo. Unit eight was directly beneath them and sat vacant, as did unit six directly beside us. The other side of the apartment building was three-quarters full, with only one vacant unit.

We successfully filled two of the three suites for the start of October, and by mid-month, we assumed the last one wouldn't go until at least November 1. But on the evening of the third Wednesday in October, while watching TV, we heard something hit our living room window. Our kittens ran over to investigate. Not thinking much of it, we continued our program. But once we heard another *ping* and the kittens started chirping at the source of the sound, my boyfriend got up to investigate.

"What the—?"

"What?" I asked.

He raised his finger to the window, as if to tell someone to wait, and walked to the door.

I got up to see who was there. A woman with badly bleached blonde hair stood below our window holding a few half-full garbage bags. She winked at me before turning to greet my boyfriend, now on the main floor holding the door open for her. She might have been around the age of my boyfriend—somewhere in her thirties, anyway. But she looked rough, weathered.

"Thanks, man," she said, as they entered our suite. "Hey there, doll," she said to me. "Aren't you a sweet thing." Her hoarse voice suggested she'd smoked since birth.

I smiled. "Hi."

"This is Fran," my boyfriend said before introducing me. "And this is my cutie, Katee."

The woman barked out a laugh that suggested she gargled with gravel. Mouth open, she gnawed on a huge wad of pink gum, blowing bubbles and smacking them dead. "That's cute. You two are cute. Great-looking couple." She raised her right eyebrow then winked. "Sorry 'bout tossing rocks at your window. Saw your 'apartment for rent' sign but don't got no fancy phone." She chucked her garbage bags at our entrance and showed herself in. Instead of taking a seat on one of the couches, she plopped down on the carpet in the middle of the room. Both kittens ran over to check her out.

She had style, homeless chic. Baggy pants tapered at the bottom. A boxy tank top covering proud braless nipples. An oversized, flowy cardigan with a ratty, tattered leopard-print scarf and a half dozen necklaces and bracelets competed for attention but completed the look. Our cats smelled her like they were huffing gas, each sniff followed by a concerned stink-face. Thankfully, all I could smell from where I sat was stale cigarette smoke.

"I'll be upfront with you 'cause I can tell you're cool cats. The fucking pigs say my conduct constitutes statutory vagrancy." She nearly rolled her eyes out of her head.

She had my boyfriend at "fucking pigs" and had me curious about whatever the rest meant.

"They don't like prostitutes, so they pick us up and hold us for bullshit stuff. That's their sick way of getting their rocks off. Twistocrites. That's why I got this made." She raised her hand and pointed at two rings on her middle finger made from a penny and a dime. "They can take you in for vagrancy if you don't got no cash on ya. So, now I always do." She gargled up another throaty laugh, as she wiggled her digits to show off her clever fuck-you finger. "But lately they've been BS-ing me about having no," she air-quoted, "'established residence and wandering idly from place to place without lawful or visible means of support.'" Fran rolled her eyes again, smacked her gum, and said, "Fucking cocksuckers. Anyway, the charge won't stick if you're not a vagrant, but it could be enough to hold you for a while and give you a hard time. So, that's where you fine folks come in. I need an address and someone to vouch that I live at it."

Fran talked for hours about her unjust treatment at the hands of the police. She and my boyfriend bonded over their contempt for all forms of authority. Her sad stories won over my bleeding heart. I wanted to help her, and we were in the position to gift her a break. After all, we'd stumbled upon this place when our luck had nearly run out. The least we could do was pay it forward.

Her stories of mistreatment at every level of the legal system fueled my boyfriend's hatred for every level of government, and he wanted to harbor her as a big "fuck you" to the big man. At close to 1 a.m., the deal was made.

Fran dug into the pockets of her harem pants and pulled out crumpled cash. Her dirty fingernails counted it. "This'll cover the week. Pay ya every Sunday?"

My boyfriend nodded, and they sealed the deal with a high-five followed by a one-armed hug and a pat on the back.

Fran moved into the unit beside ours that very night, and over the next few weeks, so did half the questionables in town. The quick-to-bud friendship between us wilted into a frenemy situation almost immediately. An emergent posse of people came and went 24/7, there was never not noise, and the preteen daughter of the tenant across the hall found a used syringe amongst her clothes when she removed them from the communal laundry room downstairs. But the thing that did it for my boyfriend was Fran avoiding him when her weekly rent was due. The police, Fran, and my boyfriend began taking turns playing the role of the devil.

What started off as warnings turned to threats then escalated to 911 calls and finally fast-tracked to my boyfriend taking Fran to court. As his hatred for Fran increased, so did his hatred for the system, which had let him down once again. In addition to his obsession with taking down "Fran & Friends," he also planned on taking down the dismissive 911 operators who eventually told him to stop calling about tenancy disputes and the corrupt cops who increasingly stopped bothering to show up, and when they did, never did anything helpful. So, to collect proof and document evidence to build his case, my boyfriend demanded that the recording device connected to our landline phone was always on and taping when in use, and he somehow got ahold of a police scanner to keep tabs on the dispatch calls to RCMP as well as their whereabouts.

Months in BC had gone by without any violence, but just as I got confident and comfortable, my boyfriend became unraveled and unpredictable. One night in late November, finally fed up, he took matters into his own hands.

"Get the fuck over here, Katee!" my boyfriend screamed from the hall outside our apartment.

I went to the hall and saw Fran's door ajar. "What are you doing in there?" I asked.

"That bitch!" I heard him but couldn't see him.

"You shouldn't be in there, babe." From the doorway, all I could see was mayhem. The walls had been painted dark red and black in some areas and different shades of yellows and greens in other places. Copious amounts of garbage, clothing, and other random belongings littered the floor. I had never seen so much crap or such a mess. Everything was destroyed, either broken or rotting or stained.

"Get in here, Katee!"

I wanted no part of a break-and-enter charge. But I wanted his wrath even less. I hurried in to appease him. Shock didn't even begin to cover the sight I saw and the smells I smelled. The nauseating sour-sweet stink of a moist, festering abscess after ripping off a Band-Aid permeated the sticky air. As I braved my way in, the swelling stench morphed into that of various bodily fluids—and solids. Mirrors and windows were broken and cardboarded-up; all the cupboard doors in the bathroom and kitchen had been ripped off their hinges; the toilet bowl was literally smashed out; and scattered everywhere were drug paraphernalia and bottles, buckets, and cans full of piss and shit. It was a literal dump.

"One of those crackheads must've been so fucked up they left the door open when they left," my boyfriend said.

I finally saw him. Camera in hand, he was documenting the destruction.

After he felt he'd collected enough evidence, we vacated the unit, closed Fran's door behind us, and went back into our home.

"I'm going to be the one forced to deal with that fucking disaster. You think the bailiff will make her do it before he officially removes her? You think he'll make her clean out all that shit?"

In the days after winning our dispute resolution court hearing against her, we'd witnessed Fran and her sketchy crew removing bits and pieces from her apartment. She knew her time was running out, so she'd likely already taken her most prized possessions. We didn't know if she would come back for any more of it.

"Just leave it, babe," I said. "She got the order of possession. It's almost over. But we've gotta be patient till it's enforced. We've gotta—"

My boyfriend struck me in the face, smashed my head into the wall, and pinned me in place with a karate chop to my throat. His tightened grip constricted my breath.

I gasped at the air he screamed at me. I fought, clawed, failed.

Pinned in place, bulging eyes begged blank ones; I searched for him in the drunk. Unrecognizable. Spinning. Pounding. Breathless. *Help.*

Ragged gasps escaped. Burning. Pressure. Whirling.

Phone. Out of reach. Far away. Mom. *I want my mom.*

His chipped tooth. *Chip his tooth!* My arms contorted and reached and grasped behind me. I grabbed whatever came into my hand and brought it down on him.

Crack! Picture frame to his face. Glass shattered. Blood appeared. The stranger's eyes disappeared, and his—*he*—returned. Shocked. Stunned.

Pinging stars. Zapping.

Too late. So tired.
Knocking.
Hello?
Come back.
Don't go back.
Wake up.
I opened my eyes. He'd released me.

He was freeing the picture of his middle child from the shards of glass that had cut his face. Like father, like son. His little buddy.

I smelled something burning. Cigarette-singed carpet. My throat stung, and I tasted bile. I swallowed a chunk of vomit and winced in pain. My head pounded, affecting my vision. I heard screaming sirens going the wrong way. Farther away. *Call the cops.* Convinced he'd kill me, frantically, ferally, I crawled to the end table and grabbed the corded slimline phone.

I called 911 for both the first and last time. The police showed up and threatened to charge both of us, something called dual charging. The glass had cut his face, but the bruises on my neck had yet to develop. Some policy. It ensured I'd never again call for help. When I threatened to, my boyfriend threatened me with counter charging.

After the cops left, my boyfriend changed into his army-style cargo pants and a dark shirt and said he was going to the empty ground floor unit to wait for Fran. Thankfully, he didn't come to bed that first night. The next evening, as soon as he got home from work, he changed into the same camouflage costume and added a black hat. He didn't come back upstairs until the next morning when I was getting ready for work. I knew better than to engage. His eyes were wild and unrested. By lunchtime, I found out he hadn't shown up to his job that day when the owner of the salon he tattooed in came into my work asking his whereabouts. When I got home that evening, he was still hiding out in the empty unit. He scared the bejesus out of me when I entered the building, popping out from behind the main floor apartment door like Jack Nicholson in the chilling axe scene from *The Shining*, his crazy eyes saying, *Wheeere's Franny?*

As it got dark later that evening, I kept an eye on the downstairs unit's window, which remained pitch-black while he hid inside waiting. He came up a few times to grab various things: a snack, eye black grease, a balaclava, and copious restocks of beer.

As I got ready for bed on the third night of sleeping alone, I wondered when—and worried how—this would end. At first, I'd thought my boyfriend just wanted to scare Fran, maybe even rough her up a little. But that night, I felt certain he would kill someone. Possibly more than one person. Maybe even me. As I lay in bed, I remembered learning when we first met that my boyfriend and a few of his friends had been acquaintances of Paul Bernardo, an infamous serial rapist and serial killer. At the time, I'd thought it an unsettling coincidence; it wasn't like anyone knew what that sicko had been up to before he'd gotten caught. Now I played back the chilling conversation I'd overheard about Patrick's brother's wife being murdered for her life insurance. I considered my boyfriend's loosely connected gang affiliation since arriving in BC. I ruminated over him telling me just the other week when he came home from his friend's pig farm in Port Coquitlam that his new buddy would take care of Fran if my boyfriend brought her to the farm.

Far too many coincidences. I prayed dangerous plus deranged wouldn't equal deadly.

I heard our front door unlock. I heard the fridge door open and a bottle clank. Then I heard his bell—the booby trap he'd rigged up, alerting him to someone entering the main entrance downstairs. I heard and felt running feet stomping across our apartment toward our door, followed by a *bang*, scream, *crash*, and *thud*.

Paralyzed in bed, I regretted my life choices, which played on a movie loop in my mind. Terror poisoned me. I didn't know if he'd come back and hurt me again, too, or if he'd be taken to jail for murder and would try implicating me somehow. Of all the fear he'd ever formed in me, this act of his violence spilling outside of me was hands down the most petrifying experience of our entire relationship. Outside of me, he had always maintained meticulous control of his rage. He'd saved it all up and taken it out on me alone. This was the first time someone else had fallen victim. I feared him finally losing his grip and exposing his demons to the outside world would be a particularly dangerous escalation.

As the sirens got louder, I hid under the covers like a scared child. I squeezed my eyes shut and wished away my reality.

My boyfriend had badly injured Fran, who learned her lesson and stayed gone. Apparently, she'd been carrying her bicycle up the stairs, and my boyfriend ran down them and shoved her. Fran's head hit the wall. I saw the bloody proof the next day. But since both Fran and my boyfriend despised "pigs" and neither were "rats," Fran told the cops she fell.

Over the next few months, my boyfriend's abuse was irregular and unpredictable. Only alcohol intoxication guaranteed it. It wasn't long until I learned not to fight back. Eventually, it stopped fazing me. Every punch, insulting name, and degrading act simply symbolized another brick of my once-strong wall being shattered into pieces.

I quickly learned that regardless of what people know is happening behind closed doors, regardless of the screaming and pleading and bruises and injuries, what happens in the home is viewed as a private family matter. It didn't take long before the neighbours just turned up their music in response to our noise. Threatening to call 911 on my boyfriend only intensified and prolonged the episode, and when the police were called anonymously on my behalf, they would just tell my boyfriend to walk it off and tell me to be gone by the time he got back. My beefcake colleagues at GNC and all the bodybuilding customers buying copious amounts of muscle-enhancing supplements weren't tough enough to acknowledge much less inquire about my increasingly deteriorating appearance. Even Sean and Jill turned a blind eye the one time I intentionally did a shit job covering up a black eye in the hopes one of them would be brave enough to question me about it. It was when I was most alone that I came to realize I was not to blame and that my experience was not an individual one but part of a much bigger societal problem.

"Get up."

"What?" I struggled to open my eyes. "What time is it?"

"Get up."

I yawned and stretched my arms over my head. My boyfriend punched the duvet covering my unguarded stomach. I dropped my arms down to protect my ribs and grabbed my aching abdomen. A searing aftershock of pain throbbed throughout my body. Tears hot as lava erupted from my eyes.

"What did I do?" What day was it? Friday? Nope. Sunday. I stole a glance at the clock. 4:32 a.m. Still three hours till I had to get up for work.

My boyfriend stood at the side of our bed, his eyes glossed over. He'd been drinking.

His hand thrust out toward my neck, and I flinched then released a shallow sigh of relief when, instead of strangling me, he ripped down the covers.

He shoved his face into mine. "Clean the cat litter."

"What? I just did. Before bed."

"Either you empty it now, or I'll empty it over you."

I propped myself up and slid my feet over the side of the bed. My boyfriend jabbed the tips of his fingers hard into my chest.

"Useless bitch," he mumbled as he left the room.

I threw my housecoat over my shoulders and headed to the pantry. I dug around with the pooper scooper. The litter seemed fresh. Both cats showed up to check things out. My boyfriend came over to supervise.

"Suits ya, you lazy fuck. Pickin' up shit."

I stayed quiet. He grunted and left.

I finished tying the bag housing a bit of clean litter and turned off the light. As I stepped out of the pantry and into the kitchen, a freezing surge of liquid crashed down on me, engulfing my head and shoulders. I gasped, dropped the bag, and grabbed my head. Like brain freeze, an unbearable pressure pounded my skull. I smelled orange. A stream of liquid from my cheek rolled into my mouth and confirmed it. Orange Kool-Aid.

He was looking for a fight. I needed to stay calm.

Avoiding his stare, I picked up the bag of cat litter and walked the long way around him to put it in the garbage.

"Where are you going?" He laughed hysterically.

It took all I had not to cry or yell; that would only make things worse.

"Get in the shower, you filthy pig. Or do you need me to hose you down like an animal?"

I knew he'd get bored of me soon, pass out. "I will. I can do it myself, thanks."

As I headed toward the bathroom, I heard him chuckle and say, "Like fuck you can."

I sat on the edge of the tub and let the pain from the scalding water running over my hand burn off the humiliation. What would people say if they saw me? Helpless. Pathetic. I watched my fingers become redder and redder. I couldn't feel anything. I bet they'd think I deserved it. Maybe I did. But what could I do? If I left, he'd hurt my family.

I turned off the water, stepped into the tub, and sat down without waiting for my body to adjust to the temperature. I so badly wanted to feel something. Anything. Lately, I'd been taking a bath instead of a shower every night. Each night I'd run the water a little hotter than the evening before. I didn't know whether I did it to feel something again or to punish myself for getting into such a nightmare. Either way, I looked forward to it. I needed it.

The water was so hot, beads of sweat covered my entire face and dripped from the bun of my hair. The tub squeaked as I slid my body down. I leaned back and exhaled until the water completely submerged my face. I left my eyes open because the water burned them most. I watched the odd air bubble escape my torture chamber until my boyfriend's face popped into view. He called me to sit up with his index finger. Slowly, I obeyed.

"Hey, cutie." His face had softened. His smile boasted the tiny chip on his tooth that once upon a time had melted my heart. "God, you're sexy." He reached out and cupped my breast before twisting my nipple like a radio knob. With his other hand, he rubbed his crotch.

I looked down, breaking eye contact. "Don't."

He ran his finger around my nipple twice then continued up my chest, tracing my collarbone from one side to the other before ascending the side of my neck. He rested his finger on my lower lip.

"How'd I get so lucky, huh? Ending up with a girl as sexy as a *Maxim* model?" He leaned in and kissed me.

I didn't kiss back.

"Mmm . . . you know I love when you play hard to get, my bitter sweetheart."

I needed to play along. The sooner he got what he wanted, the sooner I could go back to bed. Keep him happy, keep myself safe.

He zigzagged his hand down my back, stopping just below my tailbone. "You know you have the power to make me happy, right? Just like you abuse that power to make me angry."

"Uh huh."

He touched my chin and gently turned it toward him. His eyes were the right colour blue, like the mood ring I used to have. "You just have no idea how much I love you. Do ya?"

I shook my head, doubting either one of us had a clue about what love really was. I tried to find all the things I loved in his face, to make the next little while bearable. He had perfect ears. Maybe I noticed them because my ears stuck out like fairy ears, or elf ears, as he loved to call them. His nose really suited his face. Not too big, not too small. Not too pointy, not too round. It certainly didn't look like a strawberry like he said mine did, with tiny, clogged pores resembling seeds. A handsome monster. When it was good, it was great. Ninety percent of the time, our relationship mirrored a romance movie. But that other ten percent . . .

"Come on, cutie. Come and do your magic on me."

He took both of my hands in his and helped me to stand. Just as I raised one foot to step out of the tub, he glanced at my hair. "You didn't wash your hair yet, did you?"

I sighed and put my foot back down. "I didn't get a chance. You came in pretty much as soon as I got the tub filled."

"Right," he said. "It's somehow my fault you're still a sticky mess?" He turned and walked toward the door. "Unbelievable. Guess I'll take care of myself then."

I sat back in the tub, grabbed the bottle of shampoo, and squeezed until it ejaculated. Excessive amounts dripped over the side of my hand and down my wrist. Gobs of shampoo blobbed into the bathwater.

I heard him yell from the bedroom, "Better hurry up, Katee. Otherwise, you'll force me to get myself off to the vixen I tattooed at the salon today."

My stomach felt like dough, and his words kneaded it. If that girl only knew. If I'd only known.

"Too late, hun. I just shot my load picturing my hard cock in between her perfect tits."

I looked down at my A cups, or fried eggs, as my boyfriend called them. My body blended a poisonous concoction of mixed feelings. I threw up all over myself; pinkish vomit, consisting of spaghetti from dinner, floated on top of the water. The chunks began to sink. I imagined the *Titanic*. So many people had taken a chance, thinking the ship was perfect, the best ship ever, meant to change lives. And it had.

I pulled the drain plug and watched my dinner and bile get sucked down into the bottomless pit. Then the bathroom light went out.

"Night," said my boyfriend through the door.

I waited for him to turn the light back on. When he didn't, I re-plugged the drain and turned on the water. Only the hot this time.

Katee,

Sure, I'm an intelligent man, but I guess I'm also hell bent on self-sabotaging the only thing I used to find satisfying, sexually fulfilling, and perfect—YOU! You are the centre of my world. YOU! My love for you is the only thing that gives my life meaning.

I get these thoughts in my head about you, us, and I need to write them down. I need you to understand how my brain works. I was just remembering that time when you and I were fighting, when we lived at the apartment in L-Pit, when you took off to your girlfriend's place, when your cat shit all over your stuff and your little Furby toy got broken, remember? Well, I want you to remember how I came to get you, brought you back, I couldn't just let you go. I'll never just let you go. I've been remembering all our old fights, when you and I were first getting to know each other. I couldn't ever go through all that crap again with anyone else. I don't want to admit that it was all for nothing because it wasn't. Was it? When you sang to me, to finally tell me you loved me too, it blew me away. I need to hear you singing to me from your heart again, and that's what I've been asking you for all along. For you to love me with meaning, heart, real love. Your real feelings. Prove to me how beautiful you really are, besides just in pictures.

I know I fucked up again. But I'm not asking for much. If you don't love me anymore, then lie to me. Fake it until you do again. Oh, and I need you to talk to me like you used to. Back when you were erotic and exciting. I could use a bit of that now too. Because I'm missing your body badly, and it's only going to get worse if you don't give it to me.

I'm missing the real you badly. Nobody's perfect, Katee. But at least I'm trying. Can you?

Xoxoxo

Chapter 32

Gabbi

Terror fills my baby sister's eyes as fluid fills her airways. Her eyes plead with mine. *Save me. Take it all away. Make it untrue.*

I lean in closer until our noses nearly touch. We exchange no words. Only begging eyes. Pleading stares. Hopelessness and helplessness consume the ICU room.

Bryanne shakes her head back and forth. She looks like a haunted angel.

"What?" I ask, my question rhetorical. My squeaky voice reveals my knowing.

She keeps shaking her head. No. No. No.

I want to shake the cancer out of her. We'd filled her with love. So much love. But love wasn't nearly enough.

Feeling blue was an understatement and the exact shade of her eyes. The colour blue that drowns you. I grab her hand and rub warmth into her once-dainty fingers, now frail, skin-covered bones. Her thirty-six-year-old body aged another hundred overnight. She is an exhausted, terrified, deeply devastated shell of herself. Her eye sockets sink her spirit down with them. The dark circles snuff her flame.

Bryanne squeezes my hand. "I thought I had more fucking time." She never cursed like I did.

I squeeze *I love you* back.

Fifteen short months ago, Bryanne went to a walk-in doctor because of a pain in her side. She ended up at the hospital for emergency surgery to remove a tumor obstructing her colon. She left with a stage-four cancer diagnosis.

Six days ago, her clinical trial doctor said she probably only had a few months left to live. Our family argued over whether he'd said *a few* or *two*. Bryanne adamantly refused from the very beginning to be given a "death date," as she called it.

An hour ago, her oncologist said she probably only had a week left to live. Our family argued over what a week meant since days ago a week had meant months.

Now, Bryanne shakes her head back and forth. Back and forth. She knows.

I think she knew the previous night. I wasn't meant to fly here until Tuesday. But last night after she was admitted back into the hospital, I asked her if she thought I should change my flight. She texted me, *It's not looking good*. She was never one to panic like I was. So, I changed my flight to first thing in the morning.

The door opens, and Tara enters the dim room. "Hi, sisters. Ready for our all-nighter?" She tosses a gift-shop toothbrush at both of us. "To brush our teeth. *Ch ch ch ch, ch ch, ch ch, let's brush our teeth*," she sings.

Bryanne and I chuckle.

"I put so many of our favourite silly childhood songs in my novel. But my editor advised I cut them. If you guys want, I could take you on a trip down memory lane and read you a few of the deleted scenes," I say.

Both of their faces turn to me.

"What?"

"How are you writing us in it?" Tara asks.

"Yeah," backs Bryanne. "Are we going to be upset?"

"No, not at all. Besides one scene where you were both understandably pissed at me for being a little shit, the rest are all our best times."

"And Mom?"

"We've had a few incredibly therapeutic conversations on the matter. She's on board. More than on board. She's fully supportive."

Their faces soften.

"The book isn't about you or Mom. It's for you guys."

Bryanne squeezes my hand. "Get it done," she says. "It'll never be too late."

Tara and I refuse to waste precious sister time accessing the visitor washroom on the opposite end of the hospital floor and re-gowning before re-entering Bryanne's ICU room. We agree to use the small toilet sitting out in the open of her otherwise private room. Nothing we haven't all seen. Since there's nothing to provide any privacy—no curtain, much less a door—we decide whichever person is not using the loo will pull the blinds on the tiny observation window and stand guard at the windowless door to the room. These missions provide comic relief during an otherwise soul-suffocating time.

Once we are ready to try and get some sleep, Bryanne takes me up on my offer to read a bedtime story. She requests I choose my favourite deleted scene from my novel.

Laptop open, I start reading out loud, and both my sisters start fading fast.

Bryanne struggles to breathe even with a full-face oxygen mask providing constant air to keep her alive. Even with this maximum level of support, she gasps for her life. I stop reading so she can get some sleep.

Tara builds a makeshift bed and crumples her six-foot frame in between two hard plastic hospital chairs. Bryanne puts in her custom ear plugs and retires her eyes. I keep watch.

I watch her skin slowly turn translucent, showing off her blue veins as they struggle to circulate her blood.

I watch the machines I can't read, beeping in a language I don't speak. I try deciphering the information they provide. This watching started out like a way I felt I could help, then it became something to pass the time, but quickly it becomes an obsession.

At some point, Tara shifts enough to scrape her chairs' legs on the floor.

"Shhh," Bryanne says without opening her eyes. She raises her pointer finger to her mouth to double down.

I learn that senses are heightened when someone is dying.

While they sleep and I keep watch, I think back through our short lives as sisters. Our Christmases and summers at the cottage. Our singing competitions and campfire songs. Our first childhood home in the city, our move to the country where our parents still live. All our first homes as adults. I thought we had more fucking time, too. As my tears threaten to disturb my little blonde-haired, blue-eyed Sleeping Beauty, I wipe them away and decide to get back to writing. Even if I can complete the first draft of my book in the mere week Bryanne's been given to live, that doesn't leave me any time to read it to her. I open my laptop and feverishly type.

"Grandma Kathy is here," Bryanne says.

Grandma Kathy died twenty-three years ago. I put my laptop on the floor and sit up, scared straight. This is it.

"She is?" Tara asks. She's got this.

I try to calm the panic on my face. I've got this.

"Yup," Bryanne says matter-of-factly.

Tara and I look at each other as our faces start to melt.

"Will you tell her we say hello?"

I start sobbing and try silencing myself.

"Yup."

Grandma Kathy's got this. She's come to collect Bryanne.

The nurse enters the room.

"What's happening?" I ask her. But I know.

"Just morning vitals."

"Should we call our parents and her husband?"

The nurse looks at her watch. "No, no."

"But it's happening."

"Oh! No, no, it's not. There's plenty of time," she says as she putters around the machinery and pokes and prods our little sister.

Tara and I look at one another. I nod. Tara calls our mom. I call Johnny.

Bryanne becomes irritable. She tries getting out of bed and ripping out her lines. "Get this *off* of me!" she yells, as she yanks and pulls at her chest.

The nurse comes back in with a cool cloth and puts it on Bryanne's stomach.

"Is it happening?" I demand, blinking tears out of my vision.

"No. But it will likely happen later today. But only once the palliative doctor comes and gives her some sedation. She'll probably pass fairly fast after that."

But I know. I know with everything in my being she is dying right now. I have a *knowing*. The nurse knows death, but she doesn't know our sister. Doesn't know her tenacity, her mind-over-matter attitude. Bryanne is all in on whatever she sets her mind to. With survival no longer an option, Bryanne doesn't waste time dying.

The nurse leaves.

Bryanne stops fussing and slowly tilts her head all the way back, lifeless eyes to the ceiling.

"What's happening? What the fuck is happening?" I shriek. I know, but I want to be wrong.

I glare at the machines. Nothing seems different. No new numbers or noises. I look back at her. She remains still and silent, her mouth and eyes open. I pull my chair right up to her face and stroke her hair and her cheek. She doesn't blink. Doesn't respond. I try to inhale her last breath.

"Tara!" I signal her closer.

Tara joins me on the other side of our baby sister's head.

The nurse runs back in—crying, apologizing, rambling white noise. She flutters about like a disoriented, desperate, failing fly. The nurse sounds so far away, like I'm leaving with my sister. Everything but Bryanne falls away, as she floats away from us.

I start singing to her, our favourite childhood song:

> *"Somewhere out there beneath the pale moonlight,*
> *Someone's thinking of me and loving me tonight.*
> *Somewhere out there someone's saying a prayer,*
> *That we'll find one another in that big somewhere out*
>   *there."*

"I love you, Bryanne. You are so strong," Tara says repeatedly. I keep singing and stroking Bryanne's hair.

> *"And even though I know how very far apart we are,*
> *It helps to think we might be wishin' on the same*
>   *bright star.*

> *And when the night wind starts to sing a lonesome lullaby,*
> *It helps to think we're sleeping underneath the same big sky."*

"Mom and Dad and Johnny are almost here, B," Tara says. "We love you so much."

> *"Somewhere out there, if love can see us through,*
> *Then we'll be together somewhere out there,*
> *Out where dreams come true."*

I crack and squeak and sing my way through the song.
Tara chokes through her comforting words.
We love our baby sister as she leaves us forever.
Bryanne refused to accept that she would die. But once she could no longer deny it, she checked out almost immediately. A hauntingly angelic death.

Chapter 33

Alex

"Yoo-hoo?" Jessica singsonged.

I cringed, knowing that voice anywhere.

"Look what I found," Jessica said, waving something white. "Return to sender," Jessica sang, "address unknown. No such number, no such zone." She jigged her way into my office, using the white envelope she held like a visor to shield her eyes from the fluorescent overhead lights. "Looks like a long-lost lover might be trying to find you, Alex."

I panicked at the sight of the letter and rolled my chair back with such force it nearly ejected me when it hit the cupboards. I yelped, startled from the impact.

Jessica giggled. "Looks like you've seen a ghost. A ghost of lover's past? And what an ar-teest," she said, as she admired the envelope. "Any man who appreciates a little Elvis is—"

"Where'd you get that?" I asked far more harshly than intended. It was from *him*.

My tone had slapped the silliness off Jessica's face. "From your mail cubby, obviously. I just happened to be walking by and noticed it peeking out begging to be hand-deliv—"

"Just leave it," I barked.

Jessica's jaw dropped.

I cleared my throat. "Please." I needed to pull it together. "Sorry,

I'm just in the middle of something rather important." How the hell had *he* found my place of work? What did *he* want from me? I quickly added, "And highly confidential." *He* was really toying with me now. I forced my unsteady legs to stand and my nervous hand to reach for the letter.

A defiant Jessica turned the envelope over and read the back. "A lover's spat? How scandalously inappropriate to have love letters delivered to your work," she scolded.

I snatched at the air in front of Jessica's hand.

Jessica flipped the envelope back over. "And from a—"

"Jessica!" I yelled.

Jessica's face flattened like a pissed-off cat, curiosity killed. She thrust the envelope at me. "Here," she hissed. Before releasing it, she said, "If it's meant to be private, probably best to keep your personal matters separate from your professional ones." She stomped off.

Larger than a standard-size envelope, it was big enough to hold not only my full name and school address, handwritten in pencil, but also close to two dozen hand-drawn two-beamed eighth notes hugging famous song lyrics like quotations.

> *(Please Do Not) Return to Sender*
> *We had a quarrel, a lover's spat,*
> *I write I'm sorry, but my letters keep coming back.*

The last line was bolded so darkly it was visible where the pencil had broken from the pressure in a few spots.

I ripped into it. Inside, I found a smaller envelope. Overtop of my name and my parents' address—written in *his* penciled printing—was my mother's defiant writing in thick black Sharpie:

> *Return to sender, address unknown.*

I thought back to the young sisters' letter asking for help.

> *Hanson is mad at me. Will Hanson kill me and Rosslynn? Will you keep us safe? Pick yes or no.*

I wondered if I could keep myself safe. Yes or no.
I tore into the returned-and-now-forwarded envelope.

Hi Bitter Sweetheart,

Peekaboo found you. A school counsellor, eh? That makes better sense than a fashionista. You always were good with school—and delinquents, weren't you? Bad girl fancies high school boys, oh how the tables have turned!

I guess your asshole parents didn't give you any of my letters. Let's face it, your parents will never accept me in your life. I wondered why you never wrote me back.

"Please excuse the interruption," Doris's voice crackled over the intercom. "Ms. Alex, you have a visitor in the main office. Ms. Alex, please come to the main office for a visitor."

A visitor? An unannounced, unplanned, unscheduled visitor. Anxiety taunted me. I could feel myself unraveling. I challenged my thinking. Visitors were not completely uncommon. It was likely a family new to the community registering their children. It could be a parent dropping their kid off late and wanting some strategies to help make morning routines easier. Most probable was a student in crisis looking for me but scooped up by another staff member and ushered to the main office to avoid commotion and chaos in the halls. The chances of it being *him* were close to impossible. Someone sent by *him*? Extremely implausible. But still somewhat—

No. Stop it. Just call and ask who it is. Yes. Good idea.

"Good aftern—"

"It's Alex. Who's wanting to see me?"

"It's a surprise," Doris said. "But a surprise I know you'll like."

Even a big beautiful bouquet of flowers wasn't a good thing depending on the sender.

"Just get down here, Alex," Doris continued. "You'll be pleasantly surprised."

I hung up and tried not to throw up.

As I approached the main office, I slowed my pace so my frantically searching eyes could try to clear the room like those of a cop—or maybe more like those of a woman tiptoeing through her own home knowing an intruder waited just around an upcoming corner.

"Come, come, come, Alex," Doris called. "Your heels always give you away."

I took a breath so deep it formally announced my arrival.

"There you are," Doris said with an impish smirk that smoothed out her smoker's lines. She dropped her chin and looked at me over her glasses. She nodded toward the principal's office. "In Theresa's."

I tried to sneak a peek, but the blinds covered the fishbowl entryway. I manifested my invisible cloak of confidence and sashayed into the room.

"Shanelle," I squealed, partly in surprise, partly in relief. "Hi, love! What are you doing here?"

I loved when past students came back to visit, but this wasn't just a past student. When she was still in high school, Shanelle had decided to follow in my professional footsteps, and in her third year of university, she'd requested I take her on as a practicum student. It'd been such a tremendous honour.

"I wanted to pop in on my way up to division office to give you this," Shanelle said, handing me an envelope.

I wished I never had to see another white envelope ever again. But at least this one was addressed to me in girly bubble printing.

"What's this?"

"A copy of the letter I'm going to give your supervisor today when she interviews me for a school counselling position," she said with a squeal of her own.

"An interview? Wow. Congrats in advance. You'll get it for sure."

"I'm so grateful for the glowing reference letter you wrote me. I wanted to write you one in return."

After a short catch-up, I started to walk Shanelle out, but the principal stopped me.

"Alex, could you stay back a minute, please?"

I agreed and said my goodbyes to my promising protégé before returning my attention to Theresa.

"I just wanted to check in with you," Theresa started. "A few staff members have reported to me that Jessica has been stirring the gossip cauldron again."

I rolled my eyes and sighed. "When is she not? Honestly, Theresa, she's worse than the kids."

"I know, I know. I'm on it. But I bring it up because her tales du jour topic is actually," Theresa paused before continuing, "it's actually you, Alex."

"Me?"

Theresa nodded.

I felt my face heat up. I swallowed down my emotions.

"She's been telling people you're acting strange, really on edge. And when I confronted her, she just doubled down and said you've been really 'off.'"

I hoped she hadn't shared specifics.

"Is everything okay?" Theresa asked.

Theresa was someone I could trust. We weren't just colleagues. We were friends. But for whatever reason, I didn't feel comfortable sharing my secret about my ex resurfacing. Not until I could be sure I was safe.

I lied to appease Theresa before heading back to my office to resume my all-consuming quest for clarity. How the hell had *he* found me? I opened my laptop and Googled myself for the millionth time. And for the first time—ta-fucking-da—there I was. A link to a full bio on the school's website. My first and last name. My title and role description. My education and credentials. My email address. My cell phone number. My picture.

I couldn't take any more. A hostile parent, another letter, a student soaked in my ex's stink, and now my details on the World Wide Web. Typically, I led the multidisciplinary team of trained professionals who conducted the school's violent risk threat assessments, but the way I marched to Jessica's room suggested I might have become the one needing to be profiled.

I barged into the room without knocking or noting its occupants. "There's a reason I've always left my bio section generic, Jessica! No name or picture for a goddamn reason! Take it down immediately!" It was too late. The damage had been done. I'd been sought and found. I had successfully made myself lost, and Jessica had managed to singlehandedly turn me over to my tormentor.

Jessica's jaw dropped, but her eyes retorted. "What the heck's gotten into you, Alex? You need to get a grip, girl. You've been loopy for months now."

"How could you?"

"Could I what?"

"Put me in danger?"

"Danger?" Jessica asked with both her words and her face. "What do you mean, danger . . .?" she asked again, this time more slowly, curiously.

"Jesus, Jessica! As per usual, it's none of your goddamn business!"

Jessica's mouth snapped shut. She pressed her lips together. She blinked back bullshit tears. "Well, I never." Her guilt trip gassed the room.

I brushed the flyaway hairs off my face and straightened my shirt.

Jessica opened her mouth then closed it. She opened it again and inhaled deeply. "The disclosure of the name, business address, and business telephone number of a staff member is not considered an unreasonable invasion of privacy, Alex. The public's right to know—"

"Is balanced against the individual's right to privacy, Jessica."

"Personal information is routinely released for the normal ongoing operations of schools and school boards, Alex."

I sighed loudly before quietly mumbling, "For fuck's sake," under my breath. "Jessica, personal information cannot be disclosed to others without consent. And when I first started working here, I contacted the Freedom of Information and Protection of Privacy Act coordinator at division office. She assured me it was within my legal right to refuse consent to disclose this information under the FOIP Act due to it putting my health and safety at risk. And that is more than the extent of what you need to know."

"This community is part of the need-to-know basis, Alex."

"Yes. And they can get my name and phone number from the school or through word-of-mouth. Because the rest of the world on the World Wide Web are not part of this need-to-know group."

Jessica grunted and put her hands on her hips.

"I have made it very clear many times over the years I've worked here that I did not want—could not have—my personal information posted online. Not under any circumstances. The school office knew this. Head office knew this. And I know even you knew this, Jessica, because I personally made you aware. I need you to immediately remove both my name and cell number from the school's webpage. In its place, please leave only 'school counsellor' and the school's phone number."

"Fine. But fair warning, Alex. You have exhibited much unprofessional behaviour over the last few months. I will be taking some time to decide whether the time has come to report it. You've been acting like the mental patient, not the mental health professional."

I teared up then ran out of the room, down the hall, and down the stairs into my office. I slammed my body as hard as I could into the back of my door to try and close it faster than the damn thing slowly closed itself. As I'd run past dozens of kids getting ready to leave for the day and a few bus drivers on their way back to their posts to drive the students home for the night, knocks and muffled concerned cries started on the other side of the door. Embarrassment overwhelmed me. I slid my butt down the back of the door and folded into a seated fetal position on the floor.

The bell rang.

The audience on the other side of the door dispersed.

I started twisting my eyelashes between my middle finger and thumb. I noticed some leftover mess under my creative activity table. I reached for an abandoned bottle of white craft glue. I twisted open its orange top, turned it upside down, and squeezed out a copious amount until it covered the back of my left hand. I set down the bottle and spread around the goopy mess with my right hand until it started to get tacky. Then I blew on the back of my left hand while I rubbed together the fingers of my right hand. Little bits of dried glue fell to the floor like sticky snow. The glue wrinkled the skin on the back of my left hand as it dried, aging it by decades in minutes.

Once translucent, I picked and peeled. Picked and peeled. Picked and peeled.

With a pile of dead-skin-like flakes on the floor, I opened my phone, found my therapist's contact card, and called the number. After all, Jessica had been right about one thing.

My therapist's voicemail recording had been updated but only to say she was now away indefinitely due to a family crisis.

What now?

Chapter 34

Katee

Sex still hurt. Just before we'd moved to BC, every time my boyfriend penetrated me, a sharp pain caused me to yelp and cry. This torture had gone on for months now. It felt like a toothpick had lodged itself into my vaginal wall, and every time he pushed or pulled his penis past it, the toothpick dug in deeper.

Not having a family doctor in BC, I was connected through a primary care centre to a condescending and dismissive gynecologist. After I described the pain as best I could, he instructed me to get undressed. He inserted a metal speculum into me, replicating the exact pain I had described. After what felt like forever, he passed me a handheld mirror and told me to look and tell him if I saw anything wrong. Wrong? Never having seen inside myself, completely opened up and on display, it all looked wrong. I started to cry. He sighed and told me there was absolutely nothing wrong with me. I didn't get an answer for the excruciating pain I'd been experiencing. But after getting the results from my bloodwork, I found out I'd wound up pregnant again.

This time, I didn't dare tell my boyfriend. I knew I had to escape or I'd be tied to him forever. He sensed the changes in me. My secrecy. My pulling back and distance. Most difficult to hide—my immense sickness. My boyfriend couldn't be less concerned nor more unaffected by my rapidly decreasing health. It felt like he wanted to keep me sick, weak, tortured. I swear, a sinister part of him relished it. But my symptoms kept him in the dark: I lost weight instead of gaining it; I struggled to eat at all instead of eating for two. I believed I was literally dying.

With no care or concern at home, I went back to Dr. Dickhead with absolute knowledge of my looming fatality. He told me the only thing wrong was me being an overreactive eighteen-year-old blowing morning sickness out of proportion. I knew better. I knew the little piece of my boyfriend inside me was killing me. I prayed to miscarry this spawn of his, too.

My boyfriend's bizarre behaviour—long disappearances, drug and alcohol benders, and erratic beatings—had started escalating again. Eerily, it seemed the little traitor growing inside me might have been transmitting GPS signals to her otherwise oblivious daddy. Somehow, he always knew my location when we weren't together. He basked in name-dropping the specific restaurants or stores I went to when out with a friend or alone. One time, Jill thought she spotted him in a mall she and I were shopping in a few cities away from home. She swore she saw him duck behind a display in the morning and disappear behind a crowd in the afternoon. I missed both these glimpses of him, but I never doubted her claim. She described him looking creepy-comical, like a clown. This was less unnerving than the time I'd caught him stalking me home from Patrick's; I found this time embarrassing but also strangely validating. My boyfriend was slipping and starting to show his crazy to the world instead of just to me.

My second ultrasound revealed no heartbeat. Relief and gratitude filled me. The fetus had shrunk significantly since the previous imaging, the remaining size suggesting it had died approximately a month prior. The rotting flesh of my boyfriend's dead baby inside me had been slowly poisoning me. I needed it out. Since my body wouldn't naturally abort it, and because I was so sick, the parasite he had impregnated me with had to be surgically removed.

Luckily for my recovery, he was gone on one of his benders, so I guessed I'd likely get a few days without him to be followed by another day or two of him sleeping it off once home.

Miraculously, my mother called me the day after my procedure; she had gotten my phone number from my grandma. Never had I needed or wanted my mother more.

The call took a quick turn. My grandfather had died two days earlier, on December 19. My mom asked if I wanted to come home to attend his funeral. Ultimately, my grandpa had saved me. As he'd ascended to Heaven, he'd gifted me a chance to be pulled from hell— the opportunity to reconnect with my family. My mom offered to pay for my flights. Plural. She had no idea I needed to escape. With two jobs to provide proper notice to and two cats I had to find a way of getting to my parents' house safely, the return flight was necessary for this trip, but going home temporarily would provide the opportunity to rebuild a relationship with my family and feel out the possibility of eventually moving back to live with them until I could get into university.

My boyfriend couldn't know. He wouldn't let me go. But once I was gone, he would have no way to contact me. He didn't allow me to have a cell phone, after all. So, I waited until he was out, wrote him a note, and called Jill to take me to the airport. She agreed to take my cats to her place until I returned.

Seeing my family for the first time in over a year proved awkward, but our grief united and distracted us from the elephant I'd brought to the funeral home. My body seemed to heal at an incredibly slow pace. The pain and sickness from my procedure lingered as the prescribed antibiotics and pain medications dwindled. A constant heating pad on my stomach provided extra relief, so I planted myself by an electrical outlet as often as possible. No one seemed to notice. No one asked, anyway, and thank God for that. I didn't take the time to think about what I'd even say if anyone asked, but it certainly wouldn't have been the truth.

I didn't really breathe my entire time home. Shame suffocated me. My grandfather had had high hopes and expectations for me. Living with the feeling that I'd let down my entire family was hard enough, but I'd thought I had time. Time to turn things around. Time to rise from the ashes of the life I'd burnt to the ground. But my time had run out. My grandpa had died without seeing my metamorphosis, before meeting the person he'd expected me to become, the person he knew I could—would—be. Losing him before he witnessed me right my wrongs snuffed my soul but whopped my ass into gear to finally initiate my exit strategy: reconnect and rebuild a relationship with my mom and hopefully be invited to rejoin my family.

Shame seeped in and stimulated sleepless nights spent scheming. I shared my grandparents' bed with my grandma. She slept on my grandpa's side. I could smell him. A mixture of oatmeal and cinnamon. I could smell my grandma's cold cream and hear her quietly crying, her tears smearing the cream down her face. Lying beside her while she grieved him gnawed at my nerves. She wanted her husband back. The biggest part of me wanted that, too. But like a loser, a puny pathetic part of me couldn't help but miss my pathetic piece-of-shit boyfriend, too. But why? I couldn't figure it out. Why did I love him, a monster? What was wrong with me?

Lying beside my grieving grandma, I felt guilty for grieving two men. My grandfather: a kind, caring, highly intelligent, determined man who always showed deep love for his family—including me. My stupid boyfriend, the opposite of my grandfather: a bully who fenced me in, held me back, shit on my dreams, crushed my plans, took away my choices and my freedom, destroyed my self-worth, broke me down, and pushed me around.

I felt overwhelmed and confused. Alongside missing my boyfriend, I felt tremendous anxiety and fear about returning to him. Terrified my boyfriend might kill me for leaving, most of me wanted to stay gone, but I couldn't just run. I had to be calculated so he wouldn't chase me, find me, and hurt my family like he'd threatened so many times. I had to get him to leave me or at least choose not to follow me. I needed to plan and play the long game. I ruminated myself to sleep.

By the end of the five days, I'd figured out a place to start trying to fix things with my family. Saying sorry wouldn't cut it. Telling the truth wasn't believable. I had to prove my commitment to bettering myself and being a better daughter and sister with actions, not empty words. I couldn't very well reveal myself as a fraud, as anything other than the strong, fiercely independent girl I'd always proved myself to be. I simply couldn't—wouldn't—ask for help until I first helped myself. In my family, a post-secondary education was an intergenerational familial prerequisite. So, getting back on that path became the first correction of my mistakes. I planted promises to my family to start there and committed wholeheartedly to myself to convert from a high-school dropout to university graduate. Before I could apply for university, I needed to take a year of high-level courses to complete my Ontario Academic Credit. And before that, I had to retake my only incomplete high school core course. I registered for the next available night class to finish Grade 12 English. I also promised to regularly stay in touch with my family to repair our relationship a day at a time. I explained the long-distance block on our landline. On the way to the airport, my dad bought me a prepaid calling card. I hadn't even known such a thing existed.

My boyfriend held a little part of me hostage. To take my power back, I had to go back. I had to return to get out. Although under tragic circumstances, that trip home turned out to be the beginning of the end of my toxic relationship. I'd spent the last year and a half feeling like a bad kid and an utter disappointment to my family. But we'd been reunited. We could rebuild our bond. Out of a death had come an opportunity to reconnect. It took being back in the armpit of Ontario, of all places, and with my family, of all people, to finally feel ready to begin ending this challenging chapter of my life. To lay it to rest once and for all. It might have been my last chance after all—before anyone else died.

Bitter Sweetheart,

I was only gone a couple of days. Now I realize the mistake I made. You played me. Waited until I was away to leave me. You're gone and I can't wrap my head around it. I know what I've put you through. And now you're making me feel the pain I caused you. This isn't how our story was supposed to end. I can't handle the pain. I pray you're just being spiteful to teach me a lesson but that you're coming back. I'm lost in love with you.

Please bring your love back to me, my cruel Katee.

Xoxoxoxo

The love letter sat in the middle of our small round table. Across it lay a long stem rose made from feathers dyed blood-red.

I had returned to a familiarly empty home.

A finger-written message appeared through the steam on the window above the kitchen sink as I filled up the basin to soak the week's worth of neglected crusted dishes.

Where's my Katee? and *I Love You* had been written inside a broken heart.

I knew where my boyfriend would most likely be. Going to find him—in public and in the early stage of the evening—was safer than waiting for him to come home to find me who knew how late, how hammered, and how angry. I had to catch him while his feelings remained frayed but friendly.

I went to collect my boyfriend.

As expected, I found him at the local pub he and his salon colleagues visited frequently. The salon sisters spotted me first. My boyfriend's back was to me. The surprised faces of his entourage gave me away. He turned around, saw me, and started to sob.

My body softened. I smiled.

He stumbled over to me and dropped to his knees.

The pub patrons clapped and whistled and hooted and hollered.

My boyfriend buried his face in my stomach and tightly embraced my hips. He mumbled apologies and gratitudes and promises into me.

Relief at his reaction washed over me. Everything in my being believed things could be forever changed for the better. I second-guessed my decision to leave, but the months of preparation my leaving called for included tasks that needed getting done regardless. I could chicken out later if I changed my mind.

He hurried me out of the pub, not looking back or even saying goodbye to his drinking and drugging buddies.

We slipped along the sidewalk, frosty from the typically temperate daytime winter weather flash-freezing at nightfall. The booze compromising my boyfriend's balance didn't help.

"I can't believe you came back! And came to the pub to find me. I dreamt of that happening every night you were gone. A true dream come true," he said, his breath condensing into clouds in the cool air.

I glanced at him before turning my attention back to the ground to steady us.

At the crosswalk, he stopped and stared at me, longing in his eyes. "I want my life back. I missed you, Katee. I missed you way more than I thought I would." He came in for a hug and, through my hair, sniffed snotty tears. "I missed your smell, your voice, your laugh, your love." He pulled away and looked deep into my eyes. "I missed everything about you."

Dread over which version of him I'd return to—sappy and sweet or sour and scorned—had consumed me. His warm words, so much better than the alternative, clouded my judgement.

"I missed you, too," I said. Not a lie. I had missed parts of him. This version of him.

The high humidity felt frigid. I wanted to get home. The crosswalk sensor beeped at us to cross the street. I grabbed his hand and tugged, guiding him forward.

He followed, continuing his remorseful rant. "There are a lot of things about you that I've taken for granted, and I realized all of them when I was without you." He started to sob. "I know I fucked up big time, Katee."

Just as we approached our apartment entrance, he stopped walking, pulling me to a halt. I turned to face his glossy eyes.

"I can't forgive myself for everything I've done to you. I've never regretted anything more." Sadness seemed to swallow him.

How could I respond to that?

"I promise I'll never hurt you again."

I always believed him. He always let me down.

"Tell me you coming back means you forgive me." His baby blues begged me.

I couldn't bear to hear myself lie to myself, so I nodded. Tears burned at the back of my eyes. Traitor.

Once home, after he made love to me, I told him what I'd decided, but I pretended my plan involved him. I pretended to plead for him to return to Ontario with me. I lied and promised it would be just for the one year it would take to get my OACs. I lied and promised to come back to attend the University of British Columbia or Simon Fraser University. I damn well knew he wouldn't go back to Ontario, but I had eight months to convince him that him staying in BC without me was his choice in place of him thinking me leaving BC without him was mine.

The following week, I started night school.

Chapter 35

Katee

Six months had passed since my trip to Ontario for my grandfather's funeral. My boyfriend proved incapable of keeping his promise to never hurt me again. With my Grade 12 English exam quickly approaching, I bided my time. Once I received confirmation that I'd passed, I would put my plan in motion. Reconnecting with my family had gone better than expected. My mom agreed to let me move home. But until I was positive it would all come together, I couldn't give a specific date to anyone—not my parents, not my workplaces, and certainly not my boyfriend. He knew I still planned on moving home to Ontario sometime within the next two summer months, but he didn't believe I'd follow through. Him calling my bluff safeguarded me. Me making a sudden, last-minute move remained the only way to ensure he didn't come up with a plan of his own.

One night at the end of June, my boyfriend brought a group of strange men back to our home. I rolled over and looked at the alarm clock. 2 a.m. Scheduled to open GNC at nine o'clock in the morning, I was already long asleep. Waking to loud male voices and music with a bass that vibrated my bed made my stomach summersault. I knew I wouldn't be allowed to remain unbothered for long.

Sure enough, my boyfriend threw open the door to our bedroom, demanding that I get out of bed and put on something sexy for his friends. His eyes were as glossy as marbles. They only got like that when he consumed enough alcohol to fill his body from his toes right up to the top of his head. I pictured his glistening eyes submerged in beer. Reminding him that I had to work only awarded me a sharp slap to my face and a warning that more were to come if I didn't obey his order and make an appearance in the living room within five minutes. Wanting to avoid not only another beating but also another missed day of work, I did as instructed. I picked out a new V-neck tank top and my black stretchy dress pants.

Strange faces filled the room, including the face of my boyfriend. He looked like a completely different person when trashed. Ugly, not handsome. His face appeared swollen and oily, he lacked the ability to make or maintain eye contact, and he stopped caring about the only thing that usually kept me safe: his image in front of others. I preferred him high on cocaine or crack over him being inebriated by alcohol. Drugs made him reminisce and storytell for hours; alcohol turned him into a dangerous, unpredictable, and uncontrollable monster. When he was high, I could do no wrong; when he was drunk, I could do no right.

The visibility in our apartment was low due to the dozen or so cigarettes burning. The smell of overflowing ashtrays pooled with staling beer and burned my throat. My boyfriend ordered me to get up on the coffee table. Warm tears silently snuck down my face. One followed the curve of my upper lip and took cover in my parted mouth. Salty. I wondered at the content of sodium in a single teardrop and how many tears a person shed on average over a lifetime. Should I replenish my body's lost sodium after crying for a long period of time?

My boyfriend raised his hand. I bowed my head and stepped up onto the table. He ordered me to take off my clothes while dancing to the music. The strange men gathered around and started clapping their filthy hands to the drops of my tears, howling like wild, rabid animals and making degrading comments.

Couldn't they see how scared I was? I darted my pleading eyes from man to man, hoping to lock eyes with someone who would help me. My pleading eyes were met only with seductive winks, the exaggerated licking of lips, and one man sucking air through his rotting yellow teeth, producing a sharp hissing sound.

When did I become worthless, nothing more than skin, not worth saving? How had things gotten so bad? When had my mechanical, numbed, and programmed body started responding to my boyfriend's demand?

I glanced at my boyfriend, praying he would stop this insanity now that he'd succeeded in terrifying me and getting his new friends all riled up. I reached out and touched his bare shoulder. "Babe? Please . . ." I looked deep into his eyes. He was the only one who could save me. The only one who could make this stop.

He jerked away from my touch, almost causing me to lose my balance and fall. He raised his hand again.

I vigorously shook my head. "Please! No!" I shrieked.

He smiled and nodded at his guests, and they began to violently rip off my clothing.

Once released back to the safety of my room, I locked the door and tried falling back to sleep to escape my reality.

3:30 a.m. Four hours—four and a half tops—till I had to get up.

I heard the men out on the driveway, my boyfriend included. Everyone thanked him for a great night. As their vehicles drove away, I heard the odd thud of my boyfriend staggering back inside. When he arrived at the locked bedroom door and tried the handle, he began to curse. Before I could get up to unlock it, he kicked it in. He jumped onto the bed and began punching me underneath the covers. The more I screamed, the harder he punched. I managed to roll myself off the bed and run for the door. I escaped into the hallway of our apartment building and tripped, falling to the ground. Remaining on my hands and knees so as not to be seen, I crawled to our neighbour's door. I knocked as quietly as possible. I thought he might kill me.

The second the door opened, I pushed my way inside and closed and locked it.

Shelly and her teenage daughter Krista were still awake. Thank

God they never slept. They claimed it was my boyfriend's partying that kept them up, but really, their lights were on almost twenty-four hours a day, seven days a week. At almost any time of the day or night, I could catch a glimpse of at least one of the mother-daughter duo peeking out from behind their dining room curtains. And my boyfriend's partying had become less frequent since we'd moved to British Columbia—it was usually only once a month or so, either whenever something stressed him out or when he'd made more money in a day than he knew what to do with.

As I loosely explained the events of the evening, both sets of eyes grew plumper than the mother's and daughter's identical short, round bodies. Their heads bobbed as they hung off my every word. Typically, they fed on this kind of drama. It excited them. But now, they looked genuinely scared.

Shelly ushered me into the living room, her daughter playing the role of her shadow and waddling inches behind her. Shelly hissed at Krista to turn off all the lights. The poor girl's body vibrated, but her feet remained planted. With a sigh, her mother darted around the apartment, turning off the lights herself. Krista remained in the entrance of the living room, her face white as a mime's. She looked terrified. I'd never seen her more than a few inches away from her mom. What if me being there had put them in danger?

I'd never made it past their front door before; their place smelled bad enough from there. In the centre of their apartment, an overpowering stench of cat urine and sour human body odour shot straight through my nostrils, triggering a few seconds of agony before my nose adjusted to the smell. The sensation disappeared as quickly as it had come. I told them I didn't know what to do or where to go but that this was the final straw. I had to get out for good. Shelly invited me to sleep on their couch until daylight and assured me she and Krista would keep watch at their perch from the front window.

I tried to focus on the movie Shelly and Krista had put on and forget, if only for a moment, what my life had become. Given my drunken boyfriend's cries for me from outside on the driveway, not to mention the constant play-by-plays announced to me by the self-appointed neighbourhood watchers, it proved impossible to get, much less keep, my mind on anything other than my real-life horror story. I curled up in the fetal position on the couch intertwined with piles of laundry, which looked like they were meant to be clean but smelled far past dirty. I dug out a sweater that reeked more of must than cat piss and balled it into a pillow. I prayed it would be over soon. I prayed I could find a way to escape.

Shelly shook me awake. It felt like hours had passed rather than mere minutes. Shelly told me my boyfriend was throwing my things out our second-story window into the rain.

It hadn't been a bad dream after all.

I groggily stumbled to their secret lookout and carefully peered through a crack in the curtain to see my clothing, my food, my blankets, and literally everything else that belonged to me scattered across the wet ground below.

Then I remembered my boys. How could I have left my cats in the apartment with him? What if he hurt or killed them? I wouldn't let that happen again.

I whipped around and ran, knocking over a kitchen chair. From behind me, I heard something break, Shelly begging me to stay, and Krista sobbing. I raced back to our apartment door but came to a standstill once I reached it. I stood there, unable to mobilize my muscles. Could I withstand another beating? Possibly the worst one yet? The last one ever?

Before I could decide, the decision was made for me; the door was thrust open.

At first, my boyfriend's glare went right past me. Then, as if caught off guard, he jolted his head to the right, took a step backwards, and locked eyes with mine.

"You fucking whore!" He spat in my face, grabbed my arm, took a few steps past me, and dragged me to the top of the common-area staircase. In one continuous motion, he let go of my arm with his left hand and punched me directly in the chest with his right, sending me flying down the stairs. My scream was silenced when my head hit the wall.

A young female officer stood over me when I came to. Shelly had called the police, and my boyfriend had been taken to the drunk tank. The police took detailed notes and a few pictures of the cuts and bruises I'd sustained. They questioned me. I refused to tell them the truth. They couldn't save me from him. No one could. Talking to them would only make things worse. Ratting him out would surely be the death of me. Terrified of his vengeful nature, I minimized, defended, and denied. I swore it was nothing. I assured them he was inebriated and totally unaware of the events that had occurred. I lied and said my injuries were from my fall down the stairs, which was due to my own klutziness in the heat of our quarrel. I convinced them that the argument was over a simple misunderstanding, a misunderstanding that I was unable to rectify given his influenced state of mind.

The stunning female officer told me, in her soothing Polish accent, not to worry, that from now on everything would be okay. But I knew nothing would be okay until I planned and executed my escape.

Once they left, I fell back to sleep for a couple of hours before having to get up for work. At 8:15 a.m., I got in the shower and prayed that the close-to-scalding water would wash away my beaten body's aches and pains. The sun shone in through the small window in the bathroom, warming my face. The time had come to take back my life.

A loud noise startled me, and I slipped, barely stopping myself from falling. Was he back already? Hopefully he was sober, or I was as good as dead. My heart sunk to the pit of my stomach as my recently recovered courage disappeared down the drain with the soap suds. I turned off the water and grabbed a towel. I opened the bathroom door and peered out into the hallway to see my still very intoxicated boyfriend, who had just kicked in our locked door, coming at me with two of my decorative collectable porcelain miniature houses. I had collected them ever since my grandparents had bought me my very first one for my seventh birthday; it looked very much like their real house, the house my mom had turned seven in. The miniature houses were, of everything I owned, what reminded me most of my grandparents—a lingering part of my grandpa that I kept alive.

I screamed and backed into the door to our linen closet at the end of the hallway. My cries were silenced by the cracking sound of the houses being smashed into pieces around my bloody and bruised head. After my boyfriend dragged me around the apartment by my hand, foot, and hair interchangeably while giving me the beating of my life, the police showed up once again. They told him to take a walk and suggested that if I didn't want to press charges, I'd better pack up and leave before he got back.

Leave my home, my belongings, and my life? And go where? I was on the other side of the country from my friends and family. I'd finally realized my literal life, not just my body and mind, was in danger. I'd run out of time and had to put my escape plan into effect immediately.

My boyfriend slept off the alcohol for the better part of two days and two nights. His shell surfaced sporadically to use the washroom or get a drink. His eyes glazed over me as if I didn't exist. A fully conscious him finally emerged on the third morning. He woke up and saw me. Sober Him truly saw me, his living piece of art: head-to-toe shiners fresh from the shower.

And I saw him. A shadow of a man.

He stared.

I dropped my towel and stood on display for him to take in all the wonder of his work, his masterpiece.

His widening eyes examined my naked body in a warped game of connect-the-black-and-blue-and-purple-dots. Revulsion consumed his face, and he gagged.

I pointed to the barf bucket I'd put beside the bed. He threw up then looked up at me again and started sobbing until he choked on his rising guilt.

"I'm so sorry, Katee."

I believed him. I knew Sober Him was sorry. I walked over and sat on the bed beside him. He reached for me. I cringed.

"Fuck. I'm such a piece of shit."

I didn't argue otherwise.

"I'm sick, Katee. I'm super sick. That's why I've been drinking so much. You know I only get like this when I drink."

I didn't believe him. I knew Addict Him was lying. "You know how you get when you drink. And you still drink."

"You'd drink, too, if you thought you were dying."

"I can't do this anymore, babe," I said.

"You're leaving me soon anyway."

Not soon enough.

"Something's seriously wrong with me, and you don't even care. Do you know what that does to a man?"

I gazed at my bruises and nodded.

"Please push off school for one more year. I'll be better. I'll make it up to you," he said.

I had no words.

He cried and cried and cried.

I knew he was sorry. Probably the only sorry he'd ever truly been.

I caught a glimpse of him. The man I rarely saw anymore. The man I'd fallen in love with once upon a time ago.

We cried together. After giving me the worst beating of our almost two-year relationship, my boyfriend finally caught a glimpse of the person I used to be—and all he'd done to me.

Chapter 36

Alex

I couldn't believe I was finally done for the holidays. Hallelujah. I was going to Australia for the first time ever to visit my sister. I might never return. I tossed my keys on the bench in my boot room, kicked off my shoes, and let my jacket hit the floor. God, I loved school breaks.

"Yoshi, I'm home," I said, as I peeked around the corner. I heard a rustle coming from the couch and tip-toed over to surprise my mini pit.

Twisty ears, squinty eyes, and a tail whipping against the back of the leather couch greeted me.

"Hi, baby Yoshi."

She rolled over, exposing her bare tummy. I blew a few raspberries on it, and Yoshi went wild, howling playful warnings.

I turned on the gas fireplace, Yoshi's favourite, and the TV to watch the news, my favourite. Realizing I hadn't checked the mail in a while, I went to the front door. The box was overflowing. Having a detached garage at the back of the house meant I rarely used my front entrance. I flipped through the mail as I walked back to the kitchen.

Then I saw it. Another letter from *him*. But with a dangerous difference. I dropped all the other mail, trying to steady myself against my swimming head and starred vision. Hyperventilation threatened my oxygen supply.

Disoriented, I slid down the side of the kitchen island to the floor to catch my breath. I heard Yoshi's nails on the hardwood getting louder. My tongue hurt. I tasted blood. Yoshi came into view and licked my face. Gross dog breath. I pushed Yoshi back and sat up straight. Mail covered the floor. One was handwritten in far too familiar printing. Addressed to my full birth name. Addressed, by *him*, to my home address.

I'd been found.

I jumped up too quickly and nearly went down again. I steadied myself against the kitchen island. The cold quartz felt good on my sweaty palms. Yoshi sniffed the mail still on the ground, and I made my way to the front door to lock it. Then to the back door to lock it. Then to every window in the house to pull the blinds. Yoshi tried to keep up. I returned to the kitchen, shakily poured myself a glass of wine, and downed it. I fumbled to open a new bottle and took the whole thing to my bedroom. I placed it on my end table and had an idea.

In my furnace room, I pulled out the Rubbermaid bin that housed the purple shoebox filled with proof of the pain he had caused me. I rummaged through it until I found what I wanted—needed. I looked through the weathered photo envelope, chose the best picture of *him* and me from a million moons before, and took it to my bedroom. I grabbed the frame by my bedside and replaced the current picture of Yoshi as a puppy with the one of us, then I turned it face down. *He* had finally found me, and if I didn't respond, eventually, *he* would likely break into my home and wait for me. Having this photograph on my nightstand might buy me time if that day came. I could claim I still loved *him* and thought about *him* and have the framed picture of us as proof of this.

God, I prayed it wouldn't come to that. I needed a plan. I crawled into bed and drank myself to sleep.

At 6:59 a.m., after being awake for what felt like hours, I finally decided to stop trying to fall back asleep. Outside my house remained dark, but inside every single light remained on from the night before, as did the music downstairs. I hadn't meant to fall asleep just like I hadn't meant to wake up. But every time Yoshi rustled around in her

little bed, and every time a song changed, and every time I tossed or turned, I startled awake thinking *he* lay there in bed with me. No sense in fighting my consciousness any longer, stalling any longer. I had to figure out a plan before *he* showed up one day.

I got dressed. I decided on black leggings so I could wear my tall, fuzzy winter boots overtop of them. An upside of having such skinny legs was having extra room to conceal things in the empty space between my legs and the sides of the boots: tampons, depending on the time of the month; my phone; ChapStick; and today, the knife. I slid my hand under my pillow until I felt the rubber grip overlay of the handle and retrieved the large, heavy switchblade. The 440 stainless-steel blade had a tab, like a modern flipper knife, which allowed one-handed opening. The whole thing measured six inches. The blade's length was just shy of four inches and its height an inch.

I headed downstairs with Yoshi following close behind. I put my pup out back to do her morning business while I went to retrieve and open the letter. On the back of the envelope, in between two hearts, it read:

> You can change your name and you can move. But you will always be mine. And I'll always find you.

Psycho stalker. I flipped over the envelope. On its front, *he* had written the same song lyrics as before but this time with a slight change. Using musical eighth notes as quotation marks, *he* wrote:

> DO NOT return to sender, address *Id* known, Definitely your number, definitely your zone.
> First, I tried your parents; then I tried your work.
> If this letter doesn't land, I'll deliver it myself, and put it right in your hand.

And *he* would. I knew that much. When playing dead didn't work, I had to play nice, placate *him*, make *him* believe it was *his* idea to leave me alone. The time had come to respond. Unsure as to which of the two jails was the most current, I checked the return address.

"Oh my God!" My heart reacted and began prepping my body to flee. Discombobulation destroyed my brain's ability to process. How could this be? Since when?

#3 – 200 Edge Street

I unlocked my phone and Googled the address. Thirty-point-seven km away. A twenty-nine-minute drive. The street view showed a three-story red brick house with white trim and green shutters. *He* was out of jail. And close. Too fucking close.

Maybe this was just a new scare tactic. I called both jails. There was no inmate by *his* name at either one. I hung up. Then threw up.

Hi Sweetie,

Surprise! I'm finally a free man. Well, mostly free. I had to move back in with my baby momma. Just a baby herself. But you know I'd kick her to the curb in a heartbeat if I could have my life with you back. I'm just here until I either get a new place of my own or she finally fucks off for good. She's just a placeholder. You will NEVER be replaceable. And yup, you read right. I have a baby. She's almost one. I didn't want to tell you until I heard back from you, but since I still haven't, I thought I'd best spill the beans. Her mom doesn't turn eighteen until August. So, you should be happy to know your old man's still got it. But she's not mature like you were at seventeen, eighteen, and nineteen. Not even close. All she wants to do is party it up and go out with friends to whore it up. I'm practically a single dad, which is fine by me. I'm going to get it right this time. Just watch me. Come and play house with me. Be a momma! My baby's true mama. This could be our second chance. I tell ya, my little girl is a real blessing. I'll die before I let her prosti-tot egg donor take her from me. There's no way she even could. She can't even take care of herself, much less my daughter. I tell you, it's like I'm raising two little girls right now. Anyway, please come and see me. Come and see what being a dad does to me. How it changes me for the better. You'll see. Please just come.

All my unconditional love forever and always

xoxoxoxoxoxox

Enclosed were six gut-knotting pictures. One of *him* looking happy with a dog. Three of *him* seducing the camera. One of *him* proudly showing off a baby. One of just the baby. Half the pictures looked like they'd been taken in one location and the rest in another. The first grouping exposed an extremely cluttered room. The second showed off a room with a much more minimalist style and nicer, newer, matching, and mature-looking furniture and décor. *He* looked significantly older in the half from the baby location. And *his* head was shaved. But that face. It was still *his* handsome fucking face. I clawed my fingernail over *his* eyes as if closing the lids on a dead man.

Since it was too early to drink, I went to my junk drawer, dug around for my Ativan supply, and popped two under my tongue. Drinking alcohol would do absolutely nothing for me, anyway. I needed to stay sharp, alert, clear. I needed laser focus, prime coordination, and rapid reflexes.

Yoshi barked at the back door. I reached down the side of my boot and pulled out the knife. Before opening the door, I peeked through the blinds. Once things looked clear, I opened the knife and raised it to eye level before opening the door just enough for my pup to shove her sausage body through. I re-locked the door and re-concealed the weapon.

I followed Yoshi over to the couch; we occupied our respective spots. I looked at the time on my phone. 7:37 a.m. So much for sleeping in on the first day of my extended Christmas holidays. I had so much packing to do before heading to Australia in a few days. But maybe instead, I should have been packing up my entire house and leaving it for good. I didn't know what I should do. I wondered if my therapist's family crisis had resolved. Unlikely, or she would have returned my call by now. I searched for her contact card and called again.

Nope. Still away indefinitely. I wasn't sure what that meant. Gone for now but coming back? Or gone forever and not coming back?

I hung up before the part of her voicemail about the therapist covering her clients. I didn't have the time necessary to fill in a newbie from the beginning of this mess. Maybe my therapist would check her email. I started constructing what was meant to be a short synopsis of my current predicament, but it ended up being the full version of the full story. Immediately after hitting "send," an out-of-office auto-response bounced back.

Chapter 37

Gabbi

Gertie, our fuzzy sphynx, scratches her chin against the corner my book while she kneads her tiny claws into the blanket covering me. Outside, thunder cracks and lightning flashes. I'm waiting for Vince to choose a Friday night show for us to binge. We're individually wrapped up like human burritos occupying perpendicular sections of the couch; our heads meet in the middle. He picks a new Netflix series: "Files of the Unexplained." He clicks on the eighth episode that focuses on the decades-long mystery of the increasing reports of dismembered human feet washing up along the beaches of the Pacific Northwest coast, primarily in British Columbia.

I remember a Burnaby Blogger post mentioning a foot washing ashore in relation to my ex. I remember thinking the way that specific post was worded and written sounded just like my husband. I turn and look at him, pulling my face into a question mark.

"Little bird?" he asks.
"Did you hear about this before now?"
"What?"
"The severed feet washing up in BC."
"Yes. It's been going on for years. Shoes with feet in them wash up along the coast of BC and Washington."

I maintain my inquisitive stare. He gives me nothing. I search his eyes, trying to see into his mischievous mind. He pauses the show. I grab my phone and Google Burnaby Blogger's blog.

> *Death certificates open to the public after 20 years in BC. Anyone can request one at any time if deemed appropriate, like a physician or for legal proceedings, but some information like the date of death would be pertinent. Sure, the assault and death in Victoria is a fair guess, but it's probably as likely he overdosed on Fentanyl and his dumpster got picked up for landfill or he's been swept out with the tide and one day all he'll amount to is just another random foot that washes up on the beach somewhere.*

"What's up?" Vince asks.

I decide to test him. "This BC true crime just has me thinking. What if *he's* not dead and word of me finally speaking out against him snakes its way to him?"

Vince tenderly touches my face and comforts my unease with his kind eyes before pulling me closer.

"I just think I should hire a private investigator. Make sure he's dead before I publish my book," I add.

"Although the rules vary slightly depending on the province, access to provincial vital statistics is on a need-to-know basis. Here in Alberta, it's fifty years, going from memory. In BC, where he likely died, it's thirty years."

"Going from memory?"

The twitch of a smile on the face of someone who's been caught exposes my husband's façade.

"It's you."

A devilish dimple asterisks his smirk.

"You wrote all that? It's been years. Why didn't you tell me?"

"You had everything under control. You didn't need help."

"Then why'd you keep tabs on him?"

"In case you ever requested backup."

Love floods me, and my smile cramps my cheeks.

"Remember the meme you sent when we first started dating?" he asks.

"I don't." But I do.

"When I told you of my Viking ancestry?"

I claim clueless and wait.

"You told me you're not a princess in need of saving," he says.

"That's right. I'm a Viking queen ready to fight side by side."

Chapter 38

Katee

I woke up to the most beautiful July day. The sun's beams radiated a tremendous amount of heat that warmed my face like the breath of a summer's breeze. The birds chirped church hymns, and the town bell made a final wake-up call. I thought I could fall back asleep for a bit, but my bedroom blinds traded sides, allowing the sun to sneak through their cracks and pry my eyelids back open. It was Canada Day. A stat holiday. But I had to spend my only day off studying for my Grade 12 English exam after finally finishing the night course. Slowly, as if the bed and I were one, I peeled the warm sheets and comforting duvet off my tired body.

"Good morning, my men," I said to my cats. "You don't make it easy for me to get up, do you? And why are you both so tired? Were you up all morning doing the dishes and housework?"

"Brumeow," replied Oakley.

Monkey walked right up to my face and gave me morning kisses. He purred as he circled me for affection.

"Monk, I love you, but I can't stay in bed with you all day." I lifted my Manx kitten and placed him beside me. As if knowing I had no time for nonsense, Oakley ran over and gave Monkey a swat that sent him flying off the bed in the direction of their food dish. Oak sauntered to the edge of the bed to receive his morning hello's before jumping down and strolling toward the breakfast headquarters. Suddenly, the cats stopped the breakfast assembly-line march, their ears contorted, and they both jumped back as the front door flew open.

My boyfriend burst in, out of breath, and gasped, "Cutie, come with me! Come on!" Not waiting for my response, he ran into our bedroom, jumped onto our king-sized bed, and dove onto my lap. "Come with me right now!" he said.

"You're such a bad influence. You know I have to study today."

"Come on, cutie. Please don't move back home just to waste an entire year getting your OACs when you could stay here with me and go to uni right here the year after next once the Ontario Academic Credit has finally phased out. Don't leave me. I love you and want to spend the rest of my life with you."

The last few days following my worst beating had been more magical than I could ever explain or anyone would ever believe. It felt like ecstasy. I felt more closely connected to my boyfriend than ever before. I truly thought he'd successfully scared himself straight and that the positive change in him could be permanent. But my mind was made up about moving home by the end of the summer to start school in September even if I was still on the fence about breaking up with him by then.

"I've told you a hundred times, I need to do this for me. If you want to stay together, then move back, too. But this exam has nothing to do with that, anyway. It's just to complete my high school diploma," I said, feeling like a broken record.

"Just forget about it for now and come with me," he said, as he got off the bed and headed to the window. He reached into his pocket and struggled to grasp something. "Make a wish," he said, as he threw a tiny red object at me. A plastic star landed in my lap. "That's for the next time you want to wish upon a star. Now grant me my wish. Stop studying and come."

"I love you, but—"

"If you really love me, you'll come with me," he said. "I have a surprise for you."

I sighed. "I'm in my pyjamas. I can't leave the house looking like this."

"We're just going to the car. Come, come, come." He grabbed my hand and pulled me, barely giving me enough time to grab a light jacket to cover my arms. He led me to the car and stopped long enough to open and close the door for me. He dashed to the driver's side door and jumped in.

"Ready?" He started the engine.

"How long is this going to take?" I asked.

He shushed me and put on our song. He started singing to me as he drove. I gave in and joined. We turned down the street that headed into the mountains. Winding, never-ending roads greeted us as we started our journey up a path to the Heavens. Wildlife filled the rainforest with energy, making the magnificent, moss-covered trees seem even more monstrous than they already were. The ten-minute drive seemed much longer, like hours passed. Once this world had been entered, time was always lost.

My boyfriend pulled off into a parking lot where some of the most beautiful trails began and parked the car. By this time, it had started to sprinkle a bit, and a disappointed look came over his face. "Plan B," he said. "Wait here a sec." He got out of the car in as quick of a hurry as he'd gotten in and went around to the trunk. I could hear him rustling around. He came back soaking wet and jumped in the car. "Here ya go," he said, as he handed me a bag. I opened it to see a packed lunch: an orange-flavoured juice box, a turkey sandwich, and a chocolate bar tempted my empty stomach. "It was supposed to be a picnic, but since the weather didn't hold, we'll just have it in the car."

"Thank you," I said. "This is very nice. What's the occasion?"

He pulled a single red rose from the side pocket in the door and handed it to me.

"What's happened?" I demanded. My boyfriend once told me he would never buy me flowers. He'd only bought flowers for two people; both had died. To him, flowers symbolized death.

"I love you, Katee," he said. "You're the best thing that's ever happened to me. You're my best friend. That's what failed in all my past relationships, the fact that we weren't still friends when the going got tough."

"When the going got tough?"

"Your purity and innocence have made me strive to be a better man . . ." His tears made it impossible for him to continue.

"Why are you crying, babe? What's going on?"

"Cutie," he started, having calmed down enough to speak, "I

have a brain tumor. I only have eight months left to live." Beads of sweat formed over his pale face.

"What? You can't be serious. Are you serious? Is this a joke? Tell me this is a twisted joke."

He looked lost.

"How?" I felt my lip quiver. "When? I don't understand."

"Don't ever forget me, cutie. I need you to promise me that."

I struggled to formulate words. "What do you mean? How did you find out?"

"I can't handle you grilling me right now, Katee. I'm trying to come to terms with dying, I can't support you. It should be the other way around." He started the car and headed home. The entire ride back was silent. Death's presence filled the car with its icy breath. My boyfriend pulled into our driveway but didn't shut off the car. "I have to go to work, and you have to start your studying," he said with his head bowed low.

"I'm sorry. I'll quit school. I'll take care of you. Eight months? Eight months? What are we going to do?"

"You chose to prioritize your schooling. But I'll still always love you."

With a shaky hand, I reached for the door handle and pulled it toward me. Then I stopped, wiped the tears from my eyes, and leaned over to kiss him. He pulled me close and hung on a little longer with a grip that was much tighter than usual. "You're my cutie, and nothing will ever change that." He kissed me one last time before I got out. As he put the car into reverse, I stared, stupefied. With one hand covering my mouth and the other waving goodbye, I watched him drive away through my tears.

Once he was out of sight, I turned to enter our building. Tripping as I walked up the stairs, I dug blindly for my keys to our apartment. I heard my cats meowing on the other side of the door as I fumbled the key into the lock. Feeling the weight of a thousand worries on my weak shoulders, I dragged myself to the couch.

I called my boyfriend's cell to tell him to come home, to say I needed him and knew he needed me.

"This cellular customer . . ."

My eyes strayed upwards. My heart pounded, echoing in my ears. One . . . two . . . three . . .

". . . is not available to take your call right now."

My hand unfurled. One . . .two . . .three . . .

The phone hit the floor. On the wall where the pictures of his kids once hung were three bare nails.

I ran to the bedroom and discovered a closet full of clothes with his favourites missing. The bathroom led to a similar discovery—everything there but his essentials. A call to his work confirmed he'd never shown up. My boyfriend was gone. This *gone* had come at least eight months before its time. He'd whisked me off to Alouette Lake, romanced me, blindsided me with the diagnosis that he was dying, then abandoned me. He'd rid me of himself but left me with punishing guilt and a breakup note.

Dear Bitter Sweetheart,

If you're reading this, then obviously I couldn't change your mind on your schooling location. I know I look pretty selfish right now, but my reasoning was exactly the opposite. For the last few months something changed in you. You were convinced to move back and continue your education; determined to get your old life back. No matter what I said, or how much I tried to change your mind, you remained firm. We both knew, although we wouldn't admit, that this would be the end of us. When I found out I had a brain tumor, I knew you'd change your plans for me. I also knew that choice would change the rest of your life. If I didn't do something, you would have stayed with me until

I died. I couldn't let you do that. I couldn't let you watch your life deteriorate along with mine. So, I left. I love you, and it took all the strength I had to do what I did. Dying doesn't scare me anymore because nothing could be worse than the pain I felt when I left you. Be strong for me. Keep our memories alive, for those are a part of me death can never take.

Remember, I love you, goodbye.

In the days after my boyfriend told me of his brain tumor diagnosis then left, I watched my life from what seemed like the back-row seat of a movie theatre. When he vanished, the essence of me vanished. I was not present, fully detached. I felt nothing. I purchased my favourite comfort foods—nachos and salsa, Kraft dinner, Alphaghetti—but I couldn't swallow much, and what I managed to swallow didn't stay down.

My boyfriend had vanished, and with him went all the tenants' rent money from the past year. The landlord position had been self-appointed. The building owner lived three provinces away and had been in a coma from a near-fatal motor vehicle accident. My boyfriend had tracked down the owner's son and convinced him not to worry, he'd manage the property and save the rent until the owner recovered and could come and collect it herself. My boyfriend told the owner's son he wouldn't release any money to him without a court order since he had no way of knowing the wishes of the owner. Essentially, my boyfriend bullshitted the owner's son into thinking he and the owner had a prior arrangement. And, like everyone, the owner's son blindly trusted my boyfriend. Now, the owner of our apartment building was two weeks away from arriving to collect the money owed. I needed to pack up and get out.

Sprawled out on the floor, arms and legs beating the ground beneath me, I yelled, "Where the hell are you? Turn on your fucking phone!" Then I bellowed out a primal scream. Contradictory feelings confused my nervous system. I felt confusion and shock, rage and hatred, grief and fear, and fleeting moments of excitement and hope.

"Katee?" said a male voice; it was followed by knocking on my front door.

I had to pull it together.

"You okay in there?"

I picked myself up off the floor, straightened my shirt, wiped my eyes, and fixed my hair. In my doorway stood Sean. He'd been packing up to clear out of his apartment, too, since I'd confided in him about my boyfriend stealing everyone's rent and warned him about the owner coming soon. A few months back, Sean's parents had agreed to help him move back to his Ontario hometown if it meant he'd go to college there in the fall. They'd bought him a one-way ticket the day he received the acceptance letter in the mail. He'd fly back next month and until then, he would stay with them.

"Oh. Hey. No. Not okay," I told Sean.

"Want a drink?"

"Yes."

I followed him outside, to the entrance of the other side of our building, and to his apartment. His place was filled with young guys, maybe a half dozen or so. All eyes in the room focused on me.

Sean outstretched his arm toward me. "This is her. Katee, this is everyone."

I wondered what *This is her* was supposed to mean, who everyone thought I was.

"Your boyfriend's a fucking asshole, sweetheart. Better off without him," said some guy with strawberry-blonde hair sitting by the window.

Bittersweet without him.

A few others sitting around the filthy kitchen table nodded their heads.

"Agreed," said one guy on the other side of the room, as he took a shot off the cluttered coffee table. Once finished, he looked at me. "If I was your man, I'd never leave you."

Embarrassment warmed my face. It was the first feeling I'd felt in days. Avoiding eye contact, I accepted the shot he handed me and downed it. He must have worked in construction, as his hands looked permanently stained.

"Another?"

I held out the shot glass. He filled it. I pounded it and gestured for a third. My eyes watered, and my throat burned. A few guys laughed and clapped.

"That a girl."

So many eyes, all on me. I wondered if I was safe.

Sean touched my shoulder. I jumped.

"Ah, I should get back to my place," I said. "I have a lot of packing to do." Packing, crying—same difference.

"How are you getting all your stuff back to Ontario, doll?" said the guy who would never leave me if he was my man.

I shrugged. "I sold our furniture to an acquaintance and am using that money to fly home. Pack what I can . . . guess I'll have to leave the rest."

"My dad's a trucker," he said. "Bet I could get him to squeeze a skid on the next load going out that way."

"Really? That'd be great."

"No problem, doll. I'll ask him and get back to you."

In just under two weeks, I wrote my exam, called my parents to arrange an airport pickup, gave less than ideal notice to my work, and packed to get the fuck outta dodge. I was on edge the entire time, wondering if my boyfriend would pop out of hiding and stop me dead in my tracks. When he didn't and the day came to escape, Jill drove me and my cats to the airport.

Chapter 39

Katee

During the two-hour drive home from the airport, an unsettling energy wriggled around in my stomach like a million worms anxiously awaiting my decay. Yet as my parents and I approached the highway's warning sign—*15 km to "L-Pit"*—the worms quickly vacated, and a weight like a lead x-ray vest enclosed my body so tightly I feared I'd suffocate. I couldn't believe I was heading 80km/hour back to the armpit of Ontario. It wasn't a myth after all; even the few lucky enough to leave eventually got sucked back in. Sure, I'd wanted and planned my escape from my boyfriend and the reunification of my family for months, but now I was coming back to the place where my life had first fallen apart, where everything bad—the isolation, incarceration, and ill-treatment—had begun. I wanted to return to my family and my schooling but not this soiled, cursed country town. I wasn't even originally from this shithole, yet I, too, was living a life sentence in it.

I swore I'd never return to the place where dirty secrets masked the stench of its bullshit and lies. The town was a small, hidden, shady speck on a map, probably mistaken by most for a stain, a splatter of food, or a hole caused by the wear and tear of unfolding and refolding. Few people in the entire province knew this place existed, and even fewer could say they'd been here.

A simple drive through the town proved extremely deceiving. The main street held the title for widest in the country—so said AMA—and framing this street were gorgeous century-old buildings renovated into locally owned shops. Their inviting storefront windows showcased award-winning displays of all the so-called "finer" things in life. It was all super expensive, useless crap, if you asked me, but they wanted to attract a different caliber of customer; although, I supposed once upon a time, while I was still on the "right path," they might have considered me a prospect. The picturesque parks, trees, and flower gardens that filled the town belonged in *Town & Country Magazine*. So did the homes; they were all old, brick, and proudly placed on huge lots. To the ignorant upper-class locals and city folk who passed through each summer en route to their fancy cottages, this place resembled a stunning up-and-coming model. Yet for those of us in the know, in touch with reality, surviving in the gutters that lined her runway, that seemingly perfect, homegrown model was only close to flawless on the outside. Her angelic face and to-die-for body distracted people's attention from the dark secrets that rotted her from the inside out. These secrets were so widespread they were accepted as the norm: there was the constant violence she witnessed, fell victim to, and perpetuated; her all-too-common, serious, and in many cases fatal drug addictions; her countless abortions by desperate teenagers; and the alarming number of child and adolescent deaths caused by severe cases of neglect, vicious fights, overdoses, and suicides. People kept those deaths private, and if they were known, the reasons behind them given to the public—even the extended families—were vague and mysterious or simply "undetermined."

This place needed someone suspicious. Someone who could look past what stood out at first glance, someone willing to dig deeper to expose the secrets many would do anything to keep hidden. This pit pretended certain people didn't exist while it did whatever necessary to push them down further and keep them silent.

In the armpit of Ontario, teen pregnancy numbers multiplied like unwanted pit pubes. Just as every girl tried to shave off those pubes, this town found ways to do the same with its own coarse, dark, and embarrassing inhabitants in order to keep its quaint residents as satisfied and ignorant as possible. The head honchos attempting to run this place spent a lot of time and money constantly waxing out the unwanted growth. There was a constant pruning of the fuck-ups who came here to hide and a disguising of the ones too fucked up to leave. To maximize the growth of the pompous shops, the hoity-toity owners overpriced their merchandise to keep the unwanted locals out while still appealing to the loaded tourists passing through on their way to cottage country.

Twenty minutes from Final Destination, the last gas station before "L-Pit" appeared. I looked for the oddly shaped barn farther up on the right. It'd been meant to open as a strip joint but been shut down prematurely by the upper-class town voters who claimed to worry that its distance from town would encourage more drinking and driving. Most of us assumed the true worry was more likely that a dirty strip joint would taint the image of the quaint town.

Minutes from the centre of the armpit, I saw to the left of the road the trailer park where my friend Arleen and her mother Marilyn lived. I sighed and attempted a smile. When Arleen and I had been close, I'd felt much more connected to her mother than my own. I heard Marilyn's voice in my head: *What's the worst he can do?* If we had only known then.

But it was finally over now. The heaviness started to lift off my body, as the trailer park welcomed me back to the outskirts of town. I allowed a full smile to escape, but every muscle in my body tensed as we approached the graveyard just down the road where Marilyn's son and Arleen's fourteen-year-old brother was buried. He'd taken too much Gravol for a thrill, overheated, gone for a swim in the local river to cool off, and drowned.

Grappling with the grief, I distracted myself by looking for an old acquaintance's apartment, the after-hours party place. Being there had made me feel so grown up even though I'd been the only person in our group years younger than the legal drinking age. Thank God for fake IDs. Everyone we knew had crowded into that apartment after going out to the bar, and I had loved it. At least until a guy had taken a brick to his head before being thrown over the second-floor balcony. He was a quadriplegic now.

As we passed KFC, where I'd worked my first job, I remembered spending my fifteen-minute breaks in the refrigerated room scarfing down as many stolen Styrofoam containers of macaroni salad as I could. At sixteen, I had known better and felt totally awful about it, but living on my own, I'd justified it as something I had to do to survive. God, I'd hated that stinky, thankless job. I hadn't lasted long, but working there had taught me where not to apply in the future.

Memories of my boyfr—my *ex*-boyfriend—sucked me out of KFC. As we drove on, we passed the place where it had all started. Tears poured over my lower eyelids as if trying to obscure James's old apartment, but there it stood above The Nutty Chocolatier. I closed my eyes and tried not to remember the night we'd met.

"Honey?" interrupted my father, rescuing me from my grief.

"Yeah, Dad?"

He made eye contact with me through the rear-view mirror. "Your mother and I are so happy to finally have you home."

I smiled then glanced at my mom.

She reached her hand back and squeezed my knee.

"I promise I'll make it up to you guys." I started to cry thinking of my never-ending list of regrets. Such a bad apple. Rotten to the core. "I'm so sorry."

"You'll show us with your actions, Katee," said my mom. "Get back in school and upgrade your marks. Apply to universities. No reason you shouldn't be able to get some scholarships."

I took a deep breath. "I know. I will. I promise."

She patted my knee.

They thought I was just a bad kid. How could I ever make things right?

"Need anything in town before we head home?" my dad asked.

I shook my head. What I needed was to make amends. Make them proud. Make them trust me again. I needed to swallow my stubborn pride. Not try and explain all the things they could never possibly understand. What I needed was to keep my head down and keep myself and my family safe.

Chapter 40

Katee

"Cheers to Katee finally being home!"

Everyone raised their glasses to meet Allison's.

I'd kept a smile plastered across my face since arriving home two weeks ago. But my heart hurt. It had been a month since my boyfriend—correction, my ex—had abandoned me in British Columbia. Where was he, and why had he left me like that? Would I see him again? For closure? He still had his phone off.

My friends were all chatting, unaware of my emotional distance. I looked around the bar. This place hadn't changed at all. What a dump. I wondered what the carpet looked like in the daylight. Disgusting.

Behind the bar stood the same bartender who'd worked here before I'd left a year ago and probably before I was born. I recognized some die-hard regulars by the pool tables. Same skanky waitresses.

Everything was the same. Everyone was the same. Just I was different.

"Katee?" Allison said, squeezing my arm so tightly I elbowed her off me.

"What?" I said, turning to give her cut-eye for hurting me. But my gaze met the back of her head. I looked where she was staring and couldn't believe my eyes. Under the doorway, as ridiculously good-looking as ever, stood my ex-boyfriend.

He flashed me his award-winning grin and sauntered over. The background conversation stopped. My friends' eyes flickered back and forth between my ex and me.

"Hey, cutie." He planted a kiss on my lips. "Glad you're finally back. Was going crazy waiting for you."

Cliché, I know, but I swear my heart actually stopped. This couldn't be happening. It had to be a dream. I blinked; my jaw hung.

"Earth to Katee," said my ex in his soft, sweet voice.

Allison squeezed my arm again. "What's going on, Katee?"

"Come on, babe. Everyone's over there waiting to see you." He took my other arm, glancing at Allison as if to tell her to let go.

Still not able to find any words, I stood up and followed him. He escorted me to a crowded table in another room. All his friends—the only friends he'd allowed me to have for the eleven months before our move out West for the year—were there.

"Katee! Welcome back," said a half dozen familiar faces.

Patrick pulled out the chair beside him. "He's been driving us crazy, waiting like a dog for his owner to get back. You shoulda just driven back together. Let the fleabags suffer." He nudged the chair and gestured for me to sit.

I complied. "Hey, Patrick. Long time. Missed you." I looked at my ex, trying to wave my eyebrows to show him my utter confusion.

What had he told them? Obviously not that he had left me all alone in BC.

He just smiled at me.

He was so hot. It was good to see him. I had missed him.

As if he'd read my mind, he answered, "I told you guys, Katee had to give notice at her work. Plus, the cats wouldn't last the four-day road trip. And they'd drive us crazy. So, I drove the car back, and Katee flew home with them."

They thought we were still together. He thought we were still together. Were we? Had I gone completely insane?

I felt another squeeze on my arm. I looked up to see Allison. Just as I opened my mouth, my ex spoke for me.

"Geez, Allison. You've hogged my girl for the past twenty-four hours. Let us reunite, will ya? It's been almost a month since we've seen one another."

"Katee . . ." she started, hand on hip.

"You bar stars are gonna have to troll for dick alone tonight. You seem to forget my girl here is taken."

Taken? Did he mean taken *back*? Was the breakup just a dream? His death sentence just a nightmare? What the hell was going on?

"It's okay, Allison. I'll catch up with you guys later. Okay?"

Her lip curled as she glared at me. "Sure. See you in another couple of years."

My bladder woke me up. I had to pee so badly.

I scanned the church parking lot and looked around the car.

Thankfully, no one was in sight.

I opened the door, undid my pants, and took one last three-sixty-degree scan of our surroundings. Before finishing, I heard a noise coming from behind me. I cranked my head around to see a middle-aged man, probably the minister, standing in the doorway of the church looking right at me.

Freaked, I stopped peeing midstream, pulled up my pants, and jumped back in the car.

"Babe! We gotta go." I looked out the passenger-side window to see the man walking toward our car; luckily, he was still about three hundred feet away. It looked like he had pamphlets or something in his hand. I yanked the comforter off my boyfriend and shook his shoulder. "Hun, get up! Someone's coming."

With a groan, he pried open his eyes. "What?" he said in an annoyed tone.

"Look!" I pointed out my window.

"Shit." He sat straight up and fumbled for his keys in the console.

With the man only a hundred or so feet away now, I locked my door. "Hurry."

The engine started, and the tires squealed.

Once a safe distance from our camp-out location, my boyfriend said, "Where do ya wanna go, cutie?"

Home. To my bed. To have a shower. To eat something.

It had been two weeks since my boyfriend had found and "collected" me. Two stressful weeks of sneaking around with him behind my parents' backs when I could and staying out overnight with him on the weekends when my family was out of town. I had mixed feelings about all of it. I knew I didn't want to get back together. But part of me still wanted to spend time with him.

"Um . . . my parents will be back from the cottage tonight . . . so . . . I can't stay out with you again. Sorry."

"Yeah. Sure you are. Sorry you're a spoiled freeloader, right?"

My stomach rotted with unease. His words squeezed my heart. "Babe, don't." I placed my hand on his knee.

"Don't what, Katee? Don't be pissed you're choosing your asshole parents over me? And why? 'Cause you're a slut to the dollar? 'Cause you need someone to provide for you?" He pulled over to the side of the road. "I need someone to care for me. I'm dying, remember? And because you're so goddamn fucking selfish now, you're actually gonna let me die in a car in a parking lot somewhere. Alone."

I felt my eyes moisten. My breathing became shallow and shaky. "You left me, not the other way around."

"Oh, sure. Use the out I gave ya. I thought you'd do the right thing, Katee. Guess I never really knew you at all." He picked my hand up off his knee and dropped it back on my lap.

"Okay. I'll do it. I'll take care of you. I'm sorry."

He smiled. It warmed my heart.

"It'll probably take me four or five months to be able to save up enough money from my new job to have first and last months' rent, though."

"That's okay. I'll wait. But I want the rest of our stuff you brought back in the meantime." He'd only taken his essentials when he'd left BC.

I nodded. "Sure."

Once back at my parents' house, he gave me an awkward hug and kiss in exchange for what of our stuff I'd paid to have shipped back he could cram into the back seat of his car. A sick feeling overtook my stomach.

"Where are you going to stay tonight?" I asked, as he popped his trunk to take one last thing that wouldn't fit inside the car.

"Not sure. Wherever I end up."

I walked over to give him a hug and gasped. The trunk was full of all his essentials—the belongings he'd taken when he'd left BC six weeks ago and had been storing at Patrick's house. I started to cry. "Why is all your stuff here?"

"I have to go," he said, as he pulled away from me.

"Go where?"

He got into the car and shut the door.

"Where are you going?" I yelled through the closed window.

He reversed the car.

I ran after him, barely able to see through my tears. "Please stop."

He did as I asked. He glanced up and met my eyes for a brief second.

I shrugged my shoulders and said, "What are you doing?"

He put on his sunglasses, cranked the wheel, and disappeared.

Chapter 41

Alex

I called my most nonjudgmental—albeit craziest—friend, Tiffany.

"Hi, biatch! Excited for your big trip? Fuck, I'm jealous. I wish—"

"Can you come over?"

"Um . . ."

I glanced at the time.

"Yeah. But I'm just waking up. Late night fighting with Moe's sperm donor. Useless loser fuckface. You'll have to give me a bit to pull myself together. Need help packing?"

Shit. I kept forgetting about that. "Yes, packing."

"Okay, be over in a bit. Want me to bring anything?"

A restraining order. A moving truck. "No, thanks." My therapist. My freedom.

"Kk. I'll bring pre-drinks for our last night out before I lose you to all the thunder from Down Under you'll be getting soon. Ciao for now, bella."

I hung up. Fuck it. I walked to the fridge and popped open a bottle of sparkling wine. As I drank my orange-juice-less morning mimosa, I looked around my house. The past few months it had felt—looked—lonely. But today, it looked foreboding. It felt like a traitor. A spy for him. Like it was watching me. Reporting back to him. The block of glistening knives on the counter threatened me. Slick floors would surely slip me if I ran for my life. Wood stairs waited to trip me. Huge floor-to-ceiling, wall-to-wall, voyeur-inviting windows offered me up, pimped me out; with the blinds drawn up tight like they were in that moment—like they had been for months now—they kept me caged and blind to the happenings of the outside all around me.

"I brought booze," Tiffany said, handing me a clanking bag of wine bottles so she could remove her shoes and coat. "It's cold as a corpse's cock out there. And while we freeze our fannies off over the holidays, you'll be spending them where it's summertime at Christmas."

Already more than half in the bag, thanks to Ativan's bad influence and anxiety's peer pressure, I stumbled back a bit to make way for the tornado that was Tiffany.

"So," Tiffany started, "let's see your sluttiest summer selections." She laughed. "Honestly, I'd fuck the first guy who spoke to me in that sexy-as-fuck accent."

We headed up to my bedroom and chit-chatted about all the adventures my sister had already lined up for us. Envious, Tiffany complained about how children ruin life by sucking all the fun and spontaneity out of it.

"And don't even get me started on the toll they take on your tits," she added.

Many of my friends already had children. Smalltown folk tended to have them young. Tiffany already had three by three different fathers—or sack-of-shit sperm donors, as she called them. But I had never experienced the desire or urge to have children. My priority was love, and if having children was a dealbreaker for the man I wanted to spend my life with, then I'd have one, max two. But I didn't want kids enough to be a single married mother, as I called them. I had zero desire to be the sole raiser of children. No, thank you.

I sat back and allowed Tiffany to curate my clothing collection. As she tossed her choices to me, I folded them up and Tetris-ed them into my largest suitcase. Tiffany ranted on about the latest loser in her quest for love and how she needed to buy herself just a little more time to convince him she could be his dream girl.

"So, I told him I'm pregnant."

"Are you?"

"No. But if he thinks I am, he'll stick around, and we can fuck without condoms—since I'm already pregnant," she winked, "and hopefully I'll get actually pregnant real quick."

Although this tactic had failed three times previously, there was no convincing Tiffany out of something she already had in her hard head.

"But the fucker wanted me to pee on a stick to prove it. So, I went to the local high school at lunchtime and walked around until I saw a pregnant girl."

"Oh my God, you did not."

"Sure did. Told her I had tons of old baby stuff I'd give her if she peed in a jar for me. And she agreed."

Tiffany's craziness—resourcefulness—never ceased to amaze me. This latest outrageous stunt reminded me of why I'd picked Tiffany, of all people, to come over today. She was a proud, self-proclaimed pursuer. Perhaps she could help me see things from *his* twisted perspective. Help me configure a plan, come up with a solution.

So, I told Tiffany everything. Well, everything that'd happened since the breakup but nothing that preceded it. Some things felt too shameful to share even with my most shameless friend.

"Yeah. So, sixteen letters in total now."

"Wow. He sure loves you."

"This isn't love, Tiffany. It's possession and power and control."

"Pffft. Well, then sign me up for some of that. Jesus, Alex. What I wouldn't give to be wanted like—"

"Tiffany. I don't want to be with him. I want him to leave me alone. But I need to play nice. He needs to believe we're on good terms, that we're friends. I need to convince him that I love and care about him but not in that way anymore. I need to be sweet but firm."

"Why? Just tell him to fuck off. Shit, I'll happily take him off your hands."

Tiffany didn't know my ex. She'd never met *him*. This was another reason for choosing her. She was unbiased, unaffected by *his* charm. Yet, here she was, somehow still under *his* spell.

"I need you to promise me you'll do no such thing. You'll stay far away from him."

"Yeah, yeah. Wouldn't want your sloppy seconds anyway." She

laughed. "Sounds like it's time for a road trip." She meant stakeout. "We need to just show up there. Catch him off guard."

I had lost count of how many times I'd ridden shotgun to one of Tiffany's stakeouts in our early twenties.

By the time we finished the packing and the rest of the liquid courage, Tiffany had convinced me to put on my big-girl panties and go see *him*. A buzzed—wasted—me decided I'd prove to *him* that I had, in fact, done all the things *he'd* assured me I'd never be capable of doing.

I had repaired my relationships with my family, completed two degrees, and gotten my dream job, and in the morning, I was moving to Australia. Okay, so that last part was a lie. But I didn't know how else to safely and surely close the door on *him* and *his* obsession with getting me back. Tiff and I decided one small embellishment wouldn't hurt. I was pretty sure I could pull off the lie, and I had the plane ticket to back it up. Safety came with strings attached: staying on *his* good side; staying *his* dream girl. I'd just pretend to do that from the safe distance of the other side of the world.

When we arrived at *his* address, I recognized the corner-lot red-brick, three-storey house from the Google Street View pictures. Not even the copious amounts of alcohol and Ativan I'd consumed could calm my nerves as Tiffany parked the car and said, "We're here."

This was a terrible idea. "I can't do this, Tiff." What the fuck had I been thinking?

"You can, and you will. And I've gotcha. You know what they say: crazy beats muscle any day." Tiffany laughed.

I cringed. The irony hit too close to home.

"This isn't a good idea. We should go."

"Nope. I've been watching you stress about this all day. We drove all the way here. We're going in and finishing this once and for all." She opened her car door and got out.

Fear paralyzed me. I watched as Tiffany marched up the forest-green stairs of the white porch. I scooched my butt forward in my seat and sank my body down as a woman appeared in the doorway after Tiffany knocked. I put my sunglasses on, not caring how dumb I looked wearing them at night. I wished they could make me invisible. I saw Tiffany walking back to the car while waving me out. I worked up the nerve to open my car door.

"He's not in there. The lady said number three is around the side and attached to the back of this house in the accessory dwelling unit or something? Come on, get out." Tiffany grabbed my hand and pulled me from the car, slamming the door behind me before yanking me forward.

The side of the corner-lot red-brick house sat on Dewdney Road. In what looked like a driveway between the back of the corner house at 200 Edge Street and the side of the neighbouring house at 276 Dewdney Road sat a little finished garage of sorts. It had a flat black roof, was covered in white siding, and had a little window and a white door with a #3 beside it. Seeing that my ex was living in a driveway shed pumped me with naïve but brazen bravery.

Mistaking warning bullets for mere butterflies in my stomach, I stole the lead and pulled my friend the remaining way. I summoned *him* with my fist on the door, startling myself. The rapid cycling between feeling untouchable yet knowingly placing myself in grave danger dizzied me even more than the benzos and booze. All the rage with no place to go made my legs shake and my heart race. I psyched myself up. As I watched through the door's window for *him*, I imagined pounding my fist right through the glass and into *his* face.

"I still can't believe you're actually here," he said, grinning like a fool with tears in his eyes.

I fought to breathe without cracking my frozen core. I struggled to hear my loud friend over my pulse booming in my ears. I needed to expand my lungs and lower the volume before I passed out.

The three of us sat perpendicular to one another, creating a Bermuda Triangle that threatened to make us girls disappear under mysterious circumstances.

He focused solely on me.

I focused solely on my blabbing friend.

Tiffany focused solely on him—a novelty man to her.

He kept trying to talk to me. "So, what have you been up to for the last four years? Jesus. Can't believe it's been so long. What's new? Besides everything, I guess," he rambled. "I want to hear it all."

From frozen to numb, I tried ignoring him by staying hyper-focused on my friend's storytelling. "Oh? Right. Now I remember, yes. Tell him about the other time," I said, urging Tiffany on.

Tiffany yammered on and on, seemingly oblivious to the lack of true attention coming from either of us, much less the growing tension in the small pressure-cooker room.

He tried again. "You look great, babe. Wow. Whatever—or whoever—you're doing is sure doing you good." A suggestive hint of his Old Spice body wash flirted with my nose.

Feeling eerily composed in a way that freaked me out a bit, I chose to ignore the slut-slight and instead listed off all the things I'd achieved that he'd spent years telling me I never would. And, boy, did I embellish. Who was larger than life now? Me. Not him in his driveway shed of a shack. I boasted about how close-knit my family and I had become, that we were stronger and more bonded than ever, especially my mom and me. I bragged about applying to five of the top universities in the country and not only being accepted to but also being offered partial scholarships from all of them. I peacocked about the two degrees and the minor I'd obtained from the university I'd chosen and the fact that for both degrees, I'd attained the highest level of distinction: summa cum laude. I flaunted my adventures and travels, my explorations and escapades. When it looked like he couldn't take any more, I hit him with the "hard truth": I was moving to a place he damn well knew he couldn't follow me due to his extensive criminal record.

I flashed him my plane ticket. "And tomorrow I'm moving to Australia," I said.

Before I realized what was happening, he grabbed my knee and kissed me.

"Stop it." I jerked away. My entire body stiffened.

Tiffany cheered prematurely then read the room and silenced herself.

Feeling the warmth from his touch on my knee, I glared down and nearly gasped out loud. On the top of his right hand was a new tattoo. Medieval calligraphy spelled out the name of the gang whose leader had raped me with my boyfriend's consent many blood moons ago.

The realization of the danger I had put myself in by coming to see him rushed back with the sweat pooling under my arms and the blood surging to my head as I stood up too quickly, too urgently. I had to get the fuck out of here. I was not safe. I would never be safe.

"Tiffany—"

"Don't go, sweetie," he said.

I could taste the bitter. "We've gotta go." I nodded toward the door. I worried my trembling legs would fail me, that my knees would buckle under the pressure to balance.

Tiffany stood up and put back on her coat.

He reached for my arm. "Please stay."

Every hair on my body stood up straight, on guard. "I can't," I said. "Plus, best be gone before your girlfriend comes home." I forced a wink to mask my terror.

"She was just a side piece, a placeholder. Anyway, I kicked her out. All she does is party. I'll raise my daughter myself. She's just a dumb kid. Doesn't know her parental rights."

I grabbed my coat and turned to face the door.

"Holy shit," Tiffany said.

She and I saw the pictures at the same time.

Above the window were blown-up pictures of a very young me. A sideview shot of me in a black bra and a black boa-esque scarf around my neck. Me sitting on my bed in my pyjamas wearing far too much makeup. Me in the bathtub. Me in nothing but my dad's white-collar work shirt. I remembered the day my sister and I had taken these photographs, goofing around to get sexy glamour shots. I had only been fifteen at the time. It'd been two years before I'd met him.

"Where did you get those?"

He giggled. "You gave them to me."

I had not. He damn well knew that. More stolen property.

"Don't you think you're a little old to have such suggestive pictures of a teenager on your wall?" I said as flippantly as possible.

"You're funny. I share my bed with a teenager, share a daughter with a teenager. When I allow her those luxuries, anyway."

Rage rose to the rescue. I wanted to save the poor tortured girl.

Seventeen years young. The same age I had been when he'd first started grooming me. He'd started at least two years earlier with his latest victim. I realized I had the power to do something this time. I could do for this seventeen-year-old what no one had done for me at seventeen. I could call the police and child services and report my concerns for the girl and her baby's safety. I could share my own relationship history and my knowledge of his criminal record and convictions: break-and-enter and theft, escape from lawful custody, theft, possession of weapons, forcible confinement, aggravated assault, possession of a narcotic, failure to comply with a recognizance and with probation, assault causing bodily harm, obstruction of police, unlawfully in a dwelling, and failure to appear in court. I could also report all the crimes he'd committed for which he'd not yet been charged: ephebophilia, child abuse, sex trafficking, and making and distributing child pornography. And, lastly, I could share what he'd just told me about his current underage girlfriend's experience, show them the letter in which he bragged to me about "trading me in for a younger version," and banging and impregnating a fifteen-year-old.

I wanted to save the poor tortured girl, but for now I needed to save myself and escape while I still could.

"How cruel. Take those down before she comes back."

"I had them up before she left," he said. "She needs to know her place in my life and in my dreams. You will always be number one."

Twisted sicko. It wasn't worth a fight. I needed to get the hell out of there.

"It was great catching up," I lied. I couldn't trust myself not to do something stupid, something that would cause my immediate harm.

"Don't go to Australia. Don't leave me now that we've finally reconnected."

"We haven't reconnected. We've had closure." I swallowed hard to keep the bile at bay then smiled, waved, and exited.

Chapter 42

Gabbi

Mom finishes reading our draft of Bryanne's obituary, lowers her iPad, and looks up and around at all of us. Pooled tears finally free themselves from under her glasses.

We all nod in solidarity and disbelief. We agree that the insultingly brief, boxed-up description of Bryanne's thirty-six years, closed with a neat little bow on top, would suffice for this necessary albeit generic purpose. How else can a heartbroken family summarize the entire enormous bigger-than-life existence of their deceased beloved in merely one hundred fifty-five words? It seemed cruel, criminal. It felt like robbery.

"Yup," I say, breaking the excruciating silence. "That'll have to do for that purpose. We'll do her life justice by showing, sharing, and celebrating it in other more complete and meaningful ways."

Somber faces agree.

As we flip through dozens of family photo albums and reminisce over our favourite memories, I pull out the pictures I want to use as inspiration for the eulogy.

"Look at this one," I say, as I pass a picture of us three girls as youngsters sporting our matching baby blue sweaters with big, bold, black letters spelling our last name and birth order: "Alexander 1," "Alexander 2," and "Alexander 3." Mom and Tara *ooh* and *aww* in unison. Tears fill my eyes as I think back to our last sisters' night with Bryanne in the ICU. We discussed signs she would send us from the other side to prove she was okay and still with us. She told us every time we saw fireflies to know it was her. I contested this. I wanted something more obvious, rarer. I suggested anything in threes since there were three of us, and, after all, she was number three. Bryanne added to this anything with our colour sequence, red, green, and blue—the individual colours assigned to us in early childhood by our mom to keep our belongings with their rightful owners. Throughout our childhood, she would sew or marker our belongings with our specific colours to nip possession arguments in the bud.

"Remember this?" Tara says, as she shows off a picture of an itty-bitty Bryanne, arms up over her head to reach the handle of her toddler stroller to push her bigger sisters around the zoo.

"Oh my gosh," says Mom. "From the time she could walk and talk, she stubbornly refused to be the baby. And you two encouraged her to take care of you."

We all laugh and share other examples of our never-a-baby baby sister.

I continue collecting pictures demonstrating examples of our family's unbreakable bond. I decide I'll write about my favourites in a tribute to Bryanne. But really, it'll be a pact. A pact between sisters to always stay connected by a love too big and deep—too cosmic—to be contained. A love transcending life and death.

But first, I must complete my book. I hear Bryanne's voice from the other evening.

Get it done. It'll never be too late.

Clearly, it *is* too late for her. I tear up. My biggest failure is the thing that matters most to me—sharing with my family all I went through, all I survived. I was unsuccessful. I couldn't complete my story in time. Clearly, time is not on my side. It is too late for my youngest sister, and our father turns eighty in a few months, for God's sake. We never know when it's going to be too late.

When I return to Calgary after Bryanne's funeral, I quit my job and go to the university library every day to write my story to completion before it's too late for anyone else.

Chapter 43

Alex

Enough was enough. I would no longer wait for *him* to release me. The time had come to free myself. I deeply regretted not having taken action earlier but felt immense relief that it wasn't too late. I started by confiding in my most protective guy friend, Jack. Even though I hadn't told anyone the full extent of what had happened during my relationship with my ex, I'd intentionally kept one hundred percent of the details from Jack, afraid he would take matters into his own hands and get seriously hurt, if not killed. Tiffany was right about one thing: crazy does beat muscle every time.

At first, Jack expressed hurt that I had kept such atrocities from him, but he quickly got over it and switched to fixing mode. Right away, Jack had me provide written notice to my landlord giving the required thirty days' notice of the termination of my lease. Being mid-month, I was on the hook for the full next month's rent, but Jack assured me all my belongings would be out within a few days and I wouldn't have to worry about paying rent elsewhere because once I returned from Australia, I'd be staying with him for the foreseeable future.

Next, Jack hired professional packers and movers to arrive the day after my departure for Australia to empty out my home and move everything to a storage unit for the interim. This temporary measure would ensure that if my ex was still keeping tabs on my house, *he* wouldn't find out where I'd end up. And if *he* followed my stuff to the storage facility, the security cameras would catch *him* violating the restraining order I would be getting against *him* within the hour—after calling child services to report *him* for having a year-old baby with a still underage mother. Jack was convinced I had enough dirt on my ex to put *him* in jail right away. Even if *he* wasn't put in jail, getting slapped with a restraining order would surely push *him* over the edge and into the trap that would be set and waiting for *him* when *he* tested me. Jack believed I needed to resign from my job, as its whereabouts had been compromised. I wasn't ready to go that far quite yet. I convinced Jack to let me wait and see how things would play out. If over the next month my ex was arrested and put back in jail, I might be able to get away without quitting the job I loved so much.

The day finally came to leave. But I was leaving on my own terms. I wasn't running this time.

The doorbell rang. Yoshi charged ballistically toward the door, smashing into it nose first.

"Oh, baby. Your poor cinderblock head," I said, as I secured my pup before opening the door to greet my friend. "Morning, Jack."

"Morning, ladies," he said, as he bent down to scratch Yoshi behind the ears, and she started singing his praises.

"You ready to spend some serious quality time with your Uncle Jack, Yosh?" I asked.

"Mom who?" Jack joked.

"Don't even," I rebutted, playfully whacking my friend in the arm. "I'm already upset enough about leaving her for so long."

"And so you should be," he continued. "We're going to have so much fun while you're gone, she'll probably only get depressed once you're back."

"Jerk!"

Jack laughed. "Oh, and Christmas came early for you. This was taped to your door. You were right. The psychopath just couldn't help himself. Called your bluff and now's in breach." He handed me an envelope.

Familiar hand-drawn music notes bookended the lyrics of our

song. I glanced up at my six-foot-six, no-bullshit, tough-as-nails best guy friend and borrowed some of his never-wavering grit. I flipped over the envelope and saw more song lyrics on the back. I tore into the envelope like I wanted to tear into its piece-of-shit sender.

Bitter Sweetheart,

I hope you see this before you leave. I'm still in shock over you coming to see me. After you guys left, I just sat here thinking. My brain was going fast forward. I'm still messed up over you. I just want you to understand, that all the bad things I ever said and did to you, are my deepest regrets in my entire life. I'm truly sorry for hurting you. Please forgive me?

Only after several years have I learned just how much you really meant to me. I can't love anyone else but you, and it's my fault that you don't trust me anymore or love me back. You are reaching for your future, but I can't help but wonder if you would have succeeded if I didn't leave you . . . ? I'm owed some credit for you growing into an incredible woman.

We both deserve to feel our love, real love. I don't think I'll ever feel that way with any other person alive, just you. We could have that special relationship again that only you and I could have: 'No Ordinary Love' that's for sure. There's a reason you went out of your way to see me, whatever that reason is, I'm grateful, and hope someday you can drop the animosity you feel toward me. I'm truly not the same person I was before. If I were given a miracle, a second chance at true love, committed, passionate, true, deep devotion . . . I would win your trust back and show you every single day how much I cherish you and would never take you for granted again.

P.S. I wasn't lying. I really do have the Sade CD on order. (I wouldn't get by without it.)

I'll always love you. I really hope this isn't farewell forever.

"You okay?" Jack asked.

Reality returned to me. A smile softened my face, and I nodded at my friend. "Let's take this to the police station on the way."

"No," Jack said. "Just call and report it. I'll drop it off after. He's not gonna make you miss this flight of all flights." He reached for my suitcases and wheeled them out the door.

I leashed Yoshi and gently tugged my pup through the door. Then, under my breath, ever so quietly, I said, "Farewell forever." With that, I locked up a piece of my past with intention and walked away from it forever.

Chapter 44

Katee

"Katee!" my little sister yelled. "Some man's at the door for you."

I ran up the stairs from the basement and slid a few feet across the hardwood floor. I gasped. "What are you doing here?"

Beth puffed and threw her hip out to one side. "If that's him, he's not allowed at our house, Katee. I'm telling Mom."

I ignored her and pushed past him outside. "You're not supposed to be here. Why'd you come here? When'd you get back?"

My ex's smile faded. His eyes frowned. "I came back for you, Katee. For us. Thought you'd be happy." The audacity.

I found his sulking gross and unattractive. "Happy?" I said, as I shut the door behind me. "You left me. Again. Almost five months ago." How dare he. What nerve. "You need to leave. You're not welcome here."

Our eyes locked for so long it became uncomfortable. His eyes appeared watery, probably because he'd been staring without blinking like a creeper.

He stepped toward me.

I stepped back.

"I just want a hug," he said, as he came a little closer.

I froze. What was I supposed to say? How was I supposed to feel?

His embrace repulsed me. He reminded me of a needy child, unwilling to let go of his mother.

I pulled away. "You need to leave. My parents will be home any minute."

"I'm not giving up on us, Katee. I flew back across Canada for you. For us. I'm gonna make this work. Whatever it takes."

I turned my back on him, went inside, and slammed the door.

Shooting my shot with my long-time crush, Anthony, was the first thing I did after my ex left for what I thought was for good. I wasn't sure of my chances being that Anthony had been friends with two of my exes years ago. Lucky for me, he didn't subscribe to bro code. Neither did anyone else in the incestuous town.

But with my ex back five months after I thought he'd finally let me go, I worried Anthony would end things with me to avoid unnecessary conflict with him. I needed to prevent that from happening at all costs. For the first time in many years, I felt truly happy. I had to talk to Anthony. I had to convince him I was worth the fight I knew was coming.

The man could not smoke enough joints. He easily went through twenty-five a day. That was a pack of cigarettes, for goodness' sake. I probably wouldn't have noticed if I wasn't highly allergic to the entire cannabis plant, all "healthy" hemp products included.

His back to me, Anthony exhaled through the fan housed in his second-storey bedroom window. Choking a little, he said, "So whatchya gonna do, sexy?"

I had no idea. I sat on his bed, fiddling with the comforter. Why did guys have such ugly bedding? Honestly, a little TLC wouldn't hurt. Maybe that was what I'd get him for Christmas.

Anthony started changing his pants. We had an hour until we had to be at the bar for him to start his shift. What if my ex went there and saw me with Anthony?

"Katee, you look so stressed about this. Who cares what he thinks?" Anthony put on a fresh bandana. I waited for him to make eye contact with me; when he did, he walked over and planted his plump lips on mine. I savored the kiss for a second before pushing him away to avoid it turning into a French kiss. I didn't feel like having an allergic reaction on top of everything else going on.

"To be honest, I'm terrified. You have no idea what he's capable of. No one does. He's crazy. Dangerous. I've told you. He killed my cat, beat me up multiple times, and has threatened to hurt my family."

Anthony gathered me in his arms, his embrace tight and comforting.

I wished he'd never let me go. I wished he'd stay with me, keep me safe.

"You got nothin' to worry 'bout. I've known him for years. He wouldn't dare cross me."

I had everything to worry about. Anthony obviously hadn't known the real him. He'd do anything to get to me.

I pulled away from Anthony's sweater, embedded with the stench of weed, before it caused my throat to itch. "I'm going to call and ask Allison to come with me. I can't hang out at the bar with you all night like I usually do. That would give us away for sure."

He sighed. "Whatever you want, Katee."

I'd hurt his feelings. He told me I'd changed since my ex first came back a few days prior. I was one hundred percent preoccupied, he said, and not with him.

If Anthony only knew. I wish I never had to be away from him. He'd been my dream guy since I was sixteen, over a year before my nightmare man had found me. I knew my ex would wreck Anthony for me. If he didn't get what he wanted—me—he'd do anything it took to destroy me. And after only five months, why would Anthony stick around? He was the most drama-free person I'd ever known. I was surprised he'd stayed with me this long after hearing about the mess I'd come from.

The Corral was dead. Three hours in, only three patrons occupied the bar. Allison and I stuck out like sore thumbs. It was obvious we were there with Anthony.

"Let's go over to Blondies instead," I said, grabbing Allison's arm to get her attention. I signaled to Anthony from across the dance floor that we'd be back later. He nodded, and we left.

The frigid air stung my bare legs. I felt new hair prickle up. Allison had left her jacket behind the bar at The Corral. I knew better than to leave any evidence of my presence anywhere near Anthony. The other bar was just down the street. We arrived before we froze up entirely.

"Arg. There's a line," I said, as we approached.

"Katee, you need to relax, buddy."

"I am relaxed."

Allison laughed. "You are so not. You're sketching out. Always looking over your shoulder, all paranoid and shit."

"Shhh. God, Allison. I don't want the whole town hearing you."

We joined the end of the line, and Allison kicked the wall, dislodging the snow stuck in her boot tread. "He's going to find out. Everyone knows you two are dating. Someone's gonna tell him."

At the door, the bouncer checked our IDs and let us in. I removed my coat as we climbed the stairs. No sooner did I have my arm free than a warm hand gripped it.

"Hey." My ex studied my face.

I couldn't breathe. I didn't know what to do or say.

"Why are you making that face, Katee?"

Had he already found out about Anthony and me?

"Hello? Aren't ya gonna say something?" He leaned in to kiss my cheek.

I backed away. "I have to go to the bathroom." I searched my surroundings. "Allison? I have to go to the bathroom. Now." I grabbed her arm and yanked her toward the dance floor in the direction of the bathroom.

She resisted, slowing us down before we got to the stairs. "Katee, relax! Fuck, man. You're gonna rip my arm off or make me fall."

I jetted around the corner into the hallway that connected the two sides of the huge bar. "What am I supposed to do? What if he knows? What do I say?"

"Why don't you just tell him, Katee? Then maybe he'll leave you alone, and you can finally move on with your life. He left you, for Christ's sake. Twice. You're allowed to have a new boyfriend, you know."

I grunted and stopped, turning to face her. "Allison, you don't get it. He won't leave me alone. I've gotta get out of here." I took her hand and whisked her down the long stairway to the lower-level bathrooms.

I stared at myself in the mirror. My eyes looked messed up; my pupils pulsed to the loud bass or maybe the out-of-control beat of my heart. What a wreck. How could I get myself out of this mess?

"I have an idea," said Allison. "I'll go up ahead of you and tell him you're not feeling good. I'll ask him to get you some water." She put her icy hand on my tense shoulder. "Wait a few seconds, then come up and walk—without stopping—directly to the sports bar entrance. Once out, run to The Corral. At least Anthony can hide you somewhere there." Allison's face had lost its colour. Her voice shook when she spoke.

"You believe me now? That this is serious?"

"Katee, the way you're acting is freaking me out. I know you're serious. I've never seen you like this."

I hugged her and held on a little longer than usual. "Thanks, Alli."

She left, and as instructed, I waited a few seconds. One, two, three, four, five, six, seven, eight, nine, ten. I headed out of the bathroom. I prayed—begged—God would get me out without my ex seeing me. I ran up the stairs, tripping on one. My hand flew out to break my uphill fall.

"Why the rush?"

No! Did the universe want me to be with him? Was this meant to be my life?

I looked at my stinging palm. Blood everywhere. Tears filled my eyes, but not from the pain in my hand. I was trapped. How could I get rid of him? I gathered myself and wiped the dirt off my knee. When I made it to the top of the stairs, he snatched my arm.

"What the fuck is wrong with you?" he whispered, squeezing my arm so tightly I yelped. "Shut up, slut. Trying to avoid me so you can get fresh—or should I say dirty—cock?"

"Get your hands off me." I pushed past him, making it to the common area.

Familiar faces were everywhere. I was safe—stuck but surrounded by acquaintances and patrons.

"Ah!" My body lurched forward. An overwhelming, hot pain rippled out from the centre of my back.

Loud male voices began rioting around me.

"You piece of shit! Who hits a girl?"

I turned to see a guy I knew confronting my ex.

Another male acquaintance piped in, "You wanna fight someone, asshole?"

My ex grabbed me by the hair and pulled me toward him. "Look at me, cunt!"

"That's it," said the first guy. "You asked for it." He picked up my ex by the neck and tossed him into the wall. My ex staggered to get to his feet. The other guy ran over to block him as he tried coming at me again.

"Anthony!" yelled Allison. I looked around to see my boyfriend under the archway leading into the pool table room.

The beginning of the end had arrived. We'd be over by the end of the night, for sure.

The guys guided me to Anthony. "Hey, man. Get her out of here. We'll deal with him."

Anthony didn't say anything. He took my hand and led me to the other side of the bar.

I followed him onto the dance floor. "Why are you here?"

"The Corral was dead. Boss cut my shift short. And I was worried about you." He sheltered me in the back corner and held me until the lights came on and everyone started leaving. We drove back to his house undisturbed.

"Katee. Phone."

I glanced at the clock. 3:30 a.m. Who would call the house at this time? Who even had this number? I cleared my throat and tried to sit up. "Hello?"

"Katee?"

"Ah, yes?"

"Are you okay? This is your father."

"Dad?"

"You sound like you're on drugs. Are you?"

Anthony turned on the light. His eyebrows crinkled.

I shrugged my shoulders, feeling as confused as he looked. "No, Dad. Gosh, we're sleeping. What's going on?"

"He called saying Anthony's a drug dealer and he drugged you up tonight. Is that true? Are you safe?"

"He *who*? And, no, Anthony's not, and he didn't. I'm fine."

"That pedophile."

I sighed.

Anthony opened his mouth and started to say something.

I raised my index finger to my lips to quiet him. "Dad. He's crazy. Anthony's amazing. You know that. I'm safe. I'm going to let you go now so we can go back to sleep. I'll talk to you in the morning, okay?"

"Okay. As long as you're safe."

"I am, Dad. Thanks for checking. Love you."

"Love you more."

Anthony moved the phone cradle off the bed. "What was that about?"

I couldn't tell him. I couldn't believe he'd lasted this long. I'd thought for sure he would've broken up with me after last night's event. I leaned over and kissed him. "Nothing, babe. My dad was just worried."

He lit a cigarette and handed me the pack.

I went to the window and pulled back the curtain to turn on the fan. "What the . . .?" No. It couldn't be. But, of course, it was. "No!"

Anthony jumped out of bed. "What?" he said. I felt him come up behind me. "Oh my God. Is that . . .?"

"Yup." I started to sob. "He's watching us." My ex was across the road, standing just off the sidewalk beside a huge tree.

Anthony yanked the fan out of the windowsill. The window pane crashed shut. He jerked the curtain closed.

Why me?

Anthony's lip curled. He ripped off his shirt and threw it across the room. "He's totally lost it." He took a deep drag. "I'll talk to him in the morning." He butted out his cigarette. "This has gotta stop."

I heard the phone ring from the bathroom. I stopped brushing my teeth to hear if it was for me.

Anthony's voice was firm. A little louder than usual. "Listen, man. You gotta back off. She doesn't wanna see you right now. And to be honest? You're freaking everyone out. Gotta chill, okay?"

Oh, no. Anthony was talking to him. I tossed my toothbrush into the sink and rushed back to the bedroom. Anthony sat on his bed, phone in hand. He glanced up at me and raised his hand as if to say he had everything under control. While Anthony listened, he rolled his eyes in response to whatever my ex was saying. He mimicked with his right hand the amount of talking my ex was doing.

What the hell could he possibly be saying?

"Okay, man. I'll tell her."

More silence on our end.

"Sure, I guess. K, talk to you soon." Anthony hung up the phone.

Feeling lightheaded, I released the breath of air my lungs had taken hostage. "What did he say?"

Anthony stood up, walked over to the window, and peered outside. "Said he wrote you a letter. Left it in between the front doors. Wants you to read it now. Then he's gonna call back."

"Call back? Why?"

Anthony turned his back to the window. "He's out there right now. Think he's been there all night. Said he wants to talk to you face-to-face when you're done reading. Go for coffee or something."

"He's outside now?" I marched to the window to confirm the craziness.

Anthony laughed. "Only thing he's missing is the music to serenade you with."

"This isn't funny. Can't you see how crazy this is?"

"Oh, come on, Katee. I kinda feel for the guy. In all the years I've known him, he's never cared about a girl the way he does you." Anthony walked over to me and took my hands in his. "I can't blame him." He kissed me. "His heart's crushed. He sounded so sad."

I wrapped my arms around Anthony and squeezed as tightly as I could. "I'm scared of him."

"Just read the letter, sexy. I'll go get it for you."

I read his letter. Most of it washed over me. It was the same delusional crap he was always writing to me about—how I was the one tormenting him—with the exception of a few lines that gave me the first feeling of hope that he might not always be lurking outside my window:

If it's over between us, let's end it the right way, if it's not, then why has it taken so long for you to find the time for me?

I'm not going to phone you anymore or write to you either. I'm leaving the ball in your court; it's up to you now.

"See? Told you. Poor guy."

"Poor guy?" I tossed the pages to the floor. "Anthony, he attacked me in the bar last night."

"Katee. It's pretty simple. Tell him you don't want him back. Be done with it. Sounds to me like he's ready to accept it."

I knew he would never accept it.

The phone rang, and I gasped and jumped what felt like a foot off the bed. I yanked it out of the cradle. "What?"

"Katee?" His voice sounded so weak. He made me sick.

"What?"

His silence infuriated me. Speak, goddammit.

"Umm . . ."

I let out an exaggerated sigh before counting to three. "What?"

"Did . . . Did you read my letter?"

"The one that said you weren't going to phone me anymore?"

"Please see me. Just for a minute? I only wanna talk."

I looked up at Anthony and begged him with my eyes not to encourage me to go.

He raised his shoulders and eyebrow simultaneously.

I mouthed the words, *He wants me to see him*. If Anthony hadn't been his friend at one point in time, I doubt he would've been so forgiving. But they had a history. In comparison, I guessed I didn't have much credibility.

Anthony's eyebrows and mouth frowned. He sat down beside me on the bed. His lips moved: *Go*.

Maybe I was being a bitch. My ex had flown across the country to try and win me back. He'd written me a sweet letter. He just wanted to talk.

I rose the phone back to my mouth. "Fine. When? Where?"

I heard a big huff of air being exhaled. He must have been holding his breath. "Thank you, Katee. Thank you."

"Where and when? It's gotta be a public place."

"Can you come now?"

I looked down at my naked body and rubbed my fingers across my bare eyes. "No. Need a half hour or so to pull myself together."

"Okay. How 'bout the Haney Place Mall?"

Pretty much kitty-corner to Anthony's building. I guessed he was still right outside. "Fine. Thirty minutes. But I'm telling Anthony and my parents that I'm going to meet you there. We can talk for fifteen minutes. If I'm not back at Anthony's by then, I'm telling them to call the cops."

"Katee . . . God, Katee. I'd never hurt you."

I laughed. "You mean never again?"

"So, thirty minutes?"

"Yes." I hung up the phone.

I saw him as soon as I entered the double glass doors, sitting on a bench in the centre of the mall. He stood as I approached. I glanced around then took a deep breath. *Come on, I can do this.*

He opened his arms and tried to embrace me. "Thanks for coming, cutie."

"Why are you really here?" I searched his eyes for some truth. They looked dull. Motionless.

He guided me back to the bench he'd been sitting on. He stood at the edge of it staring at me until I couldn't take the awkwardness anymore and sat down.

"So, you're with Anthony?" He lowered his gaze to my lap.

"Why did you come back?"

He shoved his hand into his coat pocket.

My heart started beating in anticipation. Holy shit. Knife? Gun? I scanned the area as much as I could without moving my head and warning him of my suspicion and fear. Where was the quickest exit? Was anyone in hearing range?

"Katee . . ."

Too late.

"Will you marry me?"

My attention snapped back to his eyes. Tears spilt over their rims. He held out a light grey fuzzy box. Inside rested a gold ring with small yellow diamonds.

"What?"

"You don't have to answer me now. Just promise me you'll think about it." He reached his hand out to me. I reclined my upper body, but he snapped the box shut and slipped it into the left pocket of my jacket.

He'd totally lost his mind to think I'd say yes. What would happen when I said no?

Three middle-aged, overweight, and obnoxiously loud women exited a travel centre in front of me. They headed toward us. Perfect opportunity to get chaperoned out of there.

"Sorry. I've gotta go." I stood up and bee-lined it to the exit the same way I had entered. I wished fifteen minutes had already passed, that the building was surrounded by cops to keep watch till I got back to Anthony's safely.

I speed-walked back at an Olympic level. When I crossed the finish line—Anthony's threshold—I yelled up the stairs, "Please take me home. Right now."

Chapter 45

Katee

"So, everything off that wall is three-for-ten?" The girl asking looked about fifteen trying to appear forty. In her pink-polished fingers, she held a pair of animal print socks, sunglasses that read "DIVA" down the arms, and a package of two hairclips.

Seriously, people. It wasn't rocket science. "Yup. You can mix and match any items in the whole store as long as they have the same price deal."

The blonde and her two sidekicks mumbled amongst themselves for a minute, holding up the short line behind them. "What about the body piercings?"

"What does the deal sign above those say?"

She let out an exaggerated sigh to match her exaggerated eye roll. "Two-for-ten."

"Yeah, so that's not the same deal."

"Come on." She crossed her arms and shifted her hip out to one side. "What if I get one three-for-ten and one two-for-ten? It's like a better deal for you, anyway."

I turned my attention to the next person in line: an adorable little old lady with three packages of the tackiest hair clips we carried.

"Did you find everything you were looking for?"

"Yes, thanks, dear." The old lady shook her head at the teen girls.

"This store makes it pretty simple. Just read and match the signs. Guess for some, reading is the problem."

"For others, returning phone calls is the fuckin' problem," said a familiar voice.

The old lady gasped. "Watch your language, you thug."

"Mind your business, granny." My ex grabbed my arm firmly and pulled me out of the store into the mall. I whipped my head around to make sure my co-worker saw. She had already made it behind the counter to finish ringing up the customers.

"Whadda you want? Just leave me alone, already." I wanted to pull away from him, to make a scene. But the escalation of his behaviour from only hurting me in private to stalking and attacking me in public places with witnesses alarmed me.

I sat down on the bench, and he copied. An overwhelming cloud of Eternity cologne entered my nostrils. I used to love that smell. I still did even though there were so many bad memories attached to it.

"You don't answer or return my calls. You don't go out to avoid seeing me. So, I guess if I want to talk to you, I have to come here."

"No. You can't. This is my work. You can't just keep showing up here." Though it felt safer than the alternative.

He glanced around before leaning in close. "I'm warning you, Katee. Stop ignoring me." I felt the moisture of his words land on my face. He lowered his voice. "You read these fucking letters and get back to me." He tossed a stack of folded pages in my lap. "You hear me? I'm not playing your childish games anymore."

"What games? I told you. We're done."

He stood up and stepped on my foot. He crunched it further into the ground as he leaned in overtop of me. He clunked his forehead against mine. "We're not done until you've heard all I have to say. Even then, you at least owe me one last time." He grabbed my arm and pulled it with him as he backed away from me. I rose to standing position. I followed his eyes as they looked up and down my body. He raised his hand, and I flinched. He slapped my ass. "At least one last time for being such a cocktease."

I marched back into the store right past my colleague and into the staff closet. I grabbed my cigarettes and lighter and exited the tiny room.

"I'm taking my smoke break," I said to anyone listening.

When I got out back, I went behind the mall's dumpsters and sat on the wet, slushy ground. I pulled out my lighter and burned every single page of every single one of his letters; I imagined setting fire to each word before any single one came out of his mouth.

"Merry Christmas, cutie. I gave you a few days. Have you read my letters? Know what I want for Christmas?"

"No. I burned them all."

He was mute on the other end of the phone. How appropriate. A moment of silence to grieve the end of this madness.

"Thanks, cunt-ee. Best Christmas gift ever—finally freeing me of a filthy little slut like you." He snickered into the phone. "Can't believe you actually thought I wanted you back. I just wanted to get in on the piece of ass the rest of the town is getting. Since everyone is so obsessed over my extra sloppy seconds, I thought I'd better give it another poke to see if something actually improved."

I hung up.

My face hot as fire, I ripped the photocopies into snow-sized flakes that fell on my lap.

My manager stood over me. "I need to get back out on the floor. I need you to go home till this all blows over. I canceled your shifts for the week." She glanced down, taking one last look at the shameful images, before flipping her stringy blonde hair over her shoulder and exiting the storage room.

I looked down at the remaining photocopies in my nerve-struck hands. They were playful nudes I had taken for my ex years earlier: seventeen-year-old me, thirty pounds underweight. That morning, when my boss had shown up to open the store, she'd found the photocopies taped to the storefront security gate. Written all over them were things like, "for a good time call Katee." He'd even put my parents' phone number on them. Taped alongside them had been another letter. When my manager had handed it to me, I'd pulled out my lighter and managed to light the corner of it on fire before she'd smacked it out of my hand, patted out the flame, and demanded I go home before I forced her to fire me.

Chapter 46

Katee

"Sean? Whadda you mean, he's going to kill me?" Each word I spoke caused Allison's eyes to widen more. She looked like a terrified Nicole Kidman.

I heard a gulp on the other end of the phone. "Katee, I swear, I'm telling the truth."

"I believe you. But . . . what the hell should I do?" I rolled out the computer desk chair and sat down.

Allison mouthed the word, *What?*

I shrugged my shoulders.

Sean resumed, "Whatever you do, hide. Hide good. We're still at the bar. He's fucking plastered. Ranting on and on about taking you out then fleeing Ontario for good. He's even plotting it out on some folded-up lined paper he pulled outta his pocket. He's a psycho. I'm trying to stall him. You've got at least two hours. He's making me bring him. We're coming to get you."

"Okay. Thanks. Seriously, Sean—thank you so much. I'm really sorry."

Shortly after I'd left BC, Sean had, too. He'd moved back to his hometown, where my grandma still lived, a two-hour drive from my parents' house. I'd only seen Sean once in the four and a half months since we'd both gotten back to Ontario. I wondered how my ex had gotten ahold of him. I'd made the mistake of telling my ex I wouldn't be in town on New Year's Eve, as I'd be spending it celebrating with Sean and his friends. But I'd cancelled those plans last minute when Allison had begged to do something with just the two of us to make up for lost time. Thank God.

Through Sean's long pause, I heard what sounded like sniffling. Was he crying? This was exactly what I didn't want—my friends and family being pulled into this mess.

"Katee . . ."

"Yeah, hun?"

"After tonight . . ."

"Uh, huh?"

By this time, Allison had gone into the kitchen and picked up another phone to listen in on both ends of the conversation.

Ten seconds must have gone by before Sean finally answered, "After tonight . . . we're no longer . . . we can't be friends. I'm . . . I'm sorry, Katee. I just . . . it's just, I can't get caught up in whatever this is. He's a fuckin' psycho. I'm scared shitless."

"Sean—" I heard a click on the other end.

Why wouldn't my ex just leave me alone already?

Allison yelled from the other room, "What the fuck is going on, Katee?" I heard the stomp of her footsteps getting closer. I still had the receiver in my hand when she confronted me, hands on hips. "Kill you? No longer friends?"

"He told Sean he'd get one last night with me, one way or the other. Described his plan in detail." My mind felt motion sick from the roller coaster of events. I'd had almost five months of peace and stillness before my ex had come back and spun me round and round all over again.

"A plan? To kill you?" Allison swooped in close to me.

I scooted over to allow room for her to sit. "To fuck me then kill me."

She gasped. "Kill you? Chiquita! Could he actually be serious?"

My eye leaked a tear, then my jaw flinched.

When Allison saw this, her lips pressed together, and she inhaled deeply; the tendons on her neck stood out. Her eyes locked on mine.

"Yes, he's dead serious." I half-ass laughed but full-blown panicked. "No pun intended."

Living twenty minutes from the closest police station didn't offer any comfort, and it added significant risk if I waited until this crisis became crucial enough to call the cops for help. The escalation in my ex's behaviour—him openly stalking me, attacking me in public, telling people about his contempt for me and plan to kill me—terrified me and warranted this to be taken seriously. Plus, I'd had enough. I called 911.

When I hung up, I nodded at Allison to start the car and told her I needed to throw a few things in a bag.

As we pulled away from my empty house, relief washed over me with the knowledge that my family remained out of town for the night.

In the wee hours of January 1, Allison's home phone rang. A police officer informed me that my ex had been found, charged, and jailed. The constable said when they checked his pockets for weapons, they found an illegal switchblade and a letter addressed to me containing a threat on my life.

"No more fucking letters," I said before realizing what I had said and whom I had said it to.

Seemingly unphased, the officer asked if I wanted to press charges.

"Whadda ya mean?" I switched the phone to my other ear. "You said he's been charged and jailed."

The officer cleared his throat before proceeding. "We arrested him on charges related to the crime in process at the time of the call," he said cautiously.

Confused about what the officer was keeping confidential but certain of my New Year's resolution, I decided I'd finally had enough. "Yes. I'm ready."

A few days later, Sean called and filled me in on the events of New Year's Eve.

"You're one lucky star." His voice sounded back to normal—

nothing like the breathless, shaky, strained voice, unfamiliar and alarming, I had heard days earlier.

My heart stuttered against my ribcage. I wanted more than anything to feel hopeful and excited, but I knew better than to let my guard down due to yet another false sense of security.

I released my breath. "So, what happened?"

"He beat the piss out of a guy and girl." He paused to yell at someone in the background. "He was raging about you and unleashed on the first randoms that crossed him."

I gasped. "No way."

"Yup. Finally back in jail where that piece of shit belongs."

Could it be? Could I finally be free?

Chapter 47

Gabbi

Driving to my therapist's office, I glance over at my mom in the passenger seat. In her lap, her hands hold a physical copy of my completed manuscript. I smile. The first draft is finally finished.

My mom flew out to Calgary to spend three days at a cozy Airbnb I rented for us in Canmore. Nestled between the Three Sisters mountains, we'll read my book together out loud. Some of Bryanne's ashes are scattered at the base, so she'll be with us, too. When I invited my mom to come out West for my book's first read, I asked if she'd be up for a preliminary therapy session to help prep us for the mess we're about to dive into. Digging up painful parts of our relationship's tumultuous past won't be easy, but hopefully it'll be healing.

I park the car and look at my mom. "Ready?"

My mom chuckles nervously then nods. "Shall I bring this?" She holds up the thick stack of coiled pages.

"Yup."

Simultaneously, we inhale deeply then laugh our breath out because of our impeccable timing.

Inside, I introduce my mom to Lisa.

"Wow. You must look like your dad, then, Gabbi."

"All five of us look completely different," I say.

"It's true," my mom chimes in.

We all sit down and get comfortable before creating an outline of our goals for the session.

"Mom, if it's okay with you," I say, "I'd like to read you the current last two pages of my book first."

Lisa tears up. I read them to her in our last session.

My mom looks at Lisa then back at me, a mix of worry and bewilderment on her face.

"I think you hearing how I feel now is essential prior to us starting at the beginning and hearing how I felt then. When the reading gets tough, we'll have these two pages to remember. We've come so far in our relationship. In our reconnection and our healing. Regression is not an option."

My mom smiles. "I agree, Magoo." She hands me my manuscript.

I turn it over, open it to the last page, and through the tears steadily streaming down my face, I read my letter to my younger family:

Dear Family from the years 1996–2001,
Mom, Dad, Tara Leigh, and Bryanne Elizabeth,

I will start this letter by saying I love you. I fiercely love you.

The next few years will rock you. Brace yourselves.

I will burn my life to the ground. Be patient with me. I eventually find my way. Right my wrongs. Make amends.

Everything I will experience shapes the woman I am now, the woman you love now.

I rise higher because I survive the hardships to come.

I use the regret, pain, and trauma I endure to better myself. To better my relationships with you.

I assure you I will be harder on myself than you could ever be. I will overanalyze myself, my choices, and my actions enough for all of you. This is not about you—and I will forever be sorry you get hurt in the process.

I end up healing myself. The part of me you don't like, I didn't like her either. I struggled with her, too. I externalized and disowned her and pretended she was someone separate from me. Her problems were no longer my truth. For years, I shamed her. Picked her apart. Overanalyzed her. But, eventually, I decide to help her, heal her. I write about her and all her painful experiences. She became my case study throughout all three of my degrees. My practice client. And I became the person she needed when she had no one else. I collected her and helped her unpack and process it all. Some thought it was too late to save her, but it wasn't. And the healing and growing continues to this day. It's lifelong.

I end up doing amazing things. I obtain two undergraduate degrees and a master's degree. I use my education and clinical training to therapize myself through the domestic violence I will survive, as well as its decades' long aftermath. I become the person I needed when I was younger. I dedicate my life to helping others. I finally reintegrate all my parts. And I write a book to finally explain all of it to you.

I end up becoming a phenomenal daughter and sister. I learn to love you right. I prove time and time again that I will drop everything to be with you and stop at nothing to love and support you.

I end up being proud of myself. Loving myself. And because of that, I end up finding TRUE love: healthy, supportive, unconditional, reciprocal, forever love with a man named Vince. You all adore him.

I will rise from the ashes I create. Be patient with me. I promise you, it'll all be worth it.

Again, I apologize for the turbulent times ahead. We will survive them. Please give grace.

I will end this letter by reminding you I love you. I wholeheartedly love you.

All my love,
Robbin (BB) Kathleen (Katee) Alexander (Alex) Gabriel (Gabbi)

Author's Note

When I was first physically free of him, the traumatic memories kept me hostage. Even the smallest reminders held the power to unravel me. Seeing a blue Cavalier triggered a panic attack; hearing our song or his first name led to uncontrollable rage; being touched or even just brushed up against activated vivid flashbacks; smelling cigarette smoke or the cologne he wore caused me to vomit; and tasting orange flavouring made me burst into tears. I found myself trapped in a constant state of hypervigilance. I tried my best to forget the memories and avoid their triggers. I finally had a panic attack so severe that I was hospitalized, diagnosed with generalized anxiety disorder, and prescribed medication that helped to numb me. I still didn't tell anyone anything that had happened to me. Had I, I likely would have been more appropriately diagnosed with post-traumatic stress disorder.

My trauma psychoeducation began in my second year of university, when I was accepted into the school of social work. I learned about domestic violence, trauma, and post-traumatic stress disorder. I learned about trauma theory and trauma-informed practice. I learned about various treatment modalities like cognitive behavioural therapy, exposure therapy, narrative therapy, dialectical behaviour therapy, creative arts therapy, and experiential therapy.

I decided to confront and overcome my own distressing memories through storytelling and by turning my trauma narrative into case studies to essentially therapize myself throughout the completion of my undergraduate and graduate degrees. I expanded upon my trauma narrative over many years. I wrote and rewrote, read and reread, each time adding more detail until it became easier to write, read, and eventually share. Sharing my story has helped me to reprocess my experience of domestic violence from a safe place, gifting me mastery and control over my traumatic past.

Much like keeping a diary, writing my trauma narrative all those years ago was, in a way, albeit unknowingly, like writing to my future self. An older, stronger, wiser, kinder, and more compassionate version of myself. Writing about the horrors I experienced at the hands and from the mouth of my ex proved extremely therapeutic. Writing helped to lessen the emotional pressure and impact of the traumatic experiences by reducing the intensity of my trauma reactions. And years later, when I was healed enough, I started rereading it all and writing back.

In response to my trauma narrative, I wrote letters to my younger self. This helped me process and work through my inner conflict to heal the wounded and traumatized younger parts of myself. I showed her kindness and compassion. I reflected on the difficult times my younger self experienced; I became the person she so desperately needed back then; and I told her now what she had needed to hear then. I considered how she and her trying experiences positively shaped the current version of myself and expressed gratitude to her for those painful but essential learnings. I acknowledged and created space for the significant emotions she experienced: regret, pain, heartbreak, trauma, fear, shame, guilt, and grief. I shared with her the invaluable lessons I have since learned and the priceless insight I have since gained, and I offered her advice to help support and love her through her tough times ahead.

I took the time to remind my younger self that she is worthy of being loved and not to doubt her self-worth. I shared with her all the qualities I appreciate and admire about her. I touched on her strength and resilience. I told my younger self how proud I am of her. I let her in on the life secret she has yet to learn; that she gets to choose the ending of her story. I told her I am her biggest fan.

And then, when I felt I'd fully healed myself, I wrote this book for my younger self.

Acknowledgments

I want to start by acknowledging my fellow survivors, whether you're still silently screaming or sharing your own story at the top of your lungs. I believe you. I support you. I stand with you.

To every single soul who has encouraged me and supported me through the seemingly never-ending years it took me to finish writing my story—thank you.

I am forever grateful for and appreciative of my first TRUE No Ordinary Loves: my parents and my sisters. You have loved me through my worst and are huge parts of who I am at my best.

To the real "Marilyn," "Miss Templeton," "James," "Tiffany," and "Allisons" of my past who loved and supported my younger self - thank you. To the real "Jack" and "Maria," and to all the other dear friends of my present who continue to love and support all parts of me in my fully integrated self—thank you—you keep me whole.

A huge thanks to the generous people who volunteered their time to be my beta readers, to my brilliant university professors, especially Dr. Sandra Preston, and to the authors of the books I read in university that made me realize I, too, had a story to share. Thanks to my critiquing clique at Alexandra Writers' Centre Society, my editor Danielle, my book reviewers and blurb writers. And to the phenomenal ladies at Writing Brave Press: my talented cover designer Karinna, my creative interior layout designer Michelle, and especially my book production manager Meg, who has been a godsend - thank you for adding the professional touch. And thanks to NO MORE and CASW for allowing me to share the valuable resources they curated.

And finally, I want to thank my last TRUE No Ordinary Love, my husband, Vince, who chooses to spend each and every day showing me what true, unconditional, and healthy love looks like, sounds like, and feels like.

To every single soul who has showered me in No Ordinary Love, I No Ordinary Love you right back - with my whole entire heart.

xx Robbin

Author Biography

BB Gabriel is a proud Canadian and registered social worker. A domestic violence survivor herself, she confronted and overcame her traumatic experience through storytelling, and turned her trauma narrative into case studies to therapize herself throughout the completion of her undergraduate and graduate degrees: BA (Gerontology), BSW (Social Work), MSW (Master of Social Work with a clinical specialization), and a minor in Women Studies. BB expanded upon her trauma narrative over many years. She wrote and rewrote, read and reread, each time adding more detail, until it became easier to write, read, and eventually share. Sharing her story has helped her reprocess her experience of domestic violence from a safe place, gifting her mastery and control over her traumatic past. BB lives with her partner and their two sphynx cats. She is a lover of spaghetti, karaoke, travel, animals, and anything family—but especially quality time spent together at her family's cottage, playing cards and swimming in the lake.

www.ingramcontent.com/pod-product-compliance
Lightning Source LLC
Chambersburg PA
CBHW051556010526
44118CB00023B/2732